An Annotated Bibliography

Of Selected Publications, 1991-2010,

On Dwight David Eisenhower

By

Jessica Ziparo and Louis Galambos

Johns Hopkins University

Baltimore, Maryland

2010

The Eisenhower Institute
2011

1

This bibliography could not have been produced without the full support of The Eisenhower Institute, the Eisenhower-Ann Whitman Committee, and the Eisenhower-Thomas A. Pappas Committee. Eugene Rossides, Roemer McPhee, and Douglas R. Price provided enthusiastic support for this effort to provide a guide to the abundant materials now available on President Dwight David Eisenhower. Because there is an excellent bibliography on publications prior to 1991, we have started at that date, though we have included a few 1990 publications that were not included in the aforementioned bibliography, and we closed our search in June 2010. Given the interest we see in Eisenhower's military and presidential careers, we are certain there will in the future be a need for additional bibliographic guides.

Please note that our information on authors is the best that we could locate currently. In most cases, it is drawn from the World Wide Web or from the publications themselves. We are certain that the information is not entirely up-to-date in many cases. This is particularly true where academic or government appointments are involved. We apologize for any errors or omissions. We will collect information on omissions and errors for the next digital edition, and we can be reached at galambos@jhu.edu.

Table of Contents

Keywords Index

Keyword	Entry Numbers
Early Life	8, 27, 36, 41, 58, 60, 65, 68, 82, 85, 121, 127, 133, 134, 135, 147, 157, 261.
Military- Pre WWII	36, 41, 50, 58, 61, 65, 68, 82, 85, 121, 127, 157, 219, 231, 232, 261, 285, 291.
Military—B/w the Wars	27, 36, 41, 57, 58, 59, 65, 68, 82, 99, 121, 169, 220, 231, 232, 273, 291, 292.
Military- WWII	5, 11, 14, 15, 27, 30, 33, 36, 39, 41, 50, 54, 55, 59, 60, 61, 65, 68, 73, 74, 77, 82, 83, 85, 99, 114, 115, 117, 121, 127, 128, 132, 133, 134, 135, 142, 157, 162, 221, 233, 234, 235, 236, 241, 249, 259, 291, 294.
SACEUR	14, 82, 137, 181, 290, 322.
Army Chief of Staff	30, 32, 75, 132, 304.
Columbia University	30, 62, 75, 82, 112, 192, 226.
Presidency	1, 2, 3, 4, 6, 7, 9, 10, 12, 13, 14, 16, 17, 18, 19, 20, 21, 22, 23, 24, 25, 26, 27, 28, 29, 31, 32, 34, 35, 37, 38, 42, 43, 44, 45, 46, 47, 48, 49, 51, 52, 53, 56, 59, 60, 61, 63, 64, 65, 66, 68, 69, 70, 71, 72, 73, 75, 76, 78, 79, 80, 81, 82, 83, 84, 85, 86, 87, 88, 89, 90, 91, 92, 93, 94, 95, 96, 97, 98, 99, 100, 101, 102, 103, 104, 105, 106, 107, 108, 109, 110, 111, 112, 113, 116, 118, 119, 120, 121, 122, 123, 124, 125, 126, 127, 128, 129, 130, 131, 132, 133, 134, 135, 136, 138, 139, 140, 141, 143, 144, 145, 146, 148, 149, 150, 151, 152, 153, 154, 155, 156, 158, 159, 160, 161, 163, 164, 165, 166, 167, 168, 170, 171, 172, 173, 174, 175, 176, 177, 178, 179, 180, 181, 182, 183, 184, 185, 186, 187, 188, 189, 190, 191, 193, 194, 195, 196, 197, 198, 199, 200, 201, 202, 203, 204, 205, 206, 207, 208, 209, 210, 211, 212, 213, 214, 215, 216, 217, 218, 222, 223, 224, 225, 227, 228, 229, 230, 237, 238, 239, 240, 242, 243, 244, 245, 246, 247, 248, 250, 251, 252, 253, 254, 255, 256, 257, 258, 259, 260, 262, 264, 265, 266, 267, 268, 269, 270, 271, 272, 274, 275, 276, 277, 278, 279, 280, 281, 282, 283, 284, 286, 287, 288, 289, 290, 291, 293, 294, 295, 296, 297, 298, 299, 300, 301, 302, 303, 304, 305, 306, 307, 308, 309, 310, 311, 312, 313, 314, 315, 316, 317, 318, 319, 320, 321, 322, 323, 324, 325, 326, 327, 328, 329, 330, 331, 332, 333, 334, 335, 336, 337.
Post-Presidency	27, 65, 82, 85, 99, 127, 223.
Elections	30, 86, 125, 140, 161, 176, 181, 192, 193, 226, 230, 266, 269, 280, 296, 304, 322.
Transportation	169, 292.
Politics	6, 23, 24, 30, 32, 71, 73, 81, 84, 87, 90, 92, 94, 95, 98, 100, 102, 109, 112, 125, 126, 130, 139, 140, 153, 161, 167, 168, 178, 183, 184, 185, 190, 193, 200, 202, 205, 210, 214, 226, 230, 238, 239, 251, 262, 263, 266, 269, 271, 279, 296, 301, 304, 306, 308, 315, 316, 317, 330, 335.
Civil Rights	22, 24, 44, 70, 79, 107, 108, 109, 111, 112, 149, 154, 156, 159, 164, 180, 188, 194, 227, 242, 258, 278, 282, 319, 335.

Speechmaking	17, 29, 30, 75, 76, 106, 145, 148, 191, 202, 212, 240, 262, 263, 264, 265, 266, 301, 309, 323.
Family	67, 133, 134, 135, 147.
Religion	134, 135, 163, 225, 269.
White House	92, 99, 111, 112, 153, 167, 211, 213, 251, 288, 324, 327.
NATO	137, 250, 277.
Bricker Amendment	180, 279.
Nuclear	25, 28, 29, 34, 38, 42, 49, 51, 90, 94, 104, 113, 116, 132, 172, 175, 223, 250, 314, 320, 323.
Economics	32, 53, 93, 95, 100, 110, 112, 113, 124, 138, 186, 189, 247, 275, 312, 313, 329, 331, 333.
Personal Life	39, 40, 57, 59, 67, 71, 73, 99, 133, 256, 259, 261, 269, 273, 285, 311.
Korea	26, 107, 223, 266, 270.
Middle East	2, 4, 10, 12, 13, 31, 43, 44, 49, 52, 56, 64, 69, 72, 97, 101, 103, 112, 113, 119, 122, 144, 209, 243, 245, 246, 254, 255, 275, 276, 332, 334.
Media	3, 71, 106, 111, 125, 126, 165, 170, 176, 203, 286, 287, 313.
Vietnam	6, 7, 9, 22, 101, 171, 201, 225, 295.
Cold War	1, 6, 10, 12, 17, 18, 22, 23, 24, 25, 28, 29, 30, 31, 32, 34, 37, 38, 42, 43, 44, 46, 47, 48, 49, 51, 52, 53, 56, 60, 63, 64, 66, 69, 72, 78, 80, 81, 89, 90, 91, 94, 97, 98, 101, 103, 104, 105, 106, 112, 113, 116, 119, 122, 124, 129, 131, 132, 137, 139, 141, 143, 145, 149, 151, 155, 156, 158, 159, 160, 163, 164, 166, 171, 175, 177, 178, 179, 182, 183, 184, 185, 186, 191, 201, 204, 207, 208, 209, 215, 217, 218, 222, 224, 229, 237, 240, 243, 244, 245, 246, 248, 250, 252, 253, 260, 262, 263, 266, 267, 268, 270, 272, 276, 277, 283, 284, 286, 287, 289, 290, 293, 294, 298, 300, 302, 303, 312, 313, 314, 315, 316, 317, 320, 321, 323, 325, 326, 328, 331, 332, 336, 337.
Space Exploration	37, 90, 94, 105, 111, 112, 113, 207, 208, 239, 325.
Military Policy	6, 25, 32, 38, 61, 78, 94, 98, 104, 105, 110, 113, 132, 143, 148, 158, 172, 173, 174, 175, 178, 200, 204, 206, 207, 208, 209, 215, 218, 219, 250, 252, 267, 270, 276, 277, 283, 289, 290, 291, 295, 298, 299, 320, 323, 326, 331, 336.
Foreign Relations	1, 2, 4, 7, 9, 10, 12, 13, 14, 17, 18, 19, 25, 28, 31, 37, 38, 42, 43, 44, 46, 47, 48, 49, 51, 52, 53, 56, 60, 63, 64, 66, 69, 72, 78, 80, 81, 83, 88, 89, 90, 91, 94, 97, 98, 101, 103, 106, 111, 112, 113, 116, 119, 120, 122, 124, 129, 131, 141, 143, 144, 145, 148, 149, 151, 155, 156, 160, 163, 164, 166, 171, 174, 175, 177, 179, 180, 182, 183, 184, 185, 186, 187, 188, 189, 190, 191, 197, 201, 205, 209, 217, 222, 223, 224, 229, 237, 240, 242, 243, 244, 245, 246, 247, 248, 250, 253, 254, 255, 260, 262, 263, 266, 267, 268, 270, 272, 275, 277, 279, 281, 283, 284, 289, 290, 293, 294, 298, 299, 300, 302, 303, 312, 313, 314, 315, 316, 317, 321, 323, 326, 328, 332, 336, 337.
Domestic Policy	14, 22, 23, 24, 43, 44, 70, 79, 80, 81, 84, 87, 108, 109, 111, 112, 138, 149, 154, 159, 164, 180, 188, 194, 210, 214, 239, 242, 258, 278, 279, 282, 286, 287, 305, 308, 319, 329, 330, 333, 335.
Leadership	5, 11, 16, 17, 55, 61, 64, 74, 78, 81, 94, 111, 157, 163, 167, 198, 199,

	285, 296.
Technology	25, 37, 44, 51, 78, 90, 94, 104, 113, 132, 152, 172, 173, 204, 206, 207, 208, 215, 216, 239, 241, 250, 267, 277, 320.

Books Index

Entry	Citations
1	Aldous, Richard. *MacMillan, Eisenhower, and the Cold War*. Dublin, Ireland: Four Courts Press, 2005.
2	Alin, Erika G. *The United States and the 1958 Lebanon Crisis: American Intervention in the Middle East*. Lanham, MD: University Press of America, 1994.
3	Allen, Craig. *Eisenhower and the Mass Media: Peace, Prosperity, and Prime-Time TV*. Chapel Hill & London: University of North Carolina Press, 1993.
4	Alteras, Isaac. *Eisenhower and Israel: U.S.-Israeli Relations, 1953-1960*. Gainesville, FL: University Press of Florida, 1993.
5	Ambrose, Stephen E., *The Victors: Eisenhower and His Boys: The Men of World War II*. New York: Simon & Schuster, 1999.
6	Anderson, David L. (ed.), *Shadow on the White House: Presidents and the Vietnam War, 1945-1975*. Lawrence, KS: University of Kansas Press, 1993.
7	Anderson, David L., *Trapped by Success: The Eisenhower Administration and Vietnam, 1953-1961*. New York: Columbia University Press, 1993.
8	Anderson, Lars. *Carlisle vs. Army: Jim Thorpe, Dwight Eisenhower, Pop Warner, and the Forgotten Story of Football's Greatest Battle*. New York: Random House Trade Paperback, 2007.
9	Arnold, James R. *The First Domino: Eisenhower, the Military, and America's Intervention in Vietnam*. New York: William Morrow & Co, 1991.
10	Ashton, Nigel John. *Eisenhower, Macmillan and the Problem of Nasser: Anglo-American Relations and Arab Nationalism, 1955-59*. London: MacMillan Press, 1996.
11	Axelrod, Alan. *Eisenhower on Leadership: Ike's Enduring Lessons in Total Victory Management*. San Francisco, CA: Jossey-Bass, 2006.
12	Barrett, Roby C. *The Greater Middle East and the Cold War: US Foreign Policy Under Eisenhower and Kennedy*. New York: I. B. Tauris, 2007.
13	Ben-Zvi, Abraham. *Decade of Transition: Eisenhower, Kennedy, and the Origins of the American-Israeli Alliance*. New York: Columbia University Press, 1998.
14	Bischof, Gunter and Stephen E. Ambrose, ed. *Eisenhower: A Centenary Assessment*. Baton Rouge: Louisiana State University Press, 1995.
15	Bischof, Günter and Stephen Ambrose, ed. *Eisenhower and the German POWs: Facts Against Falsehood*. Baton Rouge: Louisiana State University Press, 1992.
16	Blakesley Lance, *Presidential Leadership: From Eisenhower to Clinton*. Chicago: Nelson-Hall Publishers, 1995.
17	Bose, Meena. *Shaping and Signaling Presidential Policy: The National Security Decision Making of Eisenhower and Kennedy*. College Station: Texas A&M University Press, 1998.
18	Bowie, Robert R. and Richard H. Immerman. *Waging Peace: How Eisenhower Shaped an Enduring Cold War Strategy*. New York: Oxford University Press, 1998.
19	Boyle, Peter G., ed. *The Churchill-Eisenhower Correspondence, 1953-1955*. Chapel Hill: University of North Carolina Press, 1990.
20	Boyle, Peter G., ed. *The Eden-Eisenhower Correspondence, 1955-1957*. Chapel Hill: The University of North Carolina Press, 2005.
21	Boyle, Peter G., *Eisenhower*. Harlow, England: Pearson/Longman, 2005.

Entry	Citations
22	Brenner, Samuel, ed. *Dwight D. Eisenhower*. San Diego, CA: Greenhaven, 2002.
23	Broadwater, Jeff. *Eisenhower & the Anti-Communist Crusade*. Chapel Hill, NC: University of North Carolina Press, 1992.
24	Brownell, Herbert, with John P. Burke. *Advising Ike: The Memoirs of Attorney General Herbert Brownell*. Lawrence, KN, University Press of Kansas, 1993.
25	Brugioni, Dino A. *Eyes in the Sky: Eisenhower, the CIA and Cold War Aerial Espionage*. Annapolis, MD: Naval Institute Press, 2010.
26	Brune, Lester H., ed. *The Korean War: Handbook of the Literature and Research*. Westport, CT: Greenwood Press, 1996.
27	Burnes, Brian. *The Ike Files: Mementos of the Man and His Era From Eisenhower Presidential Library and Museum*. Kansas City, MO: Kansas City Star Books, 2008.
28	Chernus, Ira. *Apocalypse Management: Eisenhower and the Discourse of National Insecurity*. Stanford: Stanford University Press, 2008.
29	Chernus, Ira. *Eisenhower's Atoms for Peace*. College Station: Texas A&M University Press, 2002.
30	Chernus, Ira. *General Eisenhower: Ideology and Discourse*. East Lansing, MI: Michigan State University Press, 2002.
31	Citino, Nathan J. *From Arab Nationalism to OPEC: Eisenhower, King Saʻūd, and the Making of U.S.-Saudi Relations*. Bloomington & Indianapolis: Indiana University Press, 2002.
32	Clarfield, Gerald. *Security with Solvency: Dwight D. Eisenhower and the Shaping of the American Military Establishment*. Westport, CT: Praeger, 1999.
33	Coates, Tim (ed.). *D Day to VE Day 1944-45: General Eisenhower's Report on the Invasion of Europe*. London: The Stationery Office, 2000.
34	Craig, Campbell. *Destroying the Village: Eisenhower and Thermonuclear War*. New York: Columbia University Press, 1998.
35	Damms, Richard V. *The Eisenhower Presidency, 1953-1961*. London: Pearson Education Limited, 2002.
36	D'Este Carlo. *Eisenhower: A Soldier's Life*. New York: Henry Holt and Company, 2002.
37	Divine, Robert A. *The* Sputnik *Challenge*. New York: Oxford University Press, 1993.
38	Dockrill, Saki. *Eisenhower's New-Look National Security Policy, 1953-61*, London: Macmillan, 1996.
39	Eisenhower, John S. D. *General Ike: A Personal Reminiscence*. New York: Free Press, 2003.
40	Eisenhower, Susan. *Mrs. Ike: Memories and Reflections on the Life of Mamie Eisenhower*. New York: Farrar, Straus and Giroux, 1996.
41	Fromkin, David. *In the Time of the Americans: FDR, Truman, Eisenhower, Marshall, MacArthur - the Generation that Changed America's Role in the World*. New York: Alfred A. Knoff, Inc., 1995.
42	Gaddis, John Lewis, et al, ed. *Cold War Statesmen Confront the Bomb: Nuclear Diplomacy Since 1945*. New York: Oxford University Press, 1999.
43	Galambos, Louis and Daun van Ee (eds.). *Papers of Dwight David Eisenhower, Volumes 14-17: The Presidency: The Middle Way*. (Baltimore, MD: Johns Hopkins University Press, 1996).
44	Galambos, Louis and Daun van Ee (eds.). *Papers of Dwight David Eisenhower,Volumes 18-21: The Presidency: Keeping the Peace*. (Baltimore, MD: Johns Hopkins University Press,

Entry	Citations
	2001).
45	Galvin, Daniel J. *Presidential Party Building: Dwight D. Eisenhower to George W. Bush.* Princeton, NJ: Princeton University Press, 2010.
46	Gambone, Michael D. *Eisenhower, Somoza, and the Cold War in Nicaragua, 1953-1961.* Westport, CT: Praeger, 1997.
47	Garthoff, Raymond. *Assessing the Adversary: Estimates by the Eisenhower Administration of Soviet Intentions and Capabilities.* Washington: The Brooking Institution, 1991.
48	Geelhoed, E. Bruce and Anthony O. Edmonds. *Eisenhower, MacMillan and Allied Unity, 1957-61.* New York: Palgrave Macmillan, 2003.
49	Geelhoed, E. Bruce and Anthony O. Edmonds, (ed.), *The Macmillan-Eisenhower Correspondence, 1957-69.* New York: Palgrave Macmillan, 2005.
50	Gelb, Norman. *Ike and Monty: Generals at War.* New York: William Morrow and Company, Inc., 1994.
51	Greene, Benjamin P. *Eisenhower, Science Advice, and the Nuclear Test-Ban Debate, 1945-1963.* Stanford, CA: Stanford University Press, 2007.
52	Hahn, Peter. *The United States, Great Britain, and Egypt, 1945-56: Strategy and Diplomacy in the Early Cold War.* Chapel Hill, NC: University of North Carolina Press, 1991.
53	Hall, Michael R. *Sugar and Power in the Dominican Republic: Eisenhower, Kennedy and the Trujillos.* Westport CN: Greenwood Press, 2000.
54	Hauenstein, Ralph W. and Donald E. Markle. *Intelligence Was My Line: Inside Eisenhower's Other Command.* New York: Hippocrene Books, Inc., 2005.
55	Haycock, D.J. *Eisenhower and the Art of Warfare: A Critical Appraisal.* Jefferson, NC: McFarland & Company. 2004.
56	Holland, Matthew F. *America and Egypt: From Roosevelt to Eisenhower.* Westport, CT: Praeger, 1996.
57	Holland, Matthew F. *Eisenhower Between the Wars: The Making of a General and Statesman.* Westport, Connecticut: Praeger, 2001.
58	Holt, Daniel D., and James W. Leyerzapf, *Eisenhower: The Prewar Diaries and Selected Papers, 1905 - 1941.* Baltimore: The Johns Hopkins University Press, 1998.
59	Holt, Marilyn Irvin. *Mamie Doud Eisenhower: The General's First Lady.* Lawrence, KS: University Press of Kansas, 2007.
60	Humes, James C. *Eisenhower and Churchill: The Partnership That Saved the World.* New York: Three Rivers Press, 2001.
61	Jablonsky, David. *War by Land, Sea, and Air: Dwight Eisenhower and the Concept of Unified Command.* New Haven, CT: Yale University Press, 2010.
62	Jacobs, Travis. *Eisenhower at Columbia.* New Brunswick, NJ: Transaction Publishers, 2001.
63	Kahin, Audrey R., and George McT. *Subversion as Foreign Policy: The Secret Eisenhower and Dulles Debacle in Indonesia.* New York: The New Press, 1995.
64	Kingseed, Cole C. *Eisenhower and the Suez Crisis of 1956.* Baton Rouge and London: Louisiana State University Press, 1995.
65	Kinnard, Douglas. *Eisenhower: Soldier-Statesman of the American Century.* Washington D.C.: Brasseys's Inc., 2002.
66	Knorr, Lawrence. *The Relations of Dwight D Eisenhower: His Pennsylvania German Roots.* Camp Hill, PA: Sunbury Press, Inc., 2010.

Entry	Citations
67	Korda, Michael. *Ike: An American Hero*. New York, NY: HarperCollins, 2007.
68	Krebs, Ronald R. *Dueling Visions: U.S. Strategy Toward Eastern Europe Under Eisenhower*. College Station, TX: Texas A&M University Press, 2001.
69	Kunz, Diane B. *The Economic Diplomacy of the Suez Crisis*. Chapel Hill: University of North Carolina Press, 1991.
70	Ladino, Robyn Duff. *Desegregating Texas Schools: Eisenhower, Shivers, and the Crisis at Mansfield High*. Austin: University of Texas Press, 1996.
71	Lasby, Clarence G. *Eisenhower's Heart Attack: How Ike Beat Heart Disease and Held on to the Presidency*. Lawrence, Kansas: University Press of Kansas, 1997.
72	Lesch, David W. *Syria and the United States: Eisenhower's Cold War in the Middle East*. Boulder, CO: Westview Press, 1992.
73	Lewis, Catherine M. *Don't Ask What I Shot: How President Eisenhower's Love of Golf Helped Shape 1950s America*. New York: McGraw-Hill, 2007.
74	Loftus, Geoff. *Lead Like Ike: Ten Business Strategies from the CEO of D-Day*. Nashville, TN: Thomas Nelson Publishers, 2010.
75	Medhurst, Martin J. *Dwight D. Eisenhower: Strategic Communicator*. Westport, CT: Greenwood Press, 1993.
76	Medhurst, Martin J., ed. *Eisenhower's War of Words: Rhetoric and Leadership*. East Lansing, MI: Michigan State University Press, 1994.
77	Murray, G. E. Patrick. *Eisenhower Versus Montgomery: The Continuing Debate*. Westport, CN: Praeger, 1996.
78	Nash, Philip. *The Other Missiles of October: Eisenhower, Kennedy, and the Jupiters, 1957-1963*. Chapel Hill, NC: University of North Carolina Press, 1997.
79	Nichols, David A. *A Matter of Justice: Eisenhower and the Beginning of the Civil Rights Revolution*. New York: Simon & Schuster, 2007.
80	Osgood, Kenneth. *Total Cold War: Eisenhower's Secret Propaganda Battle at Home and Abroad*. Lawrence, KS: University Press of Kansas; 2006.
81	Pach, Chester J. Jr. and Elmo Richardson. *The Presidency of Dwight D. Eisenhower*. Lawrence, KS: University Press of Kansas, 1991.
82	Perret, Geoffrey. *Eisenhower*. Holbrook, MA: Adams Media Corporation, 1999.
83	Perry, Mark. *Partners in Command: George Marshall and Dwight Eisenhower in War and Peace*. New York: The Penguin Press, 2007.
84	Peterson, Mark A. *Legislating Together: The White House and Capitol Hill from Eisenhower to Reagan*. Cambridge, MA: Harvard University Press, 1990.
85	Pickett, William B. *Dwight David Eisenhower and American Power*. The American Biographical History Series, Wheeling, IL: Harlan Davidson, 1995.
86	Pickett, William B. *Eisenhower Decides to Run: Presidential Politics and Cold War Strategy*. Chicago, IL: Ivan R. Dee, 2000.
87	Pratico, Dominick. *Eisenhower and Social Security: The Origins of the Disability Program*. San Jose, CA: Writers Club Press, 2001.
88	Pruden, Caroline. *Conditional Partners: Eisenhower, the United Nations, and the Search for a Permanent Peace*. Baton Rouge: Louisiana State University Press, 1998.
89	Roadnight, Andrew. *United States Policy Towards Indonesia in the Truman and Eisenhower Years*. New York, New York: Palgrave Macmillan, 2002.

Entry	Citations
90	Roman, Peter J. *Eisenhower and the Missile Gap.* Ithaca, New York: Cornell University Press, 1995.
91	Rosenberg, Victor. *Soviet-American Relations, 1953-1960: Diplomacy and Cultural Exchange During the Eisenhower Presidency.* Jefferson, NC: McFarland & Company, 2005.
92	Sander, Alfred Dick. *Eisenhower's Executive Office.* Westport, CT: Greenwood Press, 1999.
93	Saulnier, Raymond J. *Constructive Years: The U.S. Economy Under Eisenhower.* Lanham, MD: University Press of America, Inc., 1991.
94	Showalter, Dennis E. (ed.). *Forging the Shield: Eisenhower and National Security for the 21st Century.* Chicago: Imprint Publications, 2005.
95	Sloan, John W. *Eisenhower and the Management of Prosperity.* Lawrence, KS: University Press of Kansas, 1991.
96	Smith, Neal. *Mr. Smith Went to Washington: From Eisenhower to Clinton.* Ames: Iowa State University Press, 1996.
97	Smith, Simon C. ed., *Reassessing Suez 1956: New Perspectives on the Crisis and its Aftermath* Burlington, VT: Ashgate, 2008.
98	Snead, David L. *The Gaither Committee, Eisenhower, and the Cold War.* Columbus, OH: Ohio State University Press, 1999.
99	Sowell David. *Eisenhower and Golf: A President at Play.* Jefferson, NC: McFarland & Company, Inc., Publishers, 2007.
100	Stans, Maurice H. *One of the Presidents' Men: Twenty Years With Eisenhower and Nixon.* Washington: Brassey's, 1995.
101	Statler, Kathryn C. and Andrew L. Johns. *The Eisenhower Administration, the Third World, and the Globalization of the Cold War.* Lanham, MD: Rowman & Littlefield Publishers, Inc., 2006.
102	Stebenne, David L. *Modern Republican: Arthur Larson and the Eisenhower Years.* Bloomington, IN: Indiana University Press, 2006.
103	Takeyh, Ray. *The Origins of the Eisenhower Doctrine: The US, Britain and Nasser's Egypt, 1953-57.* New York: St. Martin's Press, Inc., 2000.
104	Taubman, Philip. *Secret Empire: Eisenhower, the CIA, and the Hidden Story of America's Space Espionage.* New York: Simon & Schuster, 2003.
105	Terzian, Philip. *Architects of Power: Roosevelt, Eisenhower, and the American Century.* New York: Brief Encounters, 2010.
106	Tudda, Chris. *The Truth is Our Weapon: The Rhetorical Diplomacy of Dwight D. Eisenhower and John Foster Dulles.* Baton Rouge: Louisiana State University Press, 2006.
107	van Rijn Guido. *The Truman And Eisenhower Blues: African-American Blues And Gospel Songs, 1945-1960.* New York: Continuum, 2004.
108	Vestal, Theodore M. *The Eisenhower Court and Civil Liberties.* Westport, Conn: Praeger Publishers, 2002.
109	Wagner, Steven. *Eisenhower Republicanism: Pursuing the Middle Way.* DeKalb, IL: Northern Illinois University Press, 2006.
110	Walker, Gregg B. et al, ed. *The Military-Industrial Complex: Eisenhower's Warning Three Decades Later.* New York: Peter Lang Publishing Inc., 1992.
111	Warshaw, Shirley A., ed. *The Eisenhower Legacy: Discussions of Presidential Leadership.* Silver Spring, MD: Bartleby Press, 1992.

Entry	Citations
112	Warshaw, Shirley A., ed. *Reexamining the Eisenhower Presidency*. Westport, Conn: Greenwood Press, 1993.
113	Watson, Robert J. *History of the Office of the Secretary of Defense, Vol. 4: Into the Missile Age, 1956-1960*. Washington D.C.: Historical Office, Office of the Secretary of Defense, 1997.
114	Weidner, William. *Eisenhower & Montgomery at the Falaise Gap*. Xlibris Corporation, 2010.
115	Weintraub, Stanley. *15 Stars: Eisenhower, MacArthur, Marshall: Three Generals Who Saved the American Century*. New York: Free Press, 2007.
116	Wenger, Andreas. *Living with Peril: Eisenhower, Kennedy, and Nuclear Weapons*. Lanham, MD: Rowman & Littlefield Publishers, Inc., 1997.
117	Whiting, Charles. *American Deserter: General Eisenhower and the Execution of Eddie Slovik*. J Whiting Books, 2005 and York, England: Eskdale Publishing, 2005.
118	Wicker, Tom. *Dwight D. Eisenhower*. New York: Times Books, 2002.
119	Williamson, Daniel C. *Separate Agendas: Churchill, Eisenhower, and Anglo-American Relations, 1953-1955*. Lanham, MD: Lexington Books, 2006.
120	Winand, Pascaline. *Eisenhower, Kennedy, and the United States of Europe*. New York: St. Martin's Press, 1993.
121	Wukovits, John. *Eisenhower: A Biography*. New York: Palgrave Macmillan, 2006.
122	Yaqub, Salim. *Containing Arab Nationalism: The Eisenhower Doctrine and the Middle East*. Chapel Hill, NC: The University of North Carolina Press, 2004.

Articles Index

Entry	Citations
123	Abbott, Philip. "Eisenhower, King Utopus, and the Fifties Decade in America." *Presidential Studies Quarterly* 32, no. 1 (Mar, 2002): 7-29.
124	Adamson, Michael R. "Delusions of Development: The Eisenhower Administration and the Foreign Aid Program in Vietnam, 1955-1960." *Journal of American-East Asian Relations* 5, no. 2 (Summer 1996): 157-182.
125	Allen, Craig. "Eisenhower's Congressional Defeat of 1956: Limitations of Television and the GOP." *Presidential Studies Quarterly* 22, no. 1 (Winter, 1992): 57-71.
126	Allen, Craig. "News Conferences on TV: Ike-Age Politics Revisited." *Journalism Quarterly* 70, no. 1 (Spring 1993): 13-25.
127	Ambrose, Stephen E. "Eisenhower." *Miller Center Journal* 4, (January 1997): 11-21.
128	Ambrose, Stephen E. "Eisenhower's Legacy." *Prologue* 22 (Fall 1990): 227-236. Reprinted in vol. 26, (Special 25th Anniversary Issue 1994): 160-167.
129	Ambrose, Stephen E. "U.S. Foreign Policy in the 1950s" *Contemporary Austrian Studies* 3, (January 1995): 12-23.
130	Andrew, John, III. "Cracks in the Consensus: The Rockefeller Brothers Fund Special Studies Project and Eisenhower's America." *Presidential Studies Quarterly* 28, no. 3 (Summer 1998): 535-552.
131	Bacevich, A. J. "The Paradox of Professionalism: Eisenhower, Ridgway, and the Challenge to Civilian Control, 1953-1955." *The Journal of Military History* Vol. 61, No. 2 (Apr., 1997), pp. 303-333.
132	Baucom, Donald R. "Eisenhower and Ballistic Missile Defense The Formative Years, 1944-1961." *Air Power History* 51, no. 4 (Winter 2004): 4-17.
133	Benson, Maxine. "Dwight D. Eisenhower and the West." *Journal of the West* 34, no. 2 (April 1995): 58-65.
134	Bergman, Gerald. "The Influence of Religion on President Eisenhower's Upbringing." *Journal of American & Comparative Cultures* 23, no. 4 (Winter 2000): 89-107.
135	Bergman, Jerry. "Steeped in Religion: President Eisenhower and the Influence of the Jehovah's Witnesses." *Kansas History* 21, no. 3 (September 1998): 148-167.
136	Beschloss, Michael R. "A Tale of Two Presidents." *Wilson Quarterly* 24, no. 1 (Winter 2000): 60-70.
137	Bielakowski, Alexander M. "Eisenhower: The First NATO SACEUR." *War & Society* 22, no. 2 (October 2004): 95-108.
138	Biles, Roger. "Public Housing Policy in the Eisenhower Administration." *Mid America* 81, no. 1 (Winter 1999): 5-25.
139	Birkner, Michael J. "Eisenhower and the Red Menace." *Prologue* 33, no. 3 (September 2001): 196-205.
140	Birkner, Michael J. "'He's My Man': Sherman Adams and New Hampshire's Role in the 'Draft Eisenhower' Movement." *Historical New Hampshire* 58, no. 1 (February 2003): 5-25.
141	Bischof, Günter. "The Collapse of Liberation Rhetoric: The Eisenhower Administration and

	the 1956 Hungarian Crisis." *Hungarian Studies Review* 20, no. 1 (Spring 2006): 51-63.[1]
142	Blumenson, Martin. "Eisenhower Then and Now: Fireside Reflections." *Parameters: US Army War College* 21, no. 2 (June 1991): 22-34.
143	Borhi, László. "Rollback, Liberation, Containment, or Inaction?: U.S. Policy and Eastern Europe in the 1950s." *Journal of Cold War Studies* 1, no. 3 (Fall99 1999): 67-110.
144	Borzutzky, Silvia and David Berger. "Dammed If You Do, Dammed If You Don't: The Eisenhower Administration and the Aswan Dam." *Middle East Journal* 64, no. 1 (Winter 2010): 84-102.
145	Bose, Meena. "Words as Signals: Drafting Cold War Rhetoric in the Eisenhower and Kennedy Administrations." *Congress & the Presidency* 25, no. 1 (Spring 1998): 23-42.
146	Boyle, Peter G. "Eisenhower." *Historian* no. 43 (September 1994): 9-11.
147	Branigar, Thomas. "No Villains- No Heroes: The David Eisenhower-Milton Good Controversy." *Kansas History* 15, no. 3 (September 1992): 168-179.
148	Brinkley, Douglas. "Eisenhower the Dove." *American Heritage* 52, no. 6 (September 2001): 58-65.
149	Brinkley, Douglas. "The United States in the Truman and Eisenhower Years." *European Contributions to American Studies* 42, (January 1999): 15-29.
150	Broadwater, Jeff. "President Eisenhower and the Historians: Is the General in Retreat?" *Canadian Review of American Studies* 22, no. 1 (June 1991): 47-60.
151	Brogi, Alessandro. "Ike and Italy: The Eisenhower Administration and Italy's 'Neo-Atlanticist' Agenda." *Journal of Cold War Studies* 4, no. 3 (Summer 2002): 5-35.
152	Bromley, D. Allan. "Science and Technology: from Eisenhower to Bush." *Presidential Studies Quarterly* 21, no. 2 (1991): 243-250.
153	Brown, Roger G. and Carolyn R. Thompson. "Management of Political Functions in the Eisenhower White House: An Organizational Perspective." *Presidential Studies Quarterly* 24, no. 2 (Spring 1994): 299-307.
154	Brownell, Herbert. "Eisenhower's Civil Rights Program: A Personal Assessment." *Presidential Studies Quarterly* XXI, no. 2 (Spring 1991): 235-242.
155	Burr, William. "Avoiding the Slippery Slope: The Eisenhower Administration and the Berlin Crisis, November 1958 - January 1959." *Diplomatic History* 18, no. 2 (Spring 1994): 177-205.
156	Carletta, David M. "'Those White Guys are Working For Me': Dizzy Gillespie, Jazz, and the Cultural Politics of the Cold War During the Eisenhower Administration." *International Social Science Review* 82, no. 3/4 (June 2007): 115-134.
157	Carroll, Robert C. "The Making of a Leader: Dwight D. Eisenhower." *Military Review* 89, no. 1 (Jan- Feb 2009): 77-85.
158	Carter, Donald Alan. "Eisenhower Versus the Generals." *The Journal of Military History*, Vol. 71, No. 4 (Oct., 2007), pp. 1169-1199.
159	Catsam, Derek. "The Civil Rights Movement and the Presidency in the Hot Years of the Cold War: A Historical and Historiographical Assessment." *History Compass* 6, no. 1 (January 2008): 314-344.
160	Chang, Su-Ya. "Unleashing Chiang Kai-Shek? Eisenhower and the Policy of Indecision Toward Taiwan, 1953." *Bulletin of the Institute of Modern History, Academia Sinica*

---

[1] Originally had the year of this article as 1993 but copy of article says 2006. There is footnote on title but no corresponding info to that footnote.

	(Zhongyang Yanjiuyuan Xiandaishi Yanjiusuo Jikan) 20, (January 1991): 369-401.
161	Charnock, Emily Jane, James A. McCann, and Kathryn Dunn Tenpas. "Presidential Travel From Eisenhower to George W. Bush: An 'Electoral College' Strategy." *Political Science Quarterly* 124, no. 2 (Summer 2009). : 323-339.
162	Chernus, Ira. "Eisenhower's Ideology in World War II." *Armed Forces and Society* 23, no. 4 (Summer 1997): 595-613.
163	Chernus, Ira. "Operation Candor: Fear, Faith, and Flexibility." *Diplomatic History* 29, no. 5 (November 2005): 779-809.
164	Cizel, Annick. "The Eisenhower Administration and Africa: Racial Integration and the United States Foreign Service." *Annales du Monde Anglophone* no. 1 (1995): 21-38.
165	Clayman, Steven E. and John Heritage. "Questioning Presidents: Journalistic Deference and Adversarialness in the Press Conferences of U.S. Presidents Eisenhower and Reagan." *Journal of Communication* 52, no. 4 (Dec, 2002): 749-775.
166	Coleman, David G. "Eisenhower and the Berlin Problem, 1953-1954." *Journal of Cold War Studies* 2, no. 1 (Winter 2000): 3-34.
167	Collier, Ken. "Eisenhower and Congress: The Autopilot Presidency." *Presidential Studies Quarterly* 24, no. 2 (Spring 1994): 309-325.
168	Conley, Richard S. and Richard M. Yon. "The 'Hidden Hand' and White House Roll-Call Predictions: Legislative Liaison in the Eisenhower White House, 83d-84th Congresses." *Presidential Studies Quarterly* 37, no. 2 (June 2007). : 291-312.
169	Cook, Kevin L. "Ike's Road Trip." *MHQ: Quarterly Journal of Military History* 13, no. 3 (Spring 2001): 68-74.
170	Cornfield, Michael. "The 'First Rough Draft'? Reflections on Presidential Politics, Journalism and History." *Film & History* 21, no. 2/3 (May/September 1991): 77-82.
171	Cuddy, Edward. "Vietnam: Mr. Johnson's War - Or Mr. Eisenhower's?" *Review of Politics* 65, no. 4 (Autumn 2003): 351-374.
172	Damms, Richard V. "Containing the Military-Industrial-Congressional Complex: President Eisenhower's Science Advisers and the Case of the Nuclear-Powered Aircraft." *Essays in Economic & Business History* 14, (March 1996): 279-289.
173	Damms, Richard V. "James Killian, the Technological Capabilities Panel, and the Emergence of President Eisenhower's 'Scientific-Technological Elite'." *Diplomatic History* 24, no. 1 (Winter 2000): 57-78.
174	Daniel, Douglass K. "They Liked Ike: Pro-Eisenhower Publishers and His Decision to Run for President." *Journalism & Mass Communication Quarterly* 77, no. 2 (Summer 2000): 393-404.
175	Dockrill, Saki. "Cooperation and Suspicion: The United States' Alliance Diplomacy for the Security of Western Europe, 1953-54." *Diplomacy & Statecraft* 5, no. 1 (March 1994): 138-182.
176	Dockrill, Saki. "Eisenhower's New Look: A Maximum Deterrent at a Bearable Cost? A Reappraisal." *Storia delle Relazioni Internazionali* 13, no. 1 (January 1998): 11-25.
177	Duchin, Brian R. "The 'Agonizing Reappraisal': Eisenhower, Dulles, and the European Defense Community." *Diplomatic History* 16, no. 2 (April 1992): 201-221.
178	Duchin, Brian R. "'The Most Spectacular Legislative Battle of That Year:' President Eisenhower and the 1958 Reorganization of the Department of Defense." *Presidential Studies Quarterly* 24, no. 2 (Spring 1994): 243-262.
179	Eliades, George C. "Once More unto the Breach: Eisenhower, Dulles, and Public Opinion

15

	During the Offshore Islands Crisis of 1958." *Journal of American-East Asian Relations* 2, no. 4 (Winter 1993): 343-367.
180	Evans, Tony. "Hegemony, Domestic Politics, and the Project of Universal Human Rights." *Diplomacy & Statecraft* 6, no. 3 (September 1995): 616-644.
181	Ewald, William Bragg Jr. "Ike's First Move." *New York Times Magazine* (November 14, 1993): 57.
182	Foot, Rosemary. "The Eisenhower Administration's Fear of Empowering the Chinese." *Political Science Quarterly* 111, no. 3 (Autumn 1996): 505-521.
183	Førland, Tor Egil. "Eisenhower, Export Controls, and the Parochialism of Historians of American Foreign Relations." *Newsletter of the Society for Historians of American Foreign Relations* 24, no. 4 (September 1993): 4-17.
184	Førland, Tor Egil. "Eisenhower, Export Controls, and the Perils of Diplomatic History: A Reply to Spaulding." *Newsletter of the Society for Historians of American Foreign Relations* 25, no. 3 (June 1994): 9-22.
185	Førland, Tor Egil. "'Selling Firearms to the Indians': Eisenhower's Export Control Policy, 1953-54." *Diplomatic History* 15, no. 2 (April 1991): 221-244.
186	Forsberg, Aaron. "Eisenhower and Japanese Economic Recovery: The Politics of Integration with the Western Trading Bloc, 1952-1955." *Journal of American-East Asian Relations* 5, no. 1 (Spring 1996): 57-75.
187	Foyle, Douglas C. "Public Opinion and Foreign Policy: Elite Beliefs as a Mediating Variable." *International Studies Quarterly* 41, no. 1 (March 1997): 141-169.
188	Fraser, Cary. "Crossing the Color Line in Little Rock: The Eisenhower Administration and the Dilemma of Race for U.S. Foreign Policy." *Diplomatic History* 24, no. 2 (Spring 2000): 233-264.
189	Friman, H. Richard. "The Eisenhower Administration and the Demise of GATT: Dancing with Pandora." *American Journal of Economics and Sociology* 53, no. 3 (Jul, 1994): 257-272.
190	Gaskin, Thomas M. "Senator Lyndon B. Johnson, the Eisenhower Administration and U.S. Foreign Policy, 1957-60." *Presidential Studies Quarterly* 24, no. 2 (Spring 1994): 341-361.
191	Goar, Dudley C. "A Chance for Peace? The Eisenhower Administration and the Soviet Peace Offensive of 1953." *Mid America* 76, no. 3 (Fall 1994): 241-278.
192	Goldhamer, Joan D. "General Eisenhower in Academe: A Clash of Perspectives and a Study Suppressed." *Journal of the History of the Behavioral Sciences* 33, no. 3 (Summer 1997): 241-259.
193	Grant, Philip A. Jr. "The Presidential Election of 1952 in Tennessee." *West Tennessee Historical Society Papers* 48, (January 1994): 73-80.
194	Greenberg, Paul. "Eisenhower Draws the Racial Battle Lines with Orval Faubus." *The Journal of Blacks in Higher Education*, 18 (Winter, 1997-1998): 120-121.
195	Greenstein, Fred I. "Colin Powell's *American Journey* and the Eisenhower Precedent: A Review Essay." *Political Science Quarterly* 110, no. 4 (1995): 625-629.
196	Greenstein, Fred I. "Pursuing Eisenhower's Hidden Hand in the Princeton Archives." *Princeton University Library Chronicle* 67, no. 1 (Fall 2005): 114-124.
197	Greenstein, Fred I. "Taking Account of Individuals in International Political Psychology: Eisenhower, Kennedy and Indochina." *Political Psychology* 15, no. 1 (Mar, 1994): 61-74.
198	Greenstein, Fred. "The Hidden-Hand Presidency: Eisenhower as Leader, a 1994 Perspective." *Presidential Studies Quarterly* 24, no. 2 (Spring 1994): 233-241.
199	Greenstein, Fred I. "The President Who Led by Seeming Not to: A Centennial View of

	Dwight Eisenhower. *The Antioch Review*, 49, no. 1 (Winter, 1991): 39-44.
200	Greenstein, Fred I. and Richard H. Immerman. "Effective National Security Advising: Recovering the Eisenhower Legacy," *Political Science Quarterly*, Vol. 115, No. 3 (Autumn, 2000), pp. 335-345.
201	Greenstein, Fred I., and Immerman, Richard H. "What Did Eisenhower Tell Kennedy about Indochina? The Politics of Misperception." *The Journal of American History* 79, no. 2 (Sept, 1992): 568-587.
202	Griffin, Charles J. G. "New Light on Eisenhower's Farewell Address." *Presidential Studies Quarterly* 22, no. 3 (Summer, 1992): 469-479.
203	Guth, David W. "Ike's Red Scare: The Harry Dexter White Crisis." *American Journalism* 13, no. 2 (Spring 1996): 157-175.
204	Haight, David. "Ike and his Spies in the Sky." *Prologue* 41, no. 4 (Winter 2009): 14-22.
205	Hale, Frederick. "Challenging the Swedish Social Welfare State: The Case of Dwight David Eisenhower." *Swedish-American Historical Quarterly* 54, no. 1 (January 2003): 55-71.
206	Hall, R. Cargill. "Denied Territory: Eisenhower's Policy of Peacetime Aerial Overflight." *Air Power History* 56, no. 4 (Winter 2009): 4-9.
207	Hall, R. Cargill. "The Eisenhower Administration and the Cold War: Framing American Astronautics to Serve National Security." *Prologue* 27, no. 1 (Spring 1995): 58-72.
208	Hall, R. Cargill. "Sputnik, Eisenhower, and the Formation of the United States Space Program." *Quest: History of Spaceflight* 14, no. 4 (October 2007): 32-39.
209	Hahn, Peter L. "Securing the Middle East: The Eisenhower Doctrine of 1957." *Presidential Studies Quarterly* 36, no. 1 (Mar, 2006): 38-47.
210	Harris, Douglas B. "Dwight Eisenhower and the New Deal: The Politics of Preemption." *Presidential Studies Quarterly* 27, no. 2 (Spring, 1997): 333-342.
211	Hart, John. "Eisenhower & the Swelling of the Presidency," *Polity*, Vol. 24, No. 4 (Summer, 1992), pp. 673-691.
212	Hartung, William D. "Eisenhower's Warning: the Military-Industrial Complex Forty Years Later," *World Policy Journal*, 18, no. 1 (Spring, 2001): 39-44.
213	Heller, Francis H. "The Eisenhower White House." *Presidential Studies Quarterly* 23, no. 3 (1993): 509-517.
214	Hoff, Samuel B. "The President's Removal Power: Eisenhower and the War Claims Commission Controversy." *Congress & the Presidency* 18, no. 1 (Spring 1991): 37-54.
215	Hopkins, Robert S., III. "An Expanded Understanding of Eisenhower, American Policy and Overflights." *Intelligence and National Security* 11, no. 2 (Apr, 1996): 332-344.
216	Hoxie, R. Gordon. "Eisenhower and 'My Scientists'." *National Forum* 71, no. 4 (Fall 1990): 9-12.
217	Ingimundarson, Valur. "Containing the Offensive: The 'Chief of the Cold War' and the Eisenhower Administration's German Policy." *Presidential Studies Quarterly* 27, no. 3 (Summer 1997): 480-495.
218	Ingimundarson, Valur. "The Eisenhower Administration, the Adenauer Government, and the Political Uses of the East German Uprising in 1953." *Diplomatic History* 20, no. 3 (Summer 1996): 381-409.
219	Irish, Kerry E. "Apt Pupil: Dwight Eisenhower and the 1930 Industrial Mobilization Plan." *The Journal of Military History*, 70, No. 1 (Jan., 2006): 31-61.
220	Irish, Kerry E. "Dwight Eisenhower and Douglas MacArthur in the Philippines: There Must

	Be a Day of Reckoning." *Journal of Military History* 74, no. 2 (2010): 439-473.
221	Irish, Kerry E. "Hometown Support in the Midst of War: Dwight Eisenhower's Wartime Correspondence with Abilene Friends." *Kansas History* 25, no. 1 (Spring 2002): 14-37.
222	Jackson, Ian. "'The Limits of International Leadership': The Eisenhower Administration, East-West Trade and the Cold War, 1953-54." *Diplomacy & Statecraft* 11, no. 3 (November 2000): 113-138.
223	Jackson, Michael Gordon. "Beyond Brinkmanship: Eisenhower, Nuclear War Fighting, and Korea, 1953-1968." *Presidential Studies Quarterly* 35, no. 1 (Mar, 2005): 52-75.
224	Jacobs, Matt. "Unforeseen Consequences: The Eisenhower Administration and Fidel Castro's Revolutionary Nationalism in Cuba, 1959-1961." *Journal of the North Carolina Association of Historians* 17, (April 2009): 53-80.
225	Jacobs, Seth. "'A Monumental Struggle of Good Versus Evil': American Crusaders in Vietnam and Iraq." *New England Journal of History* 64, no. 1 (Fall 2007): 214-232.
226	Jacobs, Travis Beal. "Eisenhower, the American Assembly, and 1952." *Presidential Studies Quarterly* 22, no. 3 (Summer, 1992): 455-468.
227	Kahn, Michael A. "Shattering the Myth About President Eisenhower's Supreme Court Appointments." *Presidential Studies Quarterly* 22, no. 1 (Winter 1992): 47-56.
228	Kengor, Paul. "Comparing Presidents Reagan and Eisenhower." *Presidential Studies Quarterly* 28, no. 2 (Spring 1998): 366-393.
229	Khrushchev, Sergei. "The Cold War Through the Looking Glass." *American Heritage* 50, no. 6 (October 1999): 34-50.
230	King, James D., and James W. Riddlespeger, Jr. "Presidential Leadership of Congressional Civil Rights Voting: The Cases of Eisenhower and Johnson." *Policy Studies Journal* 21, no. 3 (September 1993): 544-555.
231	Kingseed, Cole C. "Dark Days of White Knights." *Military Review* 73, no. 1 (January 1993): 67-75.
232	Kingseed, Cole C. "Eisenhower's Prewar Anonymity: Myth or Reality?" *Parameters: US Army War College* 21, no. 3 (Autumn 1991): 87-98.
233	Kingseed, Cole C. "'Ike' Takes Charge." *Military Review* 72, no. 6 (June 1992): 73-76.
234	Kingseed, Cole C. "The Juggler and the Supreme Commander." *Military Review* 76, no. 6 (November 1996): 77-82.
235	Kingseed, Cole C. "Victory in Europe." *Military Review* 75, no. 3 (May 1995): 92-94.
236	Korda, Michael. "Ike at D-Day." *Smithsonian* 38, no. 9 (December 2007): 48-58.
237	Krebs, Ronald R. "Liberation à la Finland: Reexamining Eisenhower Administration Objectives in Eastern Europe." *Journal of Strategic Studies* Vol. 20 Issue 3 (Sep. 1997): 1-26.
238	LaFantasie, Glenn. "Monty and Ike Take Gettysburg." *MHQ: The Quarterly Journal of Military History*, vol. 8 (Autumn 1995): 67-73.
239	Launius, Roger D. "Eisenhower, Sputnik, and the Creation of NASA." *Prologue* 28, no. 2 (Summer 1996): 126-143.
240	Larres, Klaus. "Eisenhower and the First Forty Days after Stalin's Death: The Incompatibility of Détente and Political Warfare." *Diplomacy and Statecraft* 6, no. 2 (July, 1995): 431-469.
241	Larson, George A. "General Eisenhower's Modified B-25J Used During World War II." *American Aviation Historical Society Journal* 49, no. 1 (Spring 2004): 66-70.
242	Layton, Azza Salama. "International Pressure and the U.S. Government's Response to Little Rock." *Arkansas Historical Quarterly* 66, no. 2 (Summer 2007): 243-257.

243	Lesch, David W. "When the Relationship Went Sour: Syria and the Eisenhower Administration." *Presidential Studies Quarterly* 28, no. 1 (Winter 1998): 92-107.
244	Lehman, Kenneth. "Revolutions and Attributions: Making Sense of Eisenhower Administration Policies in Bolivia and Guatemala." *Diplomatic History* 21, no. 2 (Spring 1997): 185- 213.
245	Little, Douglas. "His Finest Hour?: Eisenhower, Lebanon, and the 1958 Middle East Crisis." *Diplomatic History* 20, no. 1 (1996): 27-54.
246	Little, Douglas. "The Making of a Special Relationship: The United States and Israel, 1957-68." *International Journal of Middle East Studies* 25, no. 4 (November 1993): 563-585.
247	Loayza, Matthew. "An 'Aladdin's Lamp' for Free Enterprise: Eisenhower, Fiscal Conservatism, and Latin American Nationalism, 1953-61." *Diplomacy & Statecraft* 14, no. 3 (September 2003): 83-105.
248	Lombardo, Johannes R. "Eisenhower, The British and the Security of Hong Kong, 1953-60." *Diplomacy & Statecraft* 9, no. 3 (November 1998): 134-153.
249	MacKenzie, S. P. "Essay and Reflection: On the 'Other Losses' Debate." *International History Review* 14, no. 4 (December 1992): 717-731.
250	Maddock, Shane. "The Fourth Country Problem: Eisenhower's Nuclear Nonproliferation Policy." *Presidential Studies Quarterly* 28, no. 3 (Summer, 1998): 553-572.
251	Maranto, Robert. "The Administrative Strategies of Republican Presidents from Eisenhower to Reagan." *Presidential Studies Quarterly* 23, no. 4 (Fall, 1993): 683-697.
252	Marchio, Jim. "Resistance Potential and Rollback: US Intelligence and the Eisenhower Administration's Policies Toward Eastern Europe, 1953-56." *Intelligence & National Security* 10, no. 2 (April 1995): 219-241.
253	Marchio, James. "The Planning Coordination Group: Bureaucratic Casualty in the Cold War Campaign to Exploit Soviet-Bloc Vulnerabilities." *Journal of Cold War Studies* 4, no. 4 (Fall 2002): 3-28.
254	Marsh, Steven. "Continuity and Change: Reinterpreting the Policies of the Truman and Eisenhower Administrations toward Iran, 1950–1954." *Journal of Cold War Studies* 7, no. 3 (Summer 2005): 79-123.
255	Marsh, Steve. "The United States, Iran and Operation 'Ajax': Inverting Interpretative Orthodoxy." *Middle Eastern Studies* 39, no. 3 (July 2003): 1-38.
256	Marston, Adrian. "Did President Eisenhower Have Crohn's Disease?" *Journal of Medical Biography* 10, no. 4 (November 2002): 237-239.
257	Martin, Don T. "Eisenhower and the Politics of Federal Aid to Education: The Watershed Years, 1953-1961." *Journal of the Midwest History of Education Society* 25, no. 1 (January 1998): 7-12.
258	Mayer, Michael S. "The Eisenhower Administration and the Desegregation of Washington, D.C." *Journal of Policy History* 3, no. 1 (January 1991): 24-41.
259	McCoy, Donald R. "Eisenhower and Truman: Their Flawed Relationship." *Midwest Quarterly* 34, no. 1 (September 1992): 30-41.
260	McIntosh, David. "In the Shadow of Giants: U.S. Policy Toward Small Nations: The Cases of Lebanon, Costa Rica, and Austria in the Eisenhower Years." *Contemporary Austrian Studies* 4, (January 1996): 222-279.
261	McManus, James. "Presidential Poker." *American History* 45, no. 1 (April 2010): 46-51.
262	Medhurst, Martin J. "Atoms for Peace and Nuclear Hegemony: The Rhetorical Structure of a Cold War Campaign." *Armed Forces & Society* 23, no. 4 (Summer 1997): 571-593.

263	Medhurst, Martin J. "Eisenhower and the Crusade for Freedom: The Rhetorical Origins of a Cold War Campaign." *Presidential Studies Quarterly* 27, no. 4 (Fall 1997): 646-661.
264	Medhurst, Martin J. "Reconceptualizing Rhetorical History: Eisenhower's Farewell Address." *Quarterly Journal of Speech* 80, no. 2 (May 1994): 195-218.
265	Medhurst, Martin J. "Robert L. Scott plays Dwight D. Eisenhower." *Quarterly Journal of Speech* 81, no. 4 (November 1995): 502-506.
266	Medhurst, Martin J. "Text and Context in the 1952 Presidential Campaign: Eisenhower's 'I Shall Go to Korea' Speech." *Presidential Studies Quarterly* 30, no. 3 (Sep, 2000): 464-484.
267	Melissen, Jan. "The Politics of US Missile Deployment in Britain, 1955-59." *Storia delle Relazioni Internazionali* 13, no. 1 (1998): 151-185.
268	Metz, Steven. "Eisenhower and the Planning of American Grand Strategy." *Journal of Strategic Studies* 14, no. 1 (February 1991): 49-71.
269	Miller, William Lee. "Two Moralities." *Miller Center Journal* 2, (January 1995): 19-39.
270	Millett, Allan R. "Dwight D. Eisenhower and the Korean War: Cautionary Tale and Hopeful Precedent." *Journal of American-East Asian Relations* 10, no. 3/4 (Fall-Winter 2001): 155-174.
271	Milum, Betty. "Eisenhower, ALA, and the Selection of L. Quincy Mumford." *Libraries & Culture*, 30, No. 1 (Winter, 1995): 26-56.
272	Moores, Simon. "'Neutral on our Side': US Policy towards Sweden during the Eisenhower Administration." *Cold War History* 2, no. 3 (April 2002): 29-62.
273	Morgan, Thomas. "The Making of a General: Ike, the Tank, and the Interwar Years." *On Point: The Journal of Army History* 9, no. 2 (March 2003): 11-15.
274	Morris, Kenneth E. and Barry Schwartz, "Why They liked Ike: Tradition, Crisis, and Heroic Leadership, *The Sociological Quarterly*, 34, no. 1 (Spring, 1993): 133-151.
275	Morrison, Robert. "Faith Fights Communism: The United States and Islam in Saudi Arabia During the Cold War." *Journal of the North Carolina Association of Historians* 17, (April 2009): 81-113.
276	Nadaner, Jeffrey M. "Strife Among Friends and Foes: The 1958 Anglo-American Military Interventions in the Middle East." *UCLA Historical Journal* 17, (January 1997): 82-123.
277	Nash, Philip. "Jumping Jupiters: The US Search for IRBM Host Countries in NATO, 1957-59." *Diplomacy & Statecraft* 6, no. 3 (November 1995): 753-786.
278	Nichols, David A. "'The Showpiece of Our Nation': Dwight D. Eisenhower and the Desegregation of the District of Columbia." *Washington History* 16, no. 2, (Fall/Winter, 2004/2005): 44-65.
279	Nolan, Cathal J. "The Last Hurrah of Conservative Isolationism: Eisenhower, Congress, and the Bricker Amendment." *Presidential Studies Quarterly* 22, no. 2 (Spring 1992): 337-349.
280	Norpoth, Helmut. "From Eisenhower to Bush: Perceptions of Candidates and Parties." *Electoral Studies* 28, no. 4 (Dec, 2009): 523-532.
281	Nwaubani, Ebere. "Eisenhower, Nkrumah and the Congo Crisis." *Journal of Contemporary History* 36, no. 4 (Oct, 2001): 599-622.
282	O'Reilly, Kenneth. "Racial Integration: The Battle General Eisenhower Chose Not to Fight." *The Journal of Blacks in Higher Education*, No. 18 (Winter, 1997/1998): 110-119.
283	Osgood, Kenneth A. "Form before Substance: Eisenhower's Commitment to Psychological Warfare and Negotiations with the Enemy." *Diplomatic History* 24, no. 3 (Summer 2000): 405-433.

284	Parker, Jason. "Cold War II: The Eisenhower Administration, the Bandung Conference, and the Reperiodization of the Postwar Era." *Diplomatic History* 30, no. 5 (Nov, 2006): 867-892.
285	Parker IV, Jerome H. "Fox Conner and Dwight Eisenhower: Mentoring and Application." *Military Review* 85, no. 4 (July 2005): 92-95.
286	Parry-Giles, Shawn J. "'Camouflaged' Propaganda: The Truman and Eisenhower Administrations' Covert Manipulation of News." *Western Journal of Communication* 60, no. 2 (Spring 1996): 146-167.
287	Parry-Giles, Shawn J. "The Eisenhower Administration's Conceptualization of the USIA: The Development of Overt and Covert Propaganda Strategies." *Presidential Studies Quarterly* 24, no. 2 (Spring 1994): 263-276.
288	Patterson, Bradley H., Jr. "Teams and Staff: Dwight Eisenhower's Innovations in the Structure and Operations of the Modern White House. *Presidential Studies Quarterly* 24, no. 2 (Spring 1994): 277-298.
289	Payne, Rodger A. "Public Opinion and Foreign Threats: Eisenhower's Response to Sputnik." *Armed Forces and Society* 21, no. 1 (Fall 1994): 89-112.
290	Pedaliu, Effie G. H. "Truman, Eisenhower and the Mediterranean Cold War, 1947-57." *Maghreb Review* 31, no. 1/2 (2006): 2-20.
291	Perret, Geoffrey. "Ike the Pilot" *MHQ: Quarterly Journal of Military History* 12, no. 2 (Winter 2000): 70-78.
292	Pfeiffer, David A. "Ike's Interstates at 50." *Prologue* 38, no. 2 (Summer 2006): 13-19.
293	Pharo, Per F. I. "Revising Eisenhower Revisionism?" *Newsletter of the Society for Historians of American Foreign Relations* 30, no. 4 (September 1999): 18-22.
294	Pickett, William. "Eisenhower, Clausewitz, and American Power." *Newsletter of the Society for Historians of American Foreign Relations* 22, no. 4 (September 1991): 28-40.
295	Prados, John. "Ike, Ridgway, and Dien Bien Phu." *MHQ: Quarterly Journal of Military History* 17, no. 4 (Summer 2005): 16-23.
296	Price, Kevin S. "The Partisan Legacies of Preemptive Leadership: Assessing the Eisenhower Cohorts in the U.S. House." *Political Research Quarterly* 55, no. 3 (Sep, 2002): 609-631.
297	Rabe, Stephen G. "Eisenhower Revisionism: A Decade of Scholarship." *Diplomatic History* 17, no. 1 (January 1993): 97-115.
298	Rempe, Dennis M. "An American Trojan Horse? Eisenhower, Latin America and the Development of US Internal Security Policy 1954-196 0." *Small Wars & Insurgencies* 10, no. 1 (Spring 1999): 34-64.
299	Roman, Peter J. "Eisenhower and Ballistic Missiles Arms Control 1957-1960: A Missed Opportunity?" *Journal of Strategic Studies* 19, no. 3 (Sep, 1996): 365-380.
300	Rosenau, William. "The Eisenhower Administration, US Foreign Internal Security Assistance, and the Struggle for the Developing World, 1954-1961." *Low Intensity Conflict and Law Enforcement* 10, no. 3 (Autumn 2001): 1-32.
301	Rottinghaus, Brandon. "Rethinking Presidential Responsiveness: The Public Presidency and Rhetorical Congruency, 1953–2001." *Journal of Politics* 68, no. 3 (August 2006): 720-732.
302	Ruddy, T. Michael. "U.S. Foreign Policy, the 'Third Force,' and European Union: Eisenhower and Europe's Neutrals." *Midwest Quarterly* 42, no. 1 (September 2000): 67-80.
303	Saeki, Chizuru. "The Cancellation of Eisenhower's Visit to Japan and the U.S.-Japan Centennial Festival of 1960." *New England Journal of History* 63, no. 2 (Spring 2007): 1-14.
304	Saulnier, Raymond J. "Recollections of a 1948 Visit with General Eisenhower." *Presidential Studies Quarterly* 24, no. 4 (Fall, 1994). 865-867.

305	Schapsmeier, Edward. L. and Frederick. H. Schapsmeier. "Eisenhower and Agricultural Reform: Ike's Farm Policy Appraised." *American Journal of Economics and Sociology* 51, no. 2 (April 1992): 147-159.
306	Scheele, Henry Z. "President Dwight D. Eisenhower and the U.S. House Leader Charles A. Halleck: An Examination of an Executive-Legislative Relationship." *Presidential Studies Quarterly* 23, no. 2 (Spring 1993): 289-299.
307	Schlesinger, Arthur Jr. "Effective National Security Advising: A Most Dubious Precedent." *Political Science Quarterly* 115, no. 3 (Fall 2000): 347-351.
308	Scott, George W. "The Culmination of the Great Columbia Power War: The CVA, Governor Arthur B. Langlie and Eisenhower's 'Partnership.'" *Journal of the West* 44, no. 1 (Winter 2005): 27-37.
309	Scott, Robert L. "Eisenhower's Farewell Address: Response to Medhurst." *Quarterly Journal of Speech* 81, no. 4 (November 1995): 496-501.
310	Scowcroft, Brent. "Eisenhower and a Foreign Policy Agenda." *Presidential Studies Quarterly* 22, no. 3 (Summer 1992): 451-454.
311	Secrest, Clark. "The Picture that Reassured the World." *Colorado Heritage* (Winter 1996): 31-35.
312	Sewell, Bevan. "A Perfect (Free-Market) World? Economics, the Eisenhower Administration, and the Soviet Economic Offensive in Latin America." *Diplomatic History* 32, no. 5 (Nov, 2008): 841-868.
313	Sewell, Bevan. "The Problems of Public Relations: Eisenhower, Latin America and the Potential Lessons for the Bush Administration." *Comparative American Studies* 6, no. 3 (September 2008): 295-312.
314	Smith-Norris, Martha. "The Eisenhower Administration and the Nuclear Test Ban Talks, 1958–1960: Another Challenge to 'Revisionism'." *Diplomatic History* 27, no. 4 (September 2003): 503-541.
315	Spaulding, Robert Mark Jr. "'A Gradual and Moderate Relaxation': Eisenhower and the Revision of American Export Control Policy, 1953-1955." *Diplomatic History* 17, no. 2 (April 1993): 223-249.
316	Spaulding, Robert Mark. "Eisenhower and Export Controls Revisited: A Reply to Førland." *Newsletter of the Society for Historians of American Foreign Relations* 25, no. 1 (January 1994): 9-16.
317	Spaulding, Robert Mark. "Once Again- Eisenhower and Export Controls: A Reply to Tor Forland." *Newsletter of the Society for Historians of American Foreign Relations* 25, no. 4 (September 1994): 36-40.
318	Spiliotes, Constantine J. "Conditional Partisanship and Institutional Responsibility in Presidential Decision Making." *Presidential Studies Quarterly* 30, no. 3 (September 2000): 485-513.
319	Stern, Mark. "Eisenhower and Kennedy: A Comparison of Confrontations at Little Rock and Ole Miss." *Policy Studies Journal* 21, no. 3 (Autumn 1993): 575-588.
320	Strong, Robert A. "Eisenhower, Reagan, and Escaping the Dilemmas of Deterrence." *White House Studies* 4, no. 1 (January 2004): 19-29.
321	Suri, Jeremi. "America's Search for a Technological Solution to the Arms Race: The Surprise Attack Conference of 1958 and a Challenge for 'Eisenhower Revisionists'." *Diplomatic History* 21, no. 3 (Summer 1997): 417- 451.
322	Sylvester, John A. "Taft, Dulles and Ike: New Faces for 1952." *Mid America* 76, no. 2

	(Sprng/Summer 1994): 157-179.
323	Tal, David. "Eisenhower's Disarmament Dilemma: From Chance for Peace to Open Skies Proposal." *Diplomacy and Statecraft* 12, no. 2 (June 2001): 175-196.
324	Thompson, Robert J. "Contrasting Models of White House Staff Organization: The Eisenhower, Ford, and Carter Experiences." *Congress & the Presidency* 19, no. 2 (Autumn 1992): 113-137.
325	Trace, Howard. "In Public and Behind Closed Doors: President Eisenhower and 'Sputnik'." *Quest: History of Spaceflight* 14, no. 4 (October 2007): 46-51.
326	Tudda, Chris. "'Reenacting the Story of Tantalus': Eisenhower, Dulles, and the Failed Rhetoric of Liberation." *Journal of Cold War Studies* 7, no. 4 (Fall 2005): 3-35.
327	Walcott, Charles and Karen Hult. "White House Organization as a Problem of Governance: The Eisenhower System." *Presidential Studies Quarterly* 24, no. 2 (Spring 1994): 327-339.
328	Warner, Geoffrey. "Eisenhower and Castro: US-Cuban Relations, 1958-60." *International Affairs* [London] 75, no. 4 (October 1999): 803-817.
329	Weatherford, M. Stephen. "Presidential Leadership and Ideological Consistency: Were There 'Two Eisenhowers' in Economic Policy?" *Studies in American Political Development* 16, no. 2 (Fall 2002): 111-137.
330	Wells, Wyatt. "Public Power in the Eisenhower Administration." *Journal of Policy History* 20, no. 2 (April 2008): 227-262.
331	Wenger, Andreas. "Eisenhower, Kennedy, and the Missile Gap: Determinants of US Military Expenditure in the Wake of the Sputnik Shock." *Defense and Peace Economics* 8, no. 1 (1997): 77-100.
332	Williamson, Daniel C. "Understandable Failure: The Eisenhower Administration's Strategic Goals in Iraq, 1953-1958." *Diplomacy and Statecraft* 17, no. 3 (September 2006): 597-615.
333	Wilson, Hugh A. "President Eisenhower and the Development of Active Labor Market Policy in the United States: A Revisionist View." *Presidential Studies Quarterly* 39, no. 3 (September 2009): 519-548.
334	Yaqub, Salim. "Imperious Doctrines: U.S.–Arab Relations from Dwight D. Eisenhower to George W. Bush." *Diplomatic History* 26, no. 4 (Fall 2002): 571-591.
335	Young, Jeffrey R. "Eisenhower's Federal Judges and Civil Rights Policy: A Republican 'Southern Strategy' for the 1950s." *Georgia Historical Quarterly* 78, no. 3 (Fall 1994): 536-565.
336	Zachariou, Stelios. "The Road to the Garrison State: An Overview of Greek-American Relations During the Eisenhower and Kennedy Administrations (1952-1963)." *Modern Greek Studies Yearbook* 14, (January 1998): 241-260.
337	Zhai, Qiang. "Crisis and Confrontations: Chinese-American Relations During the Eisenhower Administration." *Journal of American-East Asian Relations* 9, no. 3/4 (September 2000): 221-249.

Book Annotations

A's

1.   Aldous, Richard. *Macmillan, Eisenhower, and the Cold War*. Dublin, Ireland: Four
      Courts Press, 2005.

Author Info	Professor at University of California, Davis. "Aldous joined UCD in 1995 and was Head of the School of History & Archives in 2006-2009. He has written widely on nineteenth and twentieth century British history. In 2009 he worked with Bertie Ahern on the former Taoiseach's memoirs. Richard's eight books as author and editor include *The Lion and the Unicorn: Gladstone vs Disraeli* (2006), *Macmillan, Eisenhower and the Cold War* (2005) and *Tunes of Glory: the life of Malcolm Sargent* (2001). He is currently writing a study of Margaret Thatcher and Ronald Reagan.... A prominent public commentator, Richard is a regular political analyst for the BBC, RTE Television and Newstalk." https://rms.ucd.ie/ufrs/w_rms_cv_show.show_public?user=richard.aldous@ucd.ie
Bibliography	No.
Index	Yes.
Notes	Yes.
Photographs	No.
Appendix	No.
Tables	No.
Key Words	Presidency, Cold War, Foreign Relations
Other Notes	
Annotation	In this diplomatic history about the "special relationship" between America and Great Britain, Aldous examines Macmillan's ascent to and work as British prime minister and his attempts at summit diplomacy with America. Macmillan hoped to recreate the type of relationship between Churchill and Roosevelt and their summits with Eisenhower. Aldous's main focus is Macmillan, and Eisenhower is examined mainly through his friendship with Macmillan, which was based on their experiences during WWII. This friendship suffered with the failure of the Paris Summit.

2.   Alin, Erika G. *The United States and the 1958 Lebanon Crisis: American Intervention in
      the Middle East*. Lanham, MD: University Press of America, 1994.

Author Info	Was a political science professor at Hamline University (Minnesota) until at least 2007.
Bibliography	Yes (select).
Index	Yes.
Notes	Yes.
Photographs	No.

Appendix	No.
Tables	No.
Key Words	Presidency, Foreign Relations, Middle East
Other Notes	
Annotation	Alin examines the causes, events, and ramifications of the 1958 Lebanon Crisis. She begins with a general review of U.S.-Middle East relations during the 1950s before turning to Lebanon specifically. Alin then examines the "perceptions and considerations that underlay the Eisenhower administration's decision to intervene militarily in Lebanon in 1958." Using secondary sources, memoirs, and foreign policy primary sources, Alin concludes: 1) America's intervention in Lebanon "can only be understood in the context of American officials' perceptions of broader developments in the Middle East in the 1950s"; 2) the "immediate impetus" for intervention was "the overthrow of the pro-Western government of Iraq"; and 3) intervention's primary objective was "to demonstrate the U.S. commitment to defending its regional and international allies in the Cold War."

3.   Allen, Craig. *Eisenhower and the Mass Media: Peace, Prosperity, and Prime-Time TV.* Chapel Hill & London: University of North Carolina Press, 1993.

Author Info	Associate professor at the Walter Cronkite School of Journalism and Mass Communication at Arizona State University. His two books include *News Is People: The Rise of Local TV News* (2001) and *Eisenhower and the Mass Media* (1993). Teaches classes on reporting, communication, and media. *Eisenhower and the Mass Media* is based on Allen's dissertation, "Peace, Prosperity and Prime Time TV: Eisenhower, Stevenson and the TV Politics of 1956 (Ohio U, 1989).
Bibliography	Yes.
Index	Yes.
Notes	Yes.
Photographs	Yes (B&W)
Appendix	No.
Tables	No.
Key Words	Presidency, Media
Other Notes	
Annotation	Allen traces Eisenhower's deliberate use of the media, especially television, in a roughly chronological manner, from his election campaign through his two terms as President, and beyond. Allen finds that Eisenhower and his Administration skillfully and successfully used the media to Ike's advantage, and that they had many "firsts" in presidential use of mass media, especially in the realm of television, a credit often given to Kennedy. Ike's communications with the public were strategically structured to influence public opinion and increase Ike's popularity. Allen also examines the evolution of the role of media in Presidential politics.

4. Alteras, Isaac. *Eisenhower and Israel: U.S.-Israeli Relations, 1953-1960.* Gainesville, FL: University Press of Florida, 1993.

Author Info   History professor in the Jewish Studies' program at Queens College (CUNY). From his faculty profile: "My research interests are in US-Israeli relations and Modern Jewish History. In addition to research, reviews and publications in those areas, [t]each courses in Modern Jewish History, Zionism, Modern Israel and Twentieth Century European diplomatic history. I presented numerous scholarly papers as well as public lectures relating to the above subjects. My current research deals with US role in Arab-Israeli conflict from 1948 to the present, [t]he most recent publication, "The Palestinian - Israeli Peace Accords (1993), was published in Dictionary of American History. (Charles Scribners Sons, 1996)." http://qcpages.qc.edu/jewish_studies/alteras.html

Bibliography   Yes.

Index   Yes.

Notes   Yes.

Photographs   Yes (B&W).

Appendix   No.

Tables   No.

Key Words   Presidency, Foreign Relations, Middle East

Other Notes

Annotation   Alteras analyzes "U.S. policy toward Israel in the context of U.S. (Western) military, economic, and political interests in the Middle East as seen by [Eisenhower and Dulles]" and Israeli leaders using both American and Israeli primary sources for the period 1953-1960. He finds that in light of Cold War pressures to strengthen relations with Arab countries, the U.S. minimized its relationship with Israel between 1953 and 1957. Despite this policy of "friendly impartiality," however, Alteras stresses that Eisenhower never waivered in his, "commitment to the legitimacy, existence, and survival of the Jewish state." After the Sinai Campaign, America realized that Israel, "through its commercial and military links with non-Arab countries at the periphery of the Middle East, was serving not only its own interests but also furthering Western goals in the Middle East," and relations between the U.S. and Israel improved.

5. Ambrose, Stephen E., *The Victors: Eisenhower and His Boys: The Men of World War II.* New York: Simon & Schuster, 1999.

Author Info   Well-known Eisenhower historian. Ambrose was the Associate Editor of the Eisenhower Papers. He taught at Johns Hopkins University and University of New Orleans. For a time America's most popular biographer and historian, Ambrose's reputation sagged late in his life: there were persistent reports of plagiarism, falsification, and inaccuracies regarding his work. Ambrose died in 2002.

Bibliography	Yes.
Index	Yes.
Notes	No.
Photographs	Yes (B&W).
Appendix	No.
Tables	No.
Key Words	Military- WWII, Leadership
Other Notes	Maps.
Annotation	Ambrose weaves a narrative of war, focusing on combat soldiers and Eisenhower's command of them, based on books he had previously written, including *Eisenhower*, *Pegasus Bridge*, *Band of Brothers*, *D-Day*, and *Citizen Soldiers*. Notes have been eliminated from the text and Ambrose directs the reader to the original works for specific citations.

6.   Anderson, David L. (ed.), *Shadow on the White House: Presidents and the Vietnam War, 1945-1975.* Lawrence, KS: University of Kansas Press, 1993.

Author Info	Professor of history at California State University, Monterey Bay. Profile at https://fresca.calstate.edu/faculty/1873
Bibliography	Suggestions for Further Reading
Index	Yes.
Notes	Yes (at the end of the chapters).
Photographs	Yes (B&W).
Appendix	No.
Tables	No.
Key Words	Presidency, Vietnam, Military Policy, Politics, Cold War
Other Notes	Map.
Annotation	Collection of essays on how Presidents placed their own unique stamps on the Vietnam issue. Authors examine the "personality, politics, priorities, and actions of the presidents," and seek to "clarify some of the interconnections between the modern presidency" and Vietnam. Truman, Eisenhower, Kennedy, and Ford are the focus of one chapter each and Nixon and Johnson each have two chapters dedicated to their presidencies. Editor David L. Anderson wrote the chapter on Eisenhower: "Dwight D. Eisenhower and Wholehearted Support for Ngo Dinh Diem." He argues that Ike's approach to Vietnam included two phases: 1) from 1954-1955 continued President Truman's tactic "of working with and through the French and other Western allies to contain communism in Southeast Asia; 2) from spring of 1955- end of presidency, Eisenhower undertook an "essentially unilateral approach in which the [US] sought to protect its strategic interests in Southeast Asia by building a new Vietnamese nation around [Ngo Dinh Diem]". Anderson describes the second phase as exhibiting "a tragic irresponsibility by enmeshing the [US] in the tangled web of Vietnamese politics and exposing Americans and American interests to considerable danger." Anderson faults Ike for failing to fully understand the sociopolitical issues Diem faced in Vietnam. He concludes that Ike's

"accomplishments in Vietnam were negative: no war, but no peace. It was a record of nonsolution and ever-narrowing options."

7. Anderson, David L., *Trapped by Success: The Eisenhower Administration and Vietnam, 1953-1961.* New York: Columbia University Press, 1993.

Author Info	Professor of history at California State University, Monterey Bay. Profile at https://fresca.calstate.edu/faculty/1873
Bibliography	Yes.
Index	Yes.
Notes	Yes.
Photographs	No.
Appendix	No.
Tables	No.
Key Words	Presidency, Vietnam, Foreign Relations
Other Notes	
Annotation	Examination of the role of the Eisenhower Administration in the origins of America's war in Vietnam using previously classified State Department records, White House files, personal papers, and government documents. Anderson chronologically traces America's involvement in Vietnam from 1941 through Eisenhower's two terms. He argues that the Eisenhower Administration and subsequent American presidents were trapped by Eisenhower's successes in staving off communism and creating an ally in South Vietnam. He argues that these successes were shallow and, "premised on superficial assumptions about the government in Saigon, its future prospects, and the importance of its survival to U.S. global strategic interests." The government in South Vietnam under Diem did not make for a viable nation, and America's commitment to an independent South Vietnamese nation, "was proving increasingly unrealistic and unachievable without greater cost and risk to the United States." Anderson concludes that, "the Eisenhower administration trapped itself and its successors into a commitment to the survival of its own counterfeit creation." Bibliography, Notes, and Index.

8. Anderson, Lars. *Carlisle vs. Army: Jim Thorpe, Dwight Eisenhower, Pop Warner, and the Forgotten Story of Football's Greatest Battle.* New York: Random House Trade Paperback, 2007.

Author Info	*Sports Illustrated* staff writer and graduate of Columbia University Graduate School of Journalism. (From book)
Bibliography	No (though note on sources).
Index	Yes.
Notes	Yes.
Photographs	Yes (B&W).
Appendix	No.

Tables	No.
Key Words	Early Life, Personal Life
Other Notes	
Annotation	In a narrative manner, sportswriter Anderson recounts the 1912 football game between the Carlisle Indian School and Jim Thorpe and West Point and Eisenhower. Anderson focuses on Thorpe, Eisenhower, and Pop Warner, and illustrates the social and cultural contexts which brought the three men to the game in 1912, especially Warner's molding of the Native American team at Carlisle. Of Eisenhower, Anderson examines his early life in Abilene and his time at West Point, focusing especially on Ike's determination.

9.   Arnold, James R. *The First Domino: Eisenhower, the Military, and America's Intervention in Vietnam*. New York: William Morrow & Co, 1991.

Author Info	Prolific author on a broad range of topics. "James R. Arnold is the author of more than twenty books, including *The First Domino... Presidents Under Fire: Commanders in Chief in Victory and Defeat*; *Jeff Davis's Own: Cavalry, Comanches, and the Battle for the Texas Frontier*; and *Crisis in the Snows: Russia Confronts Napolean, the Eylau Campaign 1806-1807*. He lives on a farm near Lexington, Virginia." From http://search.barnesandnoble.com/Jungle-of-Snakes/James-R-Arnold/e/9781596915039#TABS
Bibliography	Yes.
Index	Yes.
Notes	Yes.
Photographs	Yes (B&W).
Appendix	No.
Tables	No.
Key Words	Presidency, Vietnam, Foreign Relations
Other Notes	Map.
Annotation	Arnold argues that the domino analogy, "fits the way successive administrations made decisions regarding Southeast Asia." Once President Truman made the decision to support the French, "each subsequent decision to expand the American effort inexorably fell into place." Arnold traces America's deepening involvement in Vietnam under the Eisenhower Administration. Eisenhower's policies regarding Vietnam, including the creation of SEATO, the tying of America's prestige to events in Vietnam, and supporting Diem, "inextricably bound the United States to South Vietnam's fate" and ultimately led to the U.S. involvement in the Vietnam War.

10.   Ashton, Nigel John. *Eisenhower, Macmillan and the Problem of Nasser: Anglo-American Relations and Arab Nationalism, 1955-59*. London: MacMillan Press, 1996.

Author Info	Professor of International History at the London School of Economics.

"Professor Ashton's main fields of interest are contemporary Anglo-American relations and the modern history of the Middle East." From his profile at: http://www2.lse.ac.uk/internationalHistory/whosWho/academicStaff/ashton.as px

Bibliography	Select bibliography.
Index	Yes.
Notes	Yes.
Photographs	No.
Appendix	No.
Tables	No.
Key Words	Presidency, Middle East, Cold War, Foreign Relations
Other Notes	
Annotation	Ashton examines the motivations and strategies of the U.S. and Britain in dealing with Arab nationalism during the 1950s. He concentrates on the time post-Suez, and uses British and U.S. sources. Ashton finds that from the Western perspective, there were three main factors in the Middle East: 1) Soviet incursion; 2) oil; and 3) radical, anti-western Arab nationalists. Often, British and American interests and strategies aligned, but the countries assigned different values to these factors-- America focusing on the first and Britain on the second. This created problems in some situations, most notably in Egypt. The American relation with Nasser was pragmatic and related directly to his associations with the Soviet Union. The British, however, were staunchly anti-Nasserite. Ashton concludes that: "This was the root of the differences between the two that emerged most overtly over Suez, and more covertly over Syria, the United Arab Republic, Jordan and Iraq." Eisenhower, Dulles, Macmillan, and Lloyd are featured heavily. Contribution to a series edited by M. Dockrill in military and strategic history.

11.   Axelrod, Alan. *Eisenhower on Leadership: Ike's Enduring Lessons in Total Victory Management*. San Francisco, CA: Jossey-Bass, 2006.

Author Info	From book: Alexrod "is the author of many business and management books, including the *BusinessWeek* best-sellers *Patton on Leadership* and *Elizabeth I, CEO*, as well as books on military history, U.S history, and general history." Has a PhD in English and has served as a consultant to museums, cultural institutions, and companies.
Bibliography	No.
Index	Yes.
Notes	No.
Photographs	No.
Appendix	No.
Tables	No.
Key Words	Military- WWII, Leadership
Other Notes	
Annotation	Axelrod analogizes Ike's position as supreme Allied Commander in Europe to

that of a present day CEO or manager—Eisenhower was, "in short, a manager, in the most modern sense of the word, charged with leading, coordinating, prioritizing, judging, and cajoling others toward the common goal of total victory." He pulls 232 "lessons" from Ike, largely from the decisions he had to make during Operation Overlord. Lessons include "Never Marry an Idea" (139), "Stick To your Knitting" (125), and "Simplify" (35).

B's

12.   Barrett, Roby C. *The Greater Middle East and the Cold War: US Foreign Policy Under Eisenhower and Kennedy*. New York: I. B. Tauris, 2007.

Author Info	"Roby C. Barrett is an Adjunct Scholar at the Middle East Institute, Washington DC and an Adjunct Professor of History at Texas A&M Commerce. He has a doctorate in Middle East and South Asian history from the University of Texas at Austin and is a former US Foreign Service Officer in the Middle East. He has been an Eisenhower-Roberts Research Fellow at the Eisenhower Institute in Washington, D.C. and a Rotary International Fellow at the University of Munich Institute for Russian Studies. He is a specialist on security and defence issues and has over twenty-five years of government, business and academic experience in the Middle East. He is the president of CCOMM Corporation, a firm specializing in national security policy and advanced defense technology applications." Author profile from http://us.macmillan.com/author/robycbarrett
Bibliography	Yes.
Index	Yes.
Notes	Yes.
Photographs	Yes (B&W).
Appendix	No.
Tables	No.
Key Words	Presidency, Cold War, Foreign Relations, Middle East
Other Notes	
Annotation	Barrett "examines American foreign policy in the Middle East from 1958-1963," and to a lesser extent the period between 1953 and 1955, using archival material from multiple countries including the U.S., Britain, Australia, India, and Egypt. He defines the Greater Middle East as encompassing an area from North Africa to South Asia. Barrett compares and contrasts the strategies and tactics of the Eisenhower and Kennedy Administrations in the Greater Middle East and finds them to be surprisingly similar, the real differences being Kennedy's failure to learn from Eisenhower's mistakes, and Kennedy's activist bent. Both Administrations were primarily concerned with the containment of communism and there was a "fundamental connectivity between the Eisenhower and Kennedy policies of containment and modernization of the Greater Middle East". Barrett further demonstrates America's "susceptibility at any given time to the influence of indigenous forces, the British, oil, and

Israel."

13.   Ben-Zvi, Abraham. *Decade of Transition: Eisenhower, Kennedy, and the Origins of the American-Israeli Alliance*. New York: Columbia University Press, 1998.

Author Info	Professor at the Jaffee Center for Strategic Studies at Tel Aviv University. Has been a visiting professor at Georgetown. "Ben-Zvi has published extensively on a broad range of strategic issues and on the origins, formation and dynamics of American diplomacy in the Middle East, with particular emphasis on the American-Israeli framework." http://explore.georgetown.edu/news/?ID=1910
Bibliography	Selected bibliography.
Index	Yes.
Notes	Yes.
Photographs	No.
Appendix	No.
Tables	No.
Key Words	Presidency, Foreign Relations, Middle East
Other Notes	
Annotation	A study of the evolution of America's relationship with Israel during the Eisenhower and Kennedy Administrations using primary sources. Ben-Zvi argues against the notion that Ike's Administration was consistently hostile towards Israel and Kennedy's election inaugurated a drastically different American-Israeli relationship. Instead, he argues that the Eisenhower era was "the incubation period in which the groundwork of the American-Israeli alliance was laid, with the Kennedy Administration consolidating and accelerating processes the Eisenhower foreign policy elite had set in motion." Ben-Zvi notes a change over Eisenhower's two terms in his Administration's perception of the strategic value of Israel.

14.   Bischof, Gunter and Stephen E. Ambrose, ed. *Eisenhower: A Centenary Assessment*. Baton Rouge: Louisiana State University Press, 1995.

Author Info	Ambrose: Well-known Eisenhower historian. Ambrose was the Associate Editor of the Eisenhower Papers. He taught at Johns Hopkins University and University of New Orleans. For a time America's most popular biographer and historian, Ambrose's reputation sagged late in his life: there were persistent reports of plagiarism, falsification, and inaccuracies regarding his work. Ambrose died in 2002.
	Günter Bischof is the chair and Marshall Plan professor of history and the director of CenterAustria at the University of New Orleans. He has been teaching American and European Diplomatic History at the University of New Orleans since 1989 and is the recipient of the junior and senior research awards of the UNO Alumni Foundation; he was Executive Director of CenterAustria since its founding in 1997 and then director since 2000. He is the author of

"Austria in the First Cold War, 1945/55: The Leverage of the Weak" (1999), the co-editor... of "Contemporary Austrian Studies" (16 vols), and co-editor of a dozen other books and numerous articles on World War II, the Cold War, and contemporary Austrian history.... Biscof's current research projects deal with the U.S. (non)responses to the Soviet/Warsaw Pact invasions of the GDR (1953), Hungary (1956), Czechoslovakia (1968) and Poland (1981), as well as a prosopography of Austrian immigrants/refugees to the United States in the 20th century provisionally entitled "Quiet Invaders Revisited".

Bischof is an alumnus of both the University of Innsbruck and the University of New Orleans, and holds a Ph.D. in American history from Harvard University (1989).

Bibliography	Selected bibliography.
Index	Yes.
Notes	Yes.
Photographs	Yes (B&W).
Appendix	No.
Tables	No.
Key Words	Military- WWII, SACEUR, Presidency, Foreign Relations, Domestic Policy
Other Notes	Notes on contributors.
Annotation	A collection of essays derived from lectures given at the Eisenhower Center (University of New Orleans) during 1990 in honor of the centenary of Ike's birth by a variety of scholars. The essays cover Ike's WWII career and his work as SACEUR, but are largely focused on his Presidency, including essays on both his domestic (2 essays) and foreign (8 essays) polices. Included is a mix of general and specialized papers from younger as well as more established scholars.

15.   Bischof, Günter and Stephen Ambrose, ed. *Eisenhower and the German POWs: Facts Against Falsehood*. Baton Rouge: Louisiana State University Press, 1992.

Author Info	See information in Entry #14.
Bibliography	Selected Bibliography.
Index	Yes.
Notes	Yes.
Photographs	Yes (B &W).
Appendix	Appendices A and B.
Tables	Yes.
Key Words	Military WWII.
Other Notes	Map and Contributor's Bios.
Annotation	Collection of papers produced during a two-day symposium at the Eisenhower Center in 1990, called to investigate the allegations in James Bacque's *Other Losses* that: 1) Eisenhower and the United States and French armies engineered the deaths of up to one million German POWs after WWII; and 2) professional historians were involved in a conspiracy to cover up these deaths. Essays by multiple scholars, including the editors, challenge Bacque's research, methodology, analyses, and conclusions. The editors conclude that *Other*

Losses is "seriously—nay spectacularly—flawed in its most fundamental aspects."

16. Blakesley Lance, *Presidential Leadership: From Eisenhower to Clinton.* Chicago: Nelson-Hall Publishers, 1995.

Author Info	Political Science professor at Loyola Marymount University. "Lance Blakesley received his B.A. from the University of Illinois and his M.A. and Ph. D. from Northwestern University. His teaching and research efforts are focused on urban politics, political leadership, housing policy, and politics and educational policy. He has spent a considerable amount of time in India and is particularly interested in issues concerning the economic and political development of India." From: http://bellarmine.lmu.edu/politicalscience/faculty/Lance_Blakesley.htm
Bibliography	No.
Index	Yes.
Notes	Yes.
Photographs	No.
Appendix	No.
Tables	Figures and Tables.
Key Words	Presidency, Leadership
Other Notes	
Annotation	Using a behavioral theory of "Presidential Strategic Leadership Versatility," the author ranks the presidents on various categories, including self-awareness, effective employment of subleaders, and flexibility. Drawing upon secondary sources, the author gives Eisenhower high scores on all of the model's major categories except "promoting public policy initiatives: organizing, selling, and participating," where Ike received a medium score. President Eisenhower received a higher total score than any of the subsequent presidents through William Clinton's first administration.

17. Bose, Meena. *Shaping and Signaling Presidential Policy: The National Security Decision Making of Eisenhower and Kennedy.* College Station: Texas A&M University Press, 1998.

Author Info	Professor of Political Science at Hofstra University. Author of is a contributor to the tenth edition of the American Government: Institutions and Policies textbook. Her current research focuses on the changing role of the United Nations in American foreign policy. Teaches courses on the American Presidency, American Foreign Policy, and American Politics. She taught for six years at the United States Military Academy at West Point, where she also served as Director of American Politics in 2006. She earned her undergraduate degree in international politics from Penn State University (1990), and she received her master's (1992) and doctoral (1996) degrees in politics from Princeton University. Hofstra University profile at

http://www.hofstra.edu/academics/Colleges/HCLAS/PRSSTY/prssty_chair.ht
ml

Bibliography	Yes.
Index	Yes.
Notes	Yes.
Photographs	No.
Appendix	Yes (A & B).
Tables	No.
Key Words	Presidency, Speech Making, Cold War, Foreign Relations, Leadership
Other Notes	
Annotation	Systematic evaluation of the decision-making styles of Eisenhower and Kennedy. Part One compares the Cold War foreign policy decision-making processes of Eisenhower and Kennedy, focusing on their leadership styles and their advisory systems. Part Two examines how Eisenhower and Kennedy communicated their national security strategies to both domestic and international audiences. She concludes: 1) while one can say that Eisenhower's decision making processes were largely formal and Kennedy's largely informal, classification of presidential leadership styles and advisory systems is difficult; 2) while both formal and informal processes have their drawbacks, formal processes are less risky; 3) multiple advocacy can maximize the strengths and minimizes the weaknesses in both formal and informal processes, but requires strong presidential commitment; 4) multiple advocacy can also help in presidential policy communication; 5) strategic planning, especially early in an administration, is important. Adapted from her PhD dissertation.

18. Bowie, Robert R. and Richard H. Immerman. *Waging Peace: How Eisenhower Shaped an Enduring Cold War Strategy*. New York: Oxford University Press, 1998.

Author Info	Robert R. Bowie was "director of the Policy Planning Staff of the State Department and its member on the National Security Council Planning Board from 1953-1957." (From *Waging Peace*). He is also "Emeritus Director of the Center for International Studies at Harvard University." http://www.oup.com/us/catalog/general/subject/Politics/InternationalStudies/ColdWar/?view=usa&ci=9780195140484. Richard H. Immerman (Ph.D., Boston College) is the Edward J. Buthusiem Family Distinguished Faculty Fellow and Department Chair at Temple University; Director of the Center for the Study of Force and Diplomacy.
Bibliography	No.
Index	Yes.
Notes	Yes.
Photographs	No.
Appendix	No.
Tables	No.
Key Words	Presidency, Cold War, Foreign Relations
Other Notes	
Annotation	A participant in the national security planning of the 1950s, Robert R. Bowie,

and an experienced U.S. historian, Richard H. Immerman, examine in detail the process by which the Eisenhower administration developed the basic strategy that would govern America's role in the Cold War until the collapse of the Soviet Union. The Eisenhower administration's goal was a strategy that would contain communist power and be sustainable over the long-term. Based on meticulous research in primary and secondary sources, this volume is a path-breaking contribution to national security studies.

19.   Boyle, Peter G., ed. *The Churchill-Eisenhower Correspondence, 1953-1955*. Chapel Hill: University of North Carolina Press, 1990.

Author Info	Boyle was a senior Lecturer in U.S. History at the University of Nottingham. He has written multiple books on Eisenhower.
Bibliography	No.
Index	Yes.
Notes	Yes (footnotes).
Photographs	Yes B&W.
Appendix	Yes (2).
Tables	No.
Key Words	Presidency, Foreign Relations
Other Notes	
Annotation	Eisenhower and Churchill's personal correspondence from January 1953 until Churchill's retirement in April 1955. All letters are included, save a very small number that remain classified or partially classified. Boyle provides an introduction, conclusion, and limited background information with the aim of allowing the correspondence to speak for itself. Boyle does raise a few questions in the introduction which he returns to in the conclusion, including issues such as the status of the Anglo-American "special relationship" during these years, Churchill's desire for a summit meeting with the Soviet Union, and Eisenhower's effectiveness as a statesman. The editor also notes the differences between the Churchill-Roosevelt correspondence and the Churchill-Eisenhower correspondence. The former is less reflective and more focused on the day-to-day matters of WWII. In the latter, the correspondence is "more pensive and philosophical in many places as well as concerned with everyday situations."

20.   Boyle, Peter G., ed. *The Eden-Eisenhower Correspondence, 1955-1957*. Chapel Hill: The University of North Carolina Press, 2005.

Author Info	Boyle was a senior Lecturer in U.S. History at the University of Nottingham. He has written multiple books on Eisenhower.
Bibliography	Bibliographical essay.
Index	Yes.
Notes	Yes (footnotes).
Photographs	Yes B&W.

Appendix	No.
Tables	No.
Key Words	Presidency
Other Notes	
Annotation	Correspondence between Eisenhower and Eden during the period they were simultaneously in office (April 6, 1955- January 9, 1957). Boyle breaks the correspondence into two parts: "from Eden's accession to the premiership in April 1955 to the beginning of the Suez crisis in July 1956, and from the beginning of the Suez crisis until Eden's resignation in January 1957." This chronological structure shows the strong Anglo-American relationship that existed at the beginning of the correspondence deteriorate during the Suez crisis and one can see not only "a fundamental disagreement over policy but a distrust that culminated in a total breakdown of the Anglo-American relationship at the height of the crisis." Boyle includes essays on the personalities of the men and the main issues they faced, as well as an introduction and conclusion.

21. Boyle, Peter G., *Eisenhower*. Harlow, England: Pearson/Longman, 2005.

Author Info	Boyle was a senior Lecturer in U.S. History at the University of Nottingham. He has written multiple books on Eisenhower.
Bibliography	Yes.
Index	Yes.
Notes	Yes.
Photographs	No.
Appendix	No.
Tables	No.
Key Words	Presidency, Domestic Policy, Foreign Relations
Other Notes	
Annotation	The author brings to his study of the Eisenhower presidency a full, critical knowledge of the secondary and primary sources available by the early twenty-first century. While not overwhelmingly positive, Boyle's careful appraisal of Ike's leadership, policies, and performance ends by concluding that the President had an "impressive record of achievement" (pg. 160).

22. Brenner, Samuel, ed. *Dwight D. Eisenhower*. San Diego, CA: Greenhaven, 2002.

Author Info	Brenner has PhD in history from Brown University. He earned his JD from the University of Michigan Law School. Currently clerking for judges. CV at http://www.samuelbrenner.com/Resume%20and%20Professional/Brenner%20Resume%203-25-10.pdf
Bibliography	List of books For Further Research
Index	Yes.
Notes	Very limited.
Photographs	Yes (B&W).

Appendix	Yes.
Tables	No.
Key Words	Presidency, Cold War, Vietnam, Domestic Policy, Civil Rights
Other Notes	Chronology
Annotation	Part of a series aimed at the student researcher entitled, "Presidents and Their Decisions" which examines presidents and a select number of important decisions they made while in office. This volume on Ike includes excerpts of essays from articles by various reputable historians, including Immerman and Divine, on four general issues: 1) containing communism, 2) avoiding war in Vietnam, 3) Ike and McCarthyism, and 4) school desegregation. Each excerpted essay begins with a summary of that essay. Also includes a brief biography of Eisenhower.

23.   Broadwater, Jeff. *Eisenhower & the Anti-Communist Crusade.* Chapel Hill, NC: University of North Carolina Press, 1992.

Author Info	Associate Professor of History at Barton College in Wilson, NC. "Dr. Jeff Broadwater holds a Ph.D. from Vanderbilt University. His main teaching and research interests are early American history and the history of the South. His most recent book, *George Mason, Forgotten Founder*, was published by the University of North Carolina Press in 2006." http://www2.barton.edu/cgi-bin/MySQLdb?FILE=/academics/faculty/list.html&currentprogram=1009
Bibliography	Yes.
Index	Yes.
Notes	Yes.
Photographs	Yes (B&W).
Appendix	No.
Tables	No.
Key Words	Presidency, Politics, Domestic Policy, Cold War
Other Notes	
Annotation	Broadwater argues that although Ike was opposed to McCarthy (though doing little to curb him for political reasons), Eisenhower shared with McCarthyites, "much of their obsession with internal security and their unconcern for civil liberties." Taking a broader view of "anti-communism" than simply McCarthyism, which he argues anti-communism outlasted, Broadwater examines the Eisenhower Administration's domestic anti-communist activity and finds Ike's record on anti-communism and the security field, including, "the federal employee loyalty program, the purge of the Foreign Service, the uncontrolled excesses of J. Edgar Hoover and the [FBI]," to be poor. Political Cartoons.

24.   Brownell, Herbert, with John P. Burke. *Advising Ike: The Memoirs of Attorney General Herbert Brownell.* Lawrence, KN, University Press of Kansas, 1993.

Author Info	"Herbert Brownell Jr. was attorney general under President Eisenhower from

January 21, 1953, to October 23, 1957. Brownell recieved [sic] his B.A. from the University of Nebraska in 1924 and earned a law degree from Yale in 1927…. After playing an important part in securing delegates for Eisenhower's nomination in the 1952 national convention and then during the presidential campaign, Brownell became attorney general. He often advised Eisenhower on civil rights matters. He also helped to expedite the electrocution of Ethel and Julius Rosenberg, who were sentenced to death for passing secret files about the atomic bomb to the Soviet Union. He also enshrined the practice of allowing the American Bar Association to vet judicial appointments. Finally, Brownell was instrumental in advising Eisenhower to send federal troops to enforce the desegregation of Central High School in Little Rock, Arkansas. After resigning in 1957, he rejoined his old law firm as a senior partner until 1977 and then until 1989 as counsel. He died in 1996." From the Miller Center. http://millercenter.org/academic/americanpresident/eisenhower/essays/cabinet/583
John Burke: Professor at University of Vermont. He "specializes in American politics, the American presidency, and ethics and public affairs. He has published numerous articles and eight books." http://www.uvm.edu/~polisci/?Page=JohnBurke.php

Bibliography	No.
Index	Yes.
Notes	No.
Photographs	Yes (B&W).
Appendix	Yes (5).
Tables	No.
Key Words	Presidency, Domestic Policy, Civil Rights, Cold War, Politics
Other Notes	
Annotation	Memoirs of Eisenhower's attorney general from 1953 to 1957. Brownell's memoirs cover time both before and after his work with Eisenhower, but more than half of the text is reserved for his experiences with Ike, during Ike's election and beyond. He discusses advising Ike on key legal issues of the time, including Civil Rights matters, the appointment of a new chief justice of the Supreme Court, and security subjects raised by Senators McCarthy and Bricker. He also provides an assessment of Eisenhower as a president, which is overall a positive one, though not without criticisms.

25.   Brugioni, Dino A. *Eyes in the Sky: Eisenhower, the CIA and Cold War Aerial Espionage.* Annapolis, MD: Naval Institute Press, 2010.

Author Info   From book: Brugioni, " a retired senior analyst in the CIA, briefed presidents Eisenhower through Ford. He was involved in the exploitation of U-2, SR-71, satellite imagery, and discovered and analyzed World War II aerial photography taken of the Auschwitz-Birkenau death camp. During World War II, he was a bomber crew member who flew 66 bombing missions. Now a resident of Hartwood, VA, he is also the author of *Photo Fakery*."

Bibliography	No.
Index	Yes.
Notes	Yes.
Illustrations	No.
Photographs	Yes (B&W).
Appendix	No.
Tables	No.
Key Words	Presidency, Cold War, Military Policy, Foreign Relations, Nuclear, Technology
Other Notes	
Annotation	Based on the author's firsthand knowledge from his work with the CIA during the 1950s and 1960s as well as interviews with others involved, Brugioni's book details the advancements in and development of military aerial reconnaissance, and the pivotal role Eisenhower played in promoting the technology.

26.   Brune, Lester H., ed. *The Korean War: Handbook of the Literature and Research.* Westport, CT: Greenwood Press, 1996.

Author Info	Brune: "is the John and Augusta Oglesby Professor of American Heritage at Bradley University. Previous publications include the three volume *Chronological History of the United States Foreign Relations, 1776 to 1989*; *America and the Iraqi Crisis, 1990-1992*; *The Missile Crisis of October 1962*; and chapters on defense policy and diplomacy for Robin Higham and Donald J. Mrozek's *A Guide to the Sources of U.S. Military History, Supplements II and III.*
Bibliography	Yes- multiple.
Index	Author index and subject index.
Notes	No.
Photographs	No.
Appendix	No.
Tables	No.
Key Words	Presidency, Korea
Other Notes	
Annotation	This book contains multiple chapters pertaining to issues involving the Korean War. These chapters are not detailed essays on the topics, but instead are historiographical and bibliographical essays, each ending with a bibliography of references. For issues relating to Ike, see especially chapter by Edward C. Keefer: "Truman and Eisenhower: Strategic Options for Atomic War and Diplomacy in Korea."

27.   Burnes, Brian. *The Ike Files: Mementos of the Man and His Era From Eisenhower Presidential Library and Museum.* Kansas City, MO: Kansas City Star Books, 2008.

Author Info	Burnes, "has been a reporter for *The Kansas City Star* since 1978. He is the author of *High & Rising: The 1951 Kansas City Flood* and *Great Plains Originals: Historical Documents from America's Heartland...* Burnes, a native of St. Louis, received his bachelor's degree in journalism in 1976 from the University of Missouri-Columbia and his master's degree in journalism in 1998 from the University of Kansas." (From book jacket).
Bibliography	No.
Index	Yes.
Notes	No.
Photographs	Color
Appendix	No.
Tables	No.
Key Words	Early Life, Military—B/w the Wars, Military- WWII, Presidency, Post-Presidency
Other Notes	
Annotation	Colorful and interesting sample of the documents, photographs, and other materials housed at the Eisenhower Library in Abilene, Kansas. The book is organized chronologically from Ike's childhood through the post-presidency. Text is biographical and general: the focus is on the photographs and other materials.

C's

28.   Chernus, Ira. *Apocalypse Management: Eisenhower and the Discourse of National Insecurity*. Stanford: Stanford University Press, 2008.

Author Info	Professor of Religious Studies, University of Colorado, Boulder. http://spot.colorado.edu/~chernus/. Research focuses on the discourse of peace, war, foreign policy, and nationalism in the United States, especially during the cold war and the nuclear age, and how that discourse has affected our public culture and life up to the present. Completed a large project on President Dwight D. Eisenhower and his impact on our discourse. Three books came out of that project.
Bibliography	Yes.
Index	Yes.
Notes	Yes.
Photographs	No.
Appendix	No.
Tables	No.
Key Words	Presidency, Cold War, Nuclear, Foreign Relations
Other Notes	
Annotation	Chernus examines the origins and perpetuation of the "apocalypse management" structure in the Eisenhower's Administration and argues against the idea of Ike as a peacemaker. This structure holds that the "enemy threat is now a permanent fact of life [and that t]he best to hope...is to contain and

manage it forever." Thus, enduring stability is the only possible positive outcome. Eisenhower and his Administration created this new linguistic paradigm and it "profoundly influenced their policymaking process, and... came to dominate American public discourse in the 1950s." Chernus states that his most important conclusion is: "The Eisenhower presidency locked the nation into the cold war's enduring paradox: A single-minded pursuit of national security consistently undermined the nation's sense of security" and thus there was national insecurity.

29.   Chernus, Ira. *Eisenhower's Atoms for Peace*. College Station: Texas A&M University Press, 2002.

Author Info	See information in Entry #28.
Bibliography	Yes.
Index	Yes.
Notes	Yes.
Photographs	No.
Appendix	No.
Tables	No.
Key Words	Presidency, Cold War, Nuclear, Speechmaking
Other Notes	Includes text of "Atoms for Peace" Speech.
Annotation	Discursive analysis of Ike's "Atoms for Peace" Speech and how the speech fit into what Chernus refers to as Ike's "apocalypse management" structure of foreign policy. This "structure" of thought accepts that the threat of Cold War was constant and the only way to achieve a kind of peace was to manage that threat. Chernus provides a close reading of the speech and discusses Ike's use of rhetoric to manage public opinion and fear both domestically and internationally. Also teases out the meanings of the word "peace" and argues that Eisenhower never believed that the Soviet Union would accept the conditions he'd laid down. Includes text of "Atoms for Peace" Speech.

30.   Chernus, Ira. *General Eisenhower: Ideology and Discourse*. East Lansing, MI: Michigan State University Press, 2002.

Author Info	See information in Entry #28.
Bibliography	Yes.
Index	Yes.
Notes	Yes.
Photographs	No.
Appendix	No.
Tables	No.
Key Words	Military- WWII, Army Chief of Staff, Columbia University, Elections, Speechmaking, Politics, Cold War
Other Notes	
Annotation	Chernus closely examines Eisenhower's words to explore Ike's ideology. He

finds Ike's ideology and discourse were almost fully articulated by 1943, though they would continue to develop. Chernus posits that the "key to [Eisenhower's] discourse, the center of his ideological wheel, was his view of human nature, which was basically a religious view", in which every person was "permanently seized by an inner struggle between selfish desire… and the virtue of voluntary self-restraint." Eisenhower's discourse was consistent and logically coherent, and his "political, economic, and social fears, including a deep-rooted fear of communism, all grew out of his fear that unchecked selfishness would destroy civilized order." The author examines Ike's careful choices of words to convey ideas consistent with his ideology both in public and in private. Chernus argues that Eisenhower's ideology and discourse typified early Cold War discourse.

31.   Citino, Nathan J. *From Arab Nationalism to OPEC: Eisenhower, King Saʿūd, and the Making of U.S.-Saudi Relations*. Bloomington & Indianapolis: Indiana University Press, 2002.

Author Info	Associate history professor at Colorado State University. Specializing in American Foreign Relations and Modern Middle East. Profile at: http://www.colostate.edu/dept/Hist/faculty/citino.html
Bibliography	Yes.
Index	Yes.
Notes	Yes.
Photographs	B&W.
Appendix	No.
Tables	No.
Key Words	Presidency, Cold War, Middle East, Foreign Relations
Other Notes	Maps.
Annotation	Citino examines America's policy toward Saudi Arabia during the Eisenhower Administrations and the implication of those policies for America, Saudi Arabia, the Middle East, Britain, Arab nationalists, and oil producers and consumers. He details America's gradual assumption of power in the Middle East from Great Britain: the change from "British hegemony to an American capitalist order", and discusses Saudi Arabian domestic issues.

32.   Clarfield, Gerald. *Security with Solvency: Dwight D. Eisenhower and the Shaping of the American Military Establishment*. Westport, CT: Praeger, 1999.

Author Info	Professor Emeritus at University of Missouri. "He is the author of numerous books, including Nuclear America, which he co-authored with William Wiecek of Syracuse University, and a two-volume history of United States foreign policy." (From book).
Bibliography	Yes.
Index	Yes.
Notes	Yes.

Photographs	Yes (B&W).
Appendix	No.
Tables	No.
Key Words	Army Chief of Staff, Presidency, Cold War, Military Policy, Economics, Politics.
Other Notes	
Annotation	Clarfield chronicles Eisenhower's efforts to unify America's military, and thus make it more efficient, from the end of WWII through his Presidency, and ultimately the 1958 Defense Reorganization Act. The Act did not go as far as Eisenhower wanted but was still "a major legislative achievement, the culmination of years of effort on Eisenhower's part to bring a greater degree of unity to the military establishment by focusing power in the hands of the secretary of defense while weakening the individual services." Clarfield discusses resistance by branches of the military to the Eisenhower Administration's defense policies.

33.   Coates, Tim (ed.). *D Day to VE Day 1944-45: General Eisenhower's Report on the Invasion of Europe*. London: The Stationery Office, 2000.

Author Info	"[S]tudied at University College, Oxford and at the University of Stirling. After working in the theatre for a number of years, he took up bookselling and became managing director, firstly of Sherratt and Hughes bookshops, and then of Waterstone's. He is known for his support for foreign literature…The idea for 'Uncovered Editions' came while searching through the bookshelves of his late father-in-law, Air Commodore Patrick Cave, OBE." (From book).
Bibliography	No.
Index	No.
Notes	No.
Photographs	No
Appendix	No.
Tables	No.
Key Words	Military- WWII
Other Notes	Maps.
Annotation	Volume in "Uncovered Editions" which are "historic official papers which have not previously been available in popular form… created directly from the archive of The Stationary Office in London". Coates writes that this volume is a "tactical account of his understanding of enemy manoeuvres, and his [Ike's] attempts to counter their actions" and that it presents the story of an "arduous struggle against forces whose tenacity [Ike] admired and whose skills he feared." Only one page introduction. Remainder of book purports to be reports issued by Ike, but there is very little information concerning the original documents.

34.   Craig, Campbell. *Destroying the Village: Eisenhower and Thermonuclear War*. New York: Columbia University Press, 1998.

Author Info   Professor of Religious Studies, University of Colorado, Boulder. http://spot.colorado.edu/~chernus/. Research focuses on the discourse of peace, war, foreign policy, and nationalism in the United States, especially during the cold war and the nuclear age, and how that discourse has affected our public culture and life up to the present. Completed a large project on President Dwight D. Eisenhower and his impact on our discourse. Three books have come out of this project.

Bibliography   Yes.

Index   Yes.

Notes   Yes.

Photographs   No.

Appendix   No.

Tables   No.

Key Words   Presidency, Cold War, Nuclear

Other Notes   Map

Annotation   Craig examines Eisenhower's strategy to avoid nuclear war with the Soviet Union during his Administrations and its extension into Kennedy's. Ike "push[ed] through with a great exertion a military policy which [made] any war with the chief adversary of the United States an automatic, all-out thermonuclear war." Craig argues that he did this not because of budgetary concerns or as a tactic to encourage NATO allies to take greater responsibilities: "His strategy to evade nuclear war was to make American military policy so dangerous that his advisers would find it impossible to push Eisenhower toward war and away from compromise." Craig discusses implementation of the strategy, including developments during the Quemoy-Matsu crisis of 1958 and the Berlin crisis of 1958-59.

D's

35.   Damms, Richard V. *The Eisenhower Presidency, 1953-1961.* London: Pearson Education Limited, 2002.

Author Info   Associate Professor of American history at Mississippi State University. He has published articles on science and national security in the Eisenhower era and recently published "In Search of some big, imaginative plan: the Eisenhower Administration and American Strategy in the Middle East after Suez," in Simon C. Smith, ed., *Reassessing Suez 1956* (Ashgate, 2008). He has recently presented papers at international conferences in the United Kingdom and Ireland. http://www.msstate.edu/dept/history/rdamms.htm

Bibliography   Yes.

Index   Yes.

Notes   Yes, but limited.

Photographs   No.

Appendix	Yes—Documents, Who's Who, and a Guide to Further Reading.
Tables	No.
Key Words	Presidency
Other Notes	Chronology, Maps, Glossary,
Annotation	Part of a series entitled "Seminar Studies in History" which is aimed at bridging the gap between current research and general surveys. Books in the series are written by experts in their field who contribute to the latest research on the topic. This volume is meant to "provide a general introduction and critical overview of the Eisenhower presidency and synthesize much of the current scholarship." Damms covers both of Ike's presidential terms with alternating chapters on the domestic and foreign policies of that term as well as an introduction and an overall balanced "Assessment" of Ike's policies and leadership.

36.　　D'Este Carlo. *Eisenhower: A Soldier's Life*. New York: Henry Holt and Company, 2002.

Author Info	From book: "A retired U.S. Army lieutenant colonel, Carlo D'Este is a highly regarded military historian and the author of four classic works about World War II: *Decision in Normandy*; *Bitter Victory: The Battle for Sicily, 1943*; *World War II in the Mediterranean, 1942-1945*; *Fatal Decision: Anzio and the Battle for Rome*; as well as the biography *Patton: A Genius for War*."
Bibliography	Sources and selected bibliography.
Index	Yes.
Notes	Yes.
Photographs	Yes (B&W).
Appendix	No.
Tables	No.
Key Words	Early Life, Military- Pre WWII, Military—B/w the Wars, Military- WWII
Other Notes	Maps
Annotation	A biography of Eisenhower from his birth until 1945, including his personal and military experiences and struggles. D'Este characterizes Ike's ascent from poverty in Abilene, Kansas to supreme Allied commander as "improbable" and "spectacular" and argues that Ike ambitiously worked to cultivate relationships and skills that made that assent possible. Approximately one-half of the book concerns World War II and provides a major revaluation of Ike's military leadership.

37.　　Divine, Robert A. *The Sputnik Challenge: Eisenhower's Response to the Soviet Satellite*. New York: Oxford University Press, 1993.

Author Info	George W. Littlefield Professor Emeritus in American History at University of Texas, Austin. Ph.D., 1954, Yale University. http://www.utexas.edu/cola/depts/history/faculty/divinera. Leading diplomatic historian.
Bibliography	No.

Index	Yes.
Notes	Yes.
Photographs	No.
Appendix	No.
Tables	Yes.
Key Words	Presidency, Cold War, Foreign Relations, Space Exploration, Technology
Other Notes	
Annotation	Divine details the divergent reactions of Eisenhower and the public to the Soviet launching of Sputnik: the public panicked, and "Eisenhower was one of the few Americans who was not impressed by the Soviet feat." Ike was criticized by Democrats and by his own party for not responding quickly and decisively to Sputnik, and Divine faults him for failing to reassure the public. Divine describes the fear generated in America to the news of the Soviet's achievements, and the attempts to regain the scientific and technological advantage, including defense reorganization and educational reform. He also discusses the costs of those attempts and Ike's moderately successful efforts to restrain spending.

38.   Dockrill, Saki. *Eisenhower's New-Look National Security Policy, 1953-61*, London: Macmillan, 1996.

Author Info	"Saki Dockrill was an historian who blended strategy, defence policy, international relations and cultural themes. Her analysis focused primarily on the Pacific War, 1941-45, the Cold War, and relations between the West and the Pacific Rim." Taught at Kings College London. "Her authoritative study, *Eisenhower's New Look National Security Policy, 1953-1961* (1996), placed this controversial policy in a broad context and offered a sustained defence of her hero, Dwight D. Eisenhower." She also, "served as founding editor of the journal, *Cold War History*, and then sat on its editorial board, while in 1997-2004 she presided over 21 volumes as general editor of Palgrave Macmillan's Cold War History series." Dockrill died in 2009. Her obituary is at http://www.timesonline.co.uk/tol/comment/obituaries/article6817516.ece
Bibliography	Yes.
Index	Yes.
Notes	Yes.
Photographs	No.
Appendix	Yes (5).
Tables	No.
Key Words	Presidency, Cold War, Military Policy, Foreign Relations, Nuclear
Other Notes	
Annotation	Detailed examination of Ike's New Look doctrine—"the book attempts to deal with the New Look on a number of levels—as strategy, as policy, and as diplomacy, all of which are part of a 'doctrine'." Dockrill discusses the Eisenhower Administration's implementation of the New Look, American's perceptions of the policy, and disagreements over the New Look within the executive branch. She finds that Eisenhower based the doctrine on principles

of selectivity and flexibility and sought a balance between defense and domestic financial stability. Dockrill overall praises Eisenhower for his work in foreign policy, but she notes some of the shortcomings of the New Look. She concludes that while "[T]he New Look did not provide any simple solution to the problem of regulating defense expenditures and required considerable fine tuning by the leadership" the U.S. "did not shirk from its responsibility as world leader, while at the same time keeping its economy relatively stable."

E's

39.   Eisenhower, John S. D. *General Ike: A Personal Reminiscence*. New York: Free Press, 2003.

Author Info	John Eisenhower is Ike's son. A retired U.S. Army officer, he has served as Ambassador to Belgium and various other public positions and has written several books on military history, from the U.S.-Mexican War through the Civil War, and especially on WWII.
Bibliography	Yes.
Index	Yes.
Notes	Yes.
Photographs	Yes (B&W).
Appendix	Yes.
Tables	No.
Key Words	Military WWII, Personal Life
Other Notes	Maps
Annotation	Ike's only son to survive childhood, John, has written a series of essays to correct falsehoods he had read about his father. The essays all focus on Eisenhower's military career ("military Ike") because John knows "more about his career as a soldier than [he does] his career as a civilian" and because John believes "that Ike's military career was far more important to him personally than his political life." The essays, "deal almost exclusively with Ike's relations with his associates, for the simple reasons that the facets of his personality appear differently depending on the individual he was dealing with at a given time." Included are essays concerning Ike's relationships with Patton, Fox Conner, Churchill, and Marshall. John Eisenhower utilizes his own memories as well as primary and secondary sources.

40.   Eisenhower, Susan. *Mrs. Ike: Memories and Reflections on the Life of Mamie Eisenhower*. New York: Farrar, Straus and Giroux, 1996.

Author Info	Eisenhower's granddaughter. From her website: "Susan Eisenhower is President of the Eisenhower Group, Inc, which provides strategic counsel on political, business and public affairs projects. She has consulted for Fortune

100 and Fortune 500 companies doing business in the emerging markets of the former Soviet Union and for a number of major institutions and companies engaged in the energy field. Ms. Eisenhower also serves as Chairman of the Eisenhower Institute's Leadership and Public Policy Programs. She had served as the Eisenhower Institute's president twice, and later as Chairman. During that time, she became known for her work in the former Soviet Union and in the energy field." http://www.susaneisenhower.com/about/

Bibliography	No.
Index	Yes.
Notes	Yes.
Photographs	Yes B&W.
Appendix	No.
Tables	No.
Key Words	Personal Life
Other Notes	
Annotation	Biography of Mamie Eisenhower written by Susan Eisenhower, Mamie and Ike's granddaughter. Includes personal memories, as well as the memories of John Eisenhower and other family members. Personal letters are also quoted extensively, some for the first time. Susan Eisenhower describes her grandmother's life, with a focus on her life with and marriage to, Ike, which had its challenges, including his alleged affair, the death of their son, and the problems that come with being in the public eye. Mamie is described as being "centered, confident, and unapologetic about who she was," and as a selfless wife, who had "added to [Ike's] life immeasurably." Mamie had, "in a sense, given the nation her husband, a devoted public servant, a world leader."

F's

41.   Fromkin, David. *In the Time of the Americans: FDR, Truman, Eisenhower, Marshall, MacArthur - the Generation that Changed America's Role in the World.* New York: Alfred A. Knoff, Inc., 1995.

Author Info   Professor of International Relations, History, and Law at Boston University. "Fromkin has spent most of his professional life as a practitioner attorney and a private investor. He served as the head of foreign policy for Hubert Humphrey in the 1972 presidential primary campaign. Additionally, he served for three years as a First Lieutenant in the Judge Advocate General's Corps, U.S. Army, stationed in Verdun, France, where he was a trial observer in French courts pursuant to the NATO Status of Forces Agreement…. After a varied career in law, business, and politics, he turned to writing works of history and studies of world politics… He is the author of seven books, including: *The Question of Government: An Inquiry into the Breakdown of Modern Political Systems* (1975), *The Independence of Nations* (1981), *In the Time of the Americans: FDR, Truman, Eisenhower, Marshall, MacArthur, The Generation That Changed America's Role in the World* (1995). His 1989 book, *A Peace to End*

All Peace: Creating the Modern Middle East 1914-1922 (1989), was a national bestseller, was chosen by the editors of the *New York Times Book Review* as one of the dozen best books of the year, and was shortlisted for the Pulitzer Prize. His most recent book, published in 2004, is *Europe's Last Summer: Who Started the Great War in 1914?*" From: http://www.bu.edu/ir/faculty/alphabetical/fromkin/

Bibliography	Yes.
Index	Yes.
Notes	Yes- limited.
Photographs	No.
Appendix	No.
Tables	No.
Key Words	Early Life, Military- Pre WWII, Military—B/w the Wars, Military- WWII
Other Notes	
Annotation	Based mainly on secondary sources and with limited notes, *In the Time of the Americans* is "a work of storytelling and of interpretation" and tells the story of "the American leaders who defined America's role in the international politics of the twentieth century". Fromkin sees the men he studies as, "forming a coherent generation, shaped by shared experiences that brought them to see events from a common point of view." The focus is on this generation's evolving ideas of what America's role in the world should be as the country swung from an isolationist to an internationalist posture. Collective, narrative biography.

G's

42.   Gaddis, John Lewis, et al, ed. *Cold War Statesmen Confront the Bomb: Nuclear Diplomacy Since 1945.* New York: Oxford University Press, 1999.

Author Info	Gaddis "is Robert Lovett Professor of History at Yale University. He is the author of several books on the Cold War, including, most recently *We Now Know: Rethinking Cold War History.*" (from book). Andrew P. N. Erdman wrote the essay on Ike: he is "is competing a PhD in History from Harvard University and is currently a Peace Scholar, United States Institute of Peace." (from book). Erdman currently a Consultant at McKinsey & Company, Inc. The co-editors of the book are Dr. Philip Gordon, Director for European Affairs, National Security Council; Professor Ernest May, History Department at Harvard University; and Professor Jonathon Rosenberg, from the Department of History at Florida Atlantic University.
Bibliography	No.
Index	Yes.
Notes	Yes.
Photographs	No.
Appendix	No.
Tables	No.

Key Words   Presidency, Cold War, Nuclear, Foreign Relations
Other Notes   Figure
Annotation   A collection of essays which examine how "ten Cold War statesmen thought about nuclear weapons," especially at moments when they had to consider whether or not to use them. Essays address both "Superpower" leaders such as Truman, Stalin, and Kennedy, as well as "Allies" including Churchill, Mao, and de Gaulle. Chapter by Andrew P. N. Erdman entitled: "War No Longer Has Any Logic Whatever: Dwight D. Eisenhower and the Thermonuclear Revolution" traces the development of Ike's understanding of the relationship between nuclear weapons and American national security. He finds that: "Although his belief that nuclear weapons were morally no different from any other weapon did not waver, his view of their efficacy as tools of statecraft and warfare evolved considerably." Also includes a chapter on Eisenhower's Secretary of State, John Foster Dulles.

43.   Galambos, Louis and Daun van Ee (eds.). *Papers of Dwight David Eisenhower, Volumes 14-17: The Presidency: The Middle Way.* (Baltimore, MD: Johns Hopkins University Press, 1996).

Author Info   Louis Galambos: "Chair of the Legacy Committee and a faculty member at Johns Hopkins University, he previously taught at Rice University [and Rutgers University]. A former editor of *The Journal of Economic History*, he served as President of the Economic History Association. He has written and lectured extensively on American business history, business-government relations, the history of modern institutional development, and the process of innovation in the public, private, and nonprofit sectors. His numerous publications include 'The U.S. Corporate Economy in the Twentieth Century' (in Volume Three of *The Cambridge Economic History of the United States*, 2000); *Networks of Innovation: Vaccine Development at Merck, Sharp & Dohme, and Mulford, 1895-1995*, co-authored with Jane Eliot Sewell (1998); and *Anytime, Anywhere: Entrepreneurship and the Creation of a Wireless World* (2002), co-authored with Eric John Abrahamson." He co-edited 16 (of the 21) volumes of *The Presidential Papers of Dwight David Eisenhower*.

Daun van Ee: "Historian with the Manuscript Division of the Library of Congress, Daun van Ee received his Ph.D. from Johns Hopkins. Serving in the U.S. Army in Vietnam, he won the Combat Infantryman's Badge and the Bronze Star. He was Assistant Editor of the *The Papers of Dwight David Eisenhower* from 1974 to 1977, Executive Editor from 1977 to 1995, and Editor from 1995 to 2001. He also was a member of the Editorial Board of the Model Editions Partnership, under whose auspices appeared an on-line mini-edition of Eisenhower's papers. His publications include *David Dudley Field and the Reconstruction of the Law* (Garland, 1986), and "From the New Look to the Flexible Response," in *Against All Enemies: Interpretations of American Military History* (Greenwood, 1986). He co-authored *Churchill and the Great*

Republic (2004)."

Both bios from:

http://www.eisenhowermemorial.org/legacycommittee/bios.htm

Bibliography	Yes.
Index	Yes.
Notes	Extensive annotation.
Photographs	Yes.
Appendix	Glossary and Chronology.
Tables	No.
Key Words	Presidency, Domestic Policy, Foreign Relations, Cold War, Middle East
Other Notes	
Annotation	These volumes carry forward the selective publication and annotation of Eisenhower's papers through the first Eisenhower administration, 1953-1957. As before, the editors only include materials with which Eisenhower was personally involved. They provide examples of routine correspondence such as declinations but do not publish them in their entirety. In each case, the editors describe in the notes the incoming document or situation that prompted Ike to prepare his document and use cross-references and annotations to guide the reader to additional manuscript and secondary sources. Through the courtesy of the Johns Hopkins University Press, all four of these volumes are available at no charge and in searchable form at eisenhowermemorial.org.

44.   Galambos, Louis and Daun van Ee (eds.). *Papers of Dwight David Eisenhower, Volumes 18-21: The Presidency: Keeping the Peace.* (Baltimore, MD: Johns Hopkins University Press, 2001).

Author Info	See information in Entry #43.
Bibliography	Yes.
Index	Yes.
Notes	Extensive annotation.
Photographs	Yes.
Appendix	Glossary and Chronology.
Tables	No.
Key Words	Presidency, Domestic Policy, Civil Rights, Foreign Relations, Cold War, Middle East, Technology
Other Notes	
Annotation	This set of four volumes completes *The Papers of Dwight David Eisenhower*. Here, the editors continued to follow the same basic principles that had been employed in the previous seventeen volumes of the series. They selected only those papers with which Eisenhower was personally involved in originating and/or drafting. As they note in the "Introduction," the President did not intend to make foreign policy the central mission of his second administration, but Ike had no choice in that regard. Containing communism pushed most domestic concerns into a secondary position. These volumes, like the previous four, are available courtesy of the Johns Hopkins University Press at no charge and in

searchable form at eisenhowermemorial.org.

45.   Galvin, Daniel J. *Presidential Party Building: Dwight D. Eisenhower to George W. Bush*. Princeton, NJ: Princeton University Press, 2010.

Author Info   "Daniel J. Galvin (Ph.D. Yale University) is an Assistant Professor of Political Science at Northwestern University. He is also affiliated with the Program in Comparative-Historical Social Science (CHSS) and is a Faculty Associate at the Institute for Policy Research.... Galvin is also co-editor, with Ian Shapiro and Stephen Skowronek, of *Rethinking Political Institutions: The Art of the State* (NYU Press, 2006). He has published his research in a number of journals, edited volumes, and other outlets, including *Polity*, *The Forum*, *Vox Pop*, the *Journal of Contemporary Thought*, *The New York Times*, and *Encyclopedia Britannica*.... Galvin has been the recipient of fellowships and grants from the National Science Foundation (NSF), the Miller Center of Public Affairs, the Center for the Study of the Presidency, the Lyndon B. Johnson Library, the Eisenhower Foundation, Northwestern's Weinberg College of Arts and Sciences, and Yale University." From faculty profile page at http://faculty.wcas.northwestern.edu/~djg249/

Bibliography   No.
Index   Yes.
Notes   Yes.
Photographs   No.
Appendix   Yes.
Tables   Yes.
Key Words   Presidency
Other Notes
Annotation   Explores the relationship between presidents and their political parties from Eisenhower to G. W. Bush. He argues that generally Republican presidents were party builders and, until Clinton, Democratic presidents were party predators. Of Ike Galvin finds that contrary to much literature on the subject, Eisenhower "worked tirelessly behind the scenes to build a New Republican party" and that his efforts were "persistent, aggressive, and often large in scope." Eisenhower came into office without party building organizations in place, and he had to create them. Ultimately, Ike's efforts "failed to build a new majority in his image or create a consensus around his Modern Republicanism," however, Ike did "alter the political landscape and make it more likely that future party leaders would follow in his footsteps."

46.   Gambone, Michael D. *Eisenhower, Somoza, and the Cold War in Nicaragua, 1953-1961*. Westport, CT: Praeger, 1997.

Author Info   Assistant professor of history at Kutztown University (Pennsylvania). Specializes in Latin American and U.S. History.

Bibliography	Yes.
Index	Yes.
Notes	Yes.
Photographs	No.
Appendix	No.
Tables	Figures and Tables.
Key Words	Presidency, Cold War, Foreign Relations
Other Notes	
Annotation	Gambone explores, "U.S.-Nicaraguan economic and military relations, their separate development, and interaction during the Eisenhower administration," with a dual focus on the policymaking process in both countries and the nature of the relationship between the countries. The book is divided into two parts, representing each of Eisenhower's terms and with chapters alternating in focus between the U.S. and Nicaragua. He finds that despite the power imbalance that the United States had over Nicaragua, America was not able to exert complete influence over the country and the relationship was one that could be classified "between patronage and partnership".

47.   Garthoff, Raymond. *Assessing the Adversary: Estimates by the Eisenhower Administration of Soviet Intentions and Capabilities.* Washington: The Brooking Institution, 1991.

Author Info	In 2000 listed as: "Senior Fellow Retired, foreign-policy, The Brookings Institution." The Institution gives the following bio: "Ray Garthoff is a specialist on arms control, the Cold War, the former Soviet Union and NATO. He is a former U.S. ambassador to Bulgaria and has also advised the State Department on missile treaties." http://www.brookings.edu/experts/garthoffr.aspx
Bibliography	No.
Index	No.
Notes	Yes.
Photographs	No.
Appendix	No.
Tables	No.
Key Words	Presidency, Cold War, Foreign Relations
Other Notes	
Annotation	This "Occasional Paper" analyzes the Eisenhower Administration's assessments of the Soviet Union's intentions and capabilities. Garthoff divides his paper into two parts, Part 1 covers Ike's first term ("The Post-Stalin Years") and Part 2, Ike's second ("The Post-Sputnik Years"). The paper is based on primary sources as well as Garthoff's own memories from his work for the CIA. He finds that: "The principal fault of the process of assessing the adversary... was the inability to empathize with the other side and visualize its interests in other than adversarial terms", and that a "more measured and

realistic assessment of the threat [posed by the Soviet Union]" might have led to a more successful and less costly approach than containment. Paper, "was originally prepared for a conference on the Eisenhower legacy in world affairs held in Moscow in November 1990".

48. Geelhoed, E. Bruce. and Anthony O. Edmonds. *Eisenhower, MacMillan and Allied Unity, 1957-61.* New York: Palgrave Macmillan, 2003.

Author Info	Geelhoed: Professor of History at Ball State University. His teaching and research interests are: Eisenhower Presidency; 20th-century Business history. He "is the author of *Charles E. Wilson and Controversy at the Pentagon, 1953 to 1957* (Wayne State University Press, 1979)… He is also the co-author with Anthony O. Edmonds of… *Eisenhower, Macmillan, and Allied Unity, 1957-1961* (Palgrave Macmillan, 2003). In addition, he and Dr. Edmonds are the co-editors of *The Macmillan-Eisenhower Correspondence, 1957-1969* (Palgrave Macmillan, 2005.). He served as chairperson of the History Department from 2004 until 2010. Currently he serves as the Interim Director of MA Programs in the Department." http://cms.bsu.edu/Academics/CollegesandDepartments/History/FacultyandStaff/GeelhoedE.aspx Edmonds: History Professor at Ball State University. His teaching and research specialties are 20th-century U.S., sports, America and Vietnam. He "has been the George and Frances Ball Distinguished Professor of History since 2004…. Edmonds received the 2004 Victor Lawhead Award for Outstanding Contributions to the Core Curriculum." http://cms.bsu.edu/Academics/CollegesandDepartments/History/FacultyandStaff/EdmondsAnthony.aspx
Bibliography	Yes.
Index	Yes.
Notes	Yes.
Photographs	No.
Appendix	No.
Tables	No.
Key Words	Presidency, Foreign Relations, Cold War
Other Notes	
Annotation	The authors examine the personal nature of the diplomatic partnership between Eisenhower and Macmillan from the restoration of the "special relationship" between America and Britain, which had suffered during the Suez Crisis in 1956, to the inauguration of Kennedy. Their focus is narrow and their theme simple: "personality and friendships do matter in international relations." In this particular case, "the fact that [Eisenhower and Macmillan] had known each other since the early days of World War II made a difference in the way that they and their advisors conducted foreign policy." The book does not address many international problems the men faced during the period covered. Four major chapters each cover one year of the four-year period under examination (1957-1960) and the epilogue addresses 1961. They conclude that

the men achieved a "great deal"—their partnership helped to strengthen NATO and they "introduced the important concept of moving gradually from an era of confrontation to an era of negotiation with the Soviet Union."

49.   Geelhoed, E. Bruce and Anthony O. Edmonds, (ed.), *The Macmillan-Eisenhower Correspondence, 1957-69*. New York: Palgrave Macmillan, 2005.

Author Info	See information in Entry #48.
Bibliography	"Note on Sources" (Bibliographical essay).
Index	Yes.
Notes	Yes.
Photographs	No.
Appendix	No.
Tables	No.
Key Words	Presidency, Foreign Relations, Cold War, Nuclear, Middle East
Other Notes	
Annotation	Correspondence between Eisenhower and Macmillan, collected from the Eisenhower Library in Abilene, Kansas, and from British archives. Most of the material is from the time when the two men were leaders of their respective countries. Letters are organized chronologically, with approximately one chapter per year (1957, 1958, 1959, and 1960-61). Chapters begin with brief introductions providing context.

50.   Gelb, Norman. *Ike and Monty: Generals at War*. New York: William Morrow and Company, Inc., 1994.

Author Info	"Norman Gelb graduated from Brooklyn College and did graduate work in history at the University of Minnesota and the University of Vienna. After reporting from Berlin for the Mutual Broadcasting System, he was transferred to London, where he began his history-writing career. He is the author of several highly acclaimed books." From: http://www.jewishpub.org/author.php?id=291
Bibliography	Yes.
Index	Yes.
Notes	Yes.
Photographs	No.
Appendix	No.
Tables	No.
Key Words	Military- Pre WWII, Military- WWII
Other Notes	
Annotation	Comparative biography of Eisenhower and British Field Marshal Bernard Law Montgomery, focused mainly on their service in World War II. The two men were very different in personality and temperament, had different ideas concerning strategies and tactics, and consequently struggled to form an effective working relationship. Gelb argues that this was detrimental to their

common cause in the war: "As generals at war, each had important qualities the other lacked that, had the two men been able to work together in harmony, might have compensated considerably for their respective limitations. Their discord made that impossible, with costly consequences…" He argues that while Ike was gregarious and diplomatic, he was inexperienced in combat and lacked confidence, especially in the beginning of WWII.

51.   Greene, Benjamin P. *Eisenhower, Science Advice, and the Nuclear Test-Ban Debate, 1945-1963*. Stanford, CA: Stanford University Press, 2007.

Author Info	Stanford University Press Author Bio notes that: "Benjamin P. Greene was Assistant Professor of American History at West Point from 2001 to 2004. He is now stationed in Stuttgart at Headquarters, United States European Command."
Bibliography	Yes.
Index	Yes.
Notes	Yes.
Photographs	No.
Appendix	No.
Tables	No.
Key Words	Presidency, Cold War, Nuclear, Foreign Relations, Technology.
Other Notes	
Annotation	Examines the debates amongst the scientific community and the Eisenhower Administration over the nuclear test-ban agreement. Greene concludes that: "While recent scholarship questions the sincerity of Eisenhower's efforts to ban nuclear testing… Eisenhower since 1954 was favorably inclined to accept a test-ban agreement." He finds that he failed to achieve this goal because of a distrust of the Soviet Union, his leadership style's focus on consensus which prevented him from overruling his closest advisers' opposition, a lack of pressure on the part of Congress, allies, and the American people, and "Eisenhower's understandable confusion with the complex technical issues" left him to rely on scientific advisers "strictly limited to those who opposed a test ban for the first half of his presidency." Special focus is paid to Ike's relationship with Lewis Strauss.

H's

52.   Hahn, Peter. *The United States, Great Britain, and Egypt, 1945-56: Strategy and Diplomacy in the Early Cold War*. Chapel Hill, NC: University of North Carolina Press, 1991.

Author Info	Professor at Ohio State. "Professor Hahn specializes in United States diplomatic history in the Middle East since 1940. He has won research grants from the J. William Fulbright Foreign Scholarship Board, the National

Endowment for the Humanities, the Truman Library Institute, the John F. Kennedy Library, the Lyndon Johnson Foundation, the Eisenhower World Affairs Institute, the Office of United States Air Force History, and the U.S. Army Center of Military History." Hahn's publications include *Crisis and Crossfire: The United States and the Middle East since 1945* (2005); *Caught in the Middle East: U.S. Policy toward the Arab-Israeli Conflict, 1945-1961* (2004), and (co-edited with Mary Ann Heiss) *Empire and Revolution: The United States and the Third World Since 1945* (2001). Professor Hahn is writing a book on the U.S. relationship with Iraq since World War I. From: http://history.osu.edu/people/person.cfm?id=136

Bibliography	Yes.
Index	Yes.
Notes	Yes.
Photographs	No.
Appendix	No.
Tables	No
Key Words	Presidency, Cold War, Middle East, Foreign Relations
Other Notes	
Annotation	This fully documented study draws upon the available manuscript and secondary sources to develop a better understanding of the American efforts to achieve a measure of stability in the Middle East in the immediate aftermath of World War II. Given the breakup of the colonial empires, the rise of Soviet power, and the growing force of Egyptian nationalism, the prospects for the United States were never particularly favorable, and indeed the Suez War of 1956 left a bitter heritage and, as the author notes, "rampant instability in Egypt." Soviet influence in the region became more of a problem for the United States. The strains in American-Egyptian relations persisted through the entire postwar decade, and the United States found it difficult to continue its support for Britain while satisfying the Egyptian desire for national autonomy. The U.S. position became all the more important as Britain gradually withdrew from the region. The author studies these developments primarily from a U.S. strategic and tactical perspective, leaving the Egyptian position less fully explored. Ultimately, Hahn concludes, the U.S. goals were impossible to achieve.

53. Hall, Michael R. *Sugar and Power in the Dominican Republic: Eisenhower, Kennedy and the Trujillos*. Westport CN: Greenwood Press, 2000.

Author Info	History Professor at Armstrong Atlantic State University. Teaches Latin American and Diplomatic History. Served in the Peace Corps from 1984-1987 in the Dominican Republic. http://www.armstrong.edu/Liberal_Arts/history/history_michael_hall
Bibliography	Yes.
Index	Yes.
Notes	Yes.

Photographs	No.
Appendix	No.
Tables	Yes.
Key Words	Presidency, Foreign Relations, Cold War, Economics.
Other Notes	Map.
Annotation	Using U.S. and Dominican government documents, Hall examines "the powerful impact sugar had on US-Dominican relations between 1958 and 1962." Hall explores Eisenhower and Kennedy's use of sugar quota legislation to maintain U.S. hegemony in the Dominican Republic and the Dominican's use of America's fear of communism "to justify its desire for an increased share of the preferential sugar market." The first three of the five total chapters are "background necessary to put the 1958-1962 time period into historical perspective."

54.   Hauenstein, Ralph W. and Donald E. Markle. *Intelligence Was My Line: Inside Eisenhower's Other Command*. New York: Hippocrene Books, Inc., 2005.

Author Info	"Donald E. Markle is a 1969 [University of Maryland University College] graduate, with a specialization in history. For 34 years he worked in the U.S. intelligence arena and, for 13 of those years, was stationed in Europe. Since retiring, he has concentrated on his love of history by writing and teaching. He is the author of *Spies and Spymasters of the Civil War* (Barnes and Noble, 1998) and the forthcoming *The Telegraph Goes to War* (Edmonston, 2003)." http://www.umuc.edu/fyionline/may_03/fyionline7.html
Bibliography	No.
Index	Yes.
Notes	Limited.
Photographs	Yes B&W.
Appendix	No.
Tables	No.
Key Words	Military- WWII
Other Notes	Maps.
Annotation	Memoirs of Ralph W. Hauenstein, Chief, Intelligence Branch (G-2), Hq. European Theater of Operation, U.S. Army (ETOUSA), and his service in WWII as told through Donald E. Markle from interviews. Markle weaves together Hauenstein's memories, which had been unrecorded for security purposes and are of events that occurred 50 years ago, with additional historical facts that he notes in footnotes. Hauenstein discusses his work in intelligence gathering, in Iceland, and his work as part of ETOUSA, under Eisenhower's command. Also reflects on whether or not Ike knew about the atomic bomb.

55.   Haycock, D.J. *Eisenhower and the Art of Warfare: A Critical Appraisal*. Jefferson, North Carolina: McFarland & Company. 2004.

Author Info	Book cover notes that Haycock is an English tutor, living in Los Angeles.
Bibliography	Yes.
Index	Yes.
Notes	Yes (brief).
Photographs	B&W Photographs.
Appendix	No.
Tables	No.
Key Words	Military- WWII, Leadership
Other Notes	Maps.
Annotation	Seeking "an objective portrait" and an appraisal that credits "Montgomery for his achievements," Haycock reviews the secondary literature and available memoirs. The author concludes that Eisenhower's leadership in Europe was more notable for its social rather than military skills. Ike's boss, George C. Marshall, Haycock says, was equally inept and misguided in the art of warfare. By contrast, Montgomery is described as qualified, experienced, and above all, correct about strategy.

56.   Holland, Matthew F. *America and Egypt: From Roosevelt to Eisenhower.* Westport, CT: Praeger, 1996.

Author Info	As of 2001, Holland was "Center Director at Embry-Riddle Aeronautical University in Tucson, Arizona. He was [a] former officer in the U.S. Army." From *Eisenhower Between the Wars: The Making of a General and Statesman.*
Bibliography	Selected References.
Index	Yes.
Notes	Yes.
Photographs	No.
Appendix	No.
Tables	No.
Key Words	Presidency, Cold War, Foreign Relations, Middle East
Other Notes	
Annotation	Holland draws upon the available manuscript and secondary sources to provide an even-tempered analysis of the relations between the United States and Egypt during an era of tumultuous changes. As British power in the Middle East collapsed and the United States and Soviet Union pressed forward, Egypt came to play a central role in Cold War diplomacy. Oil and strategic positioning dominated U.S. efforts to woo Gamal Abdel Nasser's government away from the Soviets. For Nasser the challenge was to remain neutral so he could bargain with both sides. The author gives more credit to the Eisenhower Administration's diplomacy than previous scholars. But as Holland points out, the Eastern Question's internal politics could not ultimately be settled by the great powers, despite their enormous fiscal and military resources. What Ike learned was how to protect America's central interests without attempting to control the region's complex, contentious political configurations.

57. Holland, Matthew F. *Eisenhower Between the Wars: The Making of a General and Statesman*. Westport, Connecticut: Praeger, 2001.

Author Info	See information in Entry #56
Bibliography	Selected Bibliography.
Index	Yes.
Notes	Yes.
Photographs	Yes (B&W).
Appendix	No.
Tables	No.
Key Words	Military—B/w the Wars, Personal Life
Other Notes	
Annotation	Holland examines Ike during the interwar years and argues that this period was essential in preparing Eisenhower for the challenges he would face as a General and as President. Holland notes that one can also see during this period traits which were crucial to Eisenhower's success—the ability to seek out outstanding mentors and learn from them, intelligence, athleticism, ambition, and creative, visionary thinking. Book is arranged topically and addresses topics including overseas assignments, politics, and schooling. Issues discussed include his work as tank commander, his drafting of the first official history of the American Expeditionary Force, his work building an army in the Philippines, and a near court martial. Also addresses personal issues including his marriage and the death of his first son.

58. Holt, Daniel D., and James W. Leyerzapf, *Eisenhower: The Prewar Diaries and Selected Papers, 1905 - 1941*. Baltimore: The Johns Hopkins University Press, 1998.

Author Info	From book: "Daniel D. Holt is director of the Dwight D. Eisenhower Presidential Library in Abilene, Kansas, where James W. Leyerzapf is an archivist." In August 2009, the George C. Marshall Foundation noted that: "Daniel D. Holt, who recently retired as director of the Eisenhower Presidential Library and Museum and is an expert in the era to be covered in the remaining [Marshall] papers, is serving as managing editor. http://www.marshallfoundation.org/news/CurrentNewsReleases.htm The Thiel College alumni page notes that Leyerzapf: "retired in October 2009 as an archivist with the Dwight D. Eisenhower Presidential Library after 37 years of service. In December, Leyerzapf received the Archivist of the Unites States Lifetime Achievement Award." http://www.thiel.edu/alumni/class-notes.htm
Bibliography	No.
Index	Yes.
Notes	Yes.
Photographs	Yes (B&W).
Appendix	No.
Tables	No.

Key Words	Early Life, Military- Pre WWII, Military—B/w the Wars
Other Notes	Chronology, Maps.
Annotation	Includes five separate prewar Eisenhower diaries and approximately one-half of all other prewar Eisenhower documents known to have survived, arranged chronologically and focused on Eisenhower's military biography and his personal development. Diaries cover much of the period between August 1929 and December 1941; only one chapter deals with the period pre-1928. The bulk of the book concerns Ike's work on the American Battle Monuments Commission, in the office of the Secretary of War, as Chief of Staff, and in the Philippines. Diary entries are candid (Eisenhower had ordered one of the diaries destroyed) and reveal much about Ike's military and political development. Editors provide chapter introductions and limited footnotes for context. Introduction by Ike's son, John S. D. Eisenhower.

59.   Holt, Marilyn Irvin. *Mamie Doud Eisenhower: The General's First Lady*. Lawrence, KS: University Press of Kansas, 2007.

Author Info	"[F]ormer director of publications at the Kansas Historical Society and has served as a research consultant for the PBS American Experience series. She is author of *The Orphan Trains: Placing Out in America* and *Linoleum, Better Babies, and the Modern Farm Woman, 1890–1930* and editor of a volume devoted to twentieth-century teenagers' diaries and journals." Bio from publisher's website (http://www.kansaspress.ku.edu/holind.html)
Bibliography	Bibliographic essay.
Index	Yes.
Notes	Yes.
Photographs	Yes (B&W).
Appendix	No.
Tables	No.
Key Words	Personal Life, Military—B/w the Wars, Military- WWII, Presidency
Other Notes	
Annotation	Biography of Mamie Eisenhower. Attention is paid to her experiences as a military wife, and how that shaped her as a First Lady. Holt argues that Mamie's personality and outward appearances of domesticity were a "perfect fit" for 1950s America, and that she, "instinctively seemed to understand the mood of the people and what they expected of her as a first lady." Her public image as a traditional wife was cast in a negative light in subsequent decades by the new women's movement, but she remained popular with the public after she and Ike left the White House. Holt also pushes past Mamie's "housewife" designation and explores her work as a general's wife and First Lady. Based on documents in the Eisenhower library. Volume is in the Modern First Ladies series published by the University Press of Kansas.

60.   Humes, James C. *Eisenhower and Churchill: The Partnership That Saved the World*. New York: Three Rivers Press, 2001.

Author Info	From his biography on Random House: "James C. Humes, a professor of language and leadership at the University of Southern Colorado, is the author of numerous books, including *Nixon's Ten Commandments of Leadership and Negotiation, Confessions of a White House Ghostwriter,* and *The Wit and Wisdom of Winston Churchill.* He served briefly in Eisenhower's White House and was a speaker, in London, for ceremonies commemorating Churchill's 125th birthday. Mr. Humes lives in Pueblo, Colorado." http://www.randomhouse.com/author/results.pperl?authorid=13819 As late as 2005, he was still at Colorado State University Pueblo, but is now not in the school's directory.
Bibliography	Yes.
Index	Yes.
Notes	No.
Photographs	No.
Appendix	No.
Tables	No.
Key Words	Early Life, Military- WWII, Presidency, Cold War, Foreign Relations
Other Notes	
Annotation	Examines Eisenhower and Churchill and the friendship between them from its origins to Churchill's death in 1965. In alternating chapters focusing on Churchill and Ike and working forward chronologically, Humes discusses the men's different backgrounds, commonalities, working relationship, and eventual friendship ("The first time Eisenhower saw Churchill was just after Christmas in 1941," Chapter 16). He attributes much to the relationship, as suggested by the subtitle, describing Eisenhower and Churchill as, "the two men who together won the war against fascism in World War II and then laid the groundwork that led to the eventual victory over communism in the Cold War." Foreword by David Eisenhower (Ike's grandson).

J's

61.　Jablonsky, David. *War by Land, Sea, and Air: Dwight Eisenhower and the Concept of Unified Command*. New Haven, CT: Yale University Press, 2010.

Author Info	External researcher at the Strategic Studies Institute. "[T]he Professor of National Security Affairs, Department of National Security and Strategy, U.S. Army War College. A graduate of Dartmouth College, Kansas University and Boston University, Dr. Jablonsky is the author of four books dealing with European history and international relations. He is a retired infantry colonel who has held the Elihu Root Chair of Strategy and the George C. Marshall Chair of Military Studies at the U.S. Army War College." Bio from http://www.strategicstudiesinstitute.army.mil/Pubs/people.cfm?authorID=354
Bibliography	No.
Index	Yes.

Notes	Yes.
Photographs	No.
Appendix	No.
Tables	No.
Key Words	Military- Pre WWII, Military- WWII, Presidency, Military Policy, Leadership
Other Notes	
Annotation	Jablonsky details Eisenhower's evolving ideas concerning, and eventual development of, a unified command system in the U.S. military. The author traces Ike's position from the beginning of his military education at West Point through World War II, and ultimately the passage of the 1958 Defense Reorganization Act. Organized chronologically, the account shows the growth of Ike as a military leader, as well as how his conceptions of unified command evolved over time. Jablonsky also addresses current events. Part of The Yale Library of Military History series, the aim of which is to present analyses of war, evaluations of political and military decision making, and "descriptive accounts of military activity that illuminate its human elements."

62.   Jacobs, Travis. *Eisenhower at Columbia*. New Brunswick, NJ: Transaction Publishers, 2001.

Author Info	Middlebury College Fletcher D. Proctor Professor Emeritus of American History. Son of a Dean at Columbia University, who was a contemporary there with Ike.
Bibliography	Yes.
Index	Yes.
Notes	Yes.
Photographs	Yes (B&W).
Appendix	No.
Tables	No.
Key Words	Columbia University
Other Notes	
Annotation	Jacobs examines a period of Ike's life that is often skimmed over: his presidency of Columbia University. Jacobs includes not only Ike's experiences with and struggles at Columbia, but also the background of the situation at Columbia University when Ike joined the school: they were disorganized and struggling financially after the tenure of an ailing President and ineffective trustees. Jacobs concludes that Eisenhower's work as President had at least limited benefits for both the school and the future U.S. President. Eisenhower's presence provided the university with much needed publicity, and Ike's work there allowed him to gain the contacts and political skills necessary for his work in the White House. The arrangement was not ideal, however, for either party, and there was a great deal of friction between Eisenhower and the academics of Columbia.

K's

63.   Kahin, Audrey R., and George McT. Kahin. *Subversion as Foreign Policy: The Secret Eisenhower and Dulles Debacle in Indonesia.* New York: The New Press, 1995.

Author Info   Audrey R. Kahin is the editor of the journal *Indonesia.* (from book) George McT. Kahin was professor emeritus of international studies at Cornell. He died in 2000. "Kahin is the namesake of Cornell's George McT. Kahin Center for Advanced Research on Southeast Asia, dedicated in his honor in 1992, and he was a seminal force in the creation of Southeast Asian studies in the United States, in general, and at Cornell, in particular." http://www.news.cornell.edu/releases/Feb00/G.McT.Kahin.Obit.html

Bibliography   No.
Index   Yes.
Notes   Yes.
Photographs   No.
Appendix   No.
Tables   No.
Key Words   Presidency, Foreign Relations, Cold War
Other Notes   Biographies of Key Figures, Note on Sources, Maps.
Annotation   The Kahins trace failed, covert operations in Indonesia under the Eisenhower Administration, operations which, "provoked and strongly abetted a major rebellion and then civil war in Indonesia that tore the country apart." Eisenhower's Administration, including the Dulles brothers, sought to overthrow the Indonesian government under Sukarno because they thought it was coming under Communist influence by way of covert military action. The authors argue that America's intervention in Indonesia was a complete failure and actually served to further entrench Sukarno's government, to the detriment of the Indonesian people. Events in Indonesia were kept "under tight wraps" in America, but "many thousands of Indonesian civilians and soldiers lost their lives" and the repercussions of America's involvement are still being felt in Indonesia. Based on American, British, and Indonesian sources, including interviews.

64.   Kingseed, Cole C. *Eisenhower and the Suez Crisis of 1956.* Baton Rouge and London: Louisiana State University Press, 1995.

Author Info   "Colonel Cole C. Kingseed, United States Army (Retired), is a thirty-year infantry veteran who commanded at the platoon, company, and battalion level. A graduate of the University of Dayton (OH) in 1971, he served in a variety of military assignments, culminating in his tenure as full professor of history and chief of military history at the U S Military Academy at West Point. Colonel Kingseed holds a Ph.D. from Ohio State University and a Master of Arts in National Security and Strategic Studies from the U.S. Naval War College. ... Cole now serves as a private leadership consultant and a Founder and Partner of Battlefield Leadership." http://www.battlefieldleadership.com/bios/colonel-cole-c-kingseed-u-s-army-retired

Bibliography	Yes.
Index	Yes.
Notes	Yes.
Photographs	No.
Appendix	No.
Tables	No.
Key Words	Presidency, Cold War, Foreign Relations, Middle East, Leadership
Other Notes	
Annotation	Uses the Suez Crisis as "a study in presidential leadership, concentrating on what Eisenhower did and how he did it." Kingseed's principal focus is not on the crisis itself, but instead Ike's crisis management. He focuses, "on the president as a decision maker and director of foreign policy." Kingseed points out correct decisions Ike made, but also mistakes: "His policy achieved his short-term goal of halting foreign aggression against Egypt, but he failed to obtain his ultimate objective of lasting regional stability to prevent the conditions that were conducive to Soviet incursions into the Middle East." Ultimately, Eisenhower is portrayed as a President who was fully in control of foreign policy and who implemented decision making processes developed during his years in the military to calmly and courageously manage the crisis. Part of the Political Traditions in Foreign Policies Series.

65.　Kinnard, Douglas. *Eisenhower: Soldier-Statesman of the American Century*. Washington D.C.: Brasseys's Inc., 2002.

Author Info	Was an emeritus professor of political science at the University of Vermont, but is no longer listed as faculty on their website.
Bibliography	Select bibliography.
Index	Yes.
Notes	Yes.
Photographs	B&W Photographs.
Appendix	No.
Tables	No.
Key Words	Early Life, Military- Pre WWII, Military—B/w the Wars, Military- WWII, Presidency, Post-Presidency.
Other Notes	Maps, Chronology.
Annotation	Having written already on Eisenhower, the author condensed his previous studies into a short book in the series on Military Profiles. Kinnard's emphasis is on the great victory in the "crusade" on the Western Front. He lauds Ike's strategy and especially his leadership of an allied force that was rife with disagreements and difficult personalities. As president, Kinnard says, Eisenhower helped to give Americans peace and prosperity, along with a touch of complacency.

66.   Knorr, Lawrence. *The Relations of Dwight D Eisenhower: His Pennsylvania German Roots*. Camp Hill, PA: Sunbury Press, Inc., 2010.

Author Info	"Lawrence Knorr, MBA PMP CCP, born in 1964, is an amateur genealogist with deep roots in the Pennsylvania Dutch Region. Lawrence's "real" jobs are as Director of Information Systems for Giant Food Stores, LLC of Carlisle, PA and as an adjunct professor at Harrisburg University, Harrisburg, PA." Lawrence, who holds a Bachelor's degree in Business/Economics (History Minor) from Wilson College and a Masters of Business Administration from Penn State, has been involved in genealogical research for fifteen years. (from book).
Bibliography	No.
Index	Yes.
Notes	No.
Photographs	Yes (B&W).
Appendix	No.
Tables	No.
Key Words	Family, Personal Life
Other Notes	
Annotation	Genealogy of Dwight Eisenhower that traces his roots back to Germany and England, with a specific focus on those relations that had some connection to Pennsylvania.

67.   Korda, Michael. *Ike: An American Hero*. New York, NY: HarperCollins, 2007.

Author Info	"Michael Korda is the former editor in chief of Simon & Schuster and is the author of many books, most recently *With Wings Like Eagles: A History of the Battle of Britain*. He served in the Royal Air Force and lives in Dutchess County, New York." (From HarperCollins website http://www.harpercollins.com/author/microsite/About.aspx?authorid=15370)
Bibliography	Yes.
Index	Yes.
Notes	Yes.
Photographs	B&W Photographs.
Appendix	No.
Tables	No.
Key Words	Early Life, Military- Pre WWII, Military—B/w the Wars, Military- WWII, Presidency
Other Notes	Maps, Illustrations
Annotation	One-volume complimentary biography of Eisenhower, which concludes that: "He was, in every sense of the words, an American hero." The book is based largely on secondary sources and memoirs, and is very readable. Though Korda covers Ike's life as a boy and during the presidency, most of the biography centers on his military career, especially the great victory during WWII; Korda's brief coverage of Ike's presidency is also positive.

68. Krebs, Ronald R. *Dueling Visions: U.S. Strategy Toward Eastern Europe Under Eisenhower*. College Station, TX: Texas A&M University Press, 2001.

Author Info	Associate professor of political science at the University of Minnesota. "Professor Ron Krebs (Ph.D., Columbia University, 2003) conducts research at the juncture of international relations and comparative politics, with a particular interest in the origins and consequences of international conflict and military service. His recently published book, *Fighting for Rights: Military Service and the Politics of Citizenship* (Cornell University Press, 2006), explores the conditions under which and the mechanisms through which military participation policies shape contestation over citizenship rights...." http://www.polisci.umn.edu/~ronkrebs/
Bibliography	Yes.
Index	Yes.
Notes	Yes.
Photographs	No.
Appendix	No.
Tables	No.
Key Words	Presidency, Foreign Relations, Cold War
Other Notes	
Annotation	Krebs's title refers to what he sees as two competing visions of Eastern European liberation policy in the Eisenhower Administration: Finlandization and rollback. Findlandization was based on the Finland model, and "imagined a tier of states that would enjoy domestic autonomy, but whose foreign policy on truly important matters would follow the Soviet line." Rollback was more aggressive, and encompassed a range of programs from radio broadcasts to covert operations aimed at forcing back the Soviet Union, "perhaps even overturning the Soviet government itself." Krebs provides two case studies, one focused on Yugoslavia and the other on Stalin's death, to show how the debate played out in Ike's Administration. He argues that the Finland model became the goal of the Administration.

69. Kunz, Diane B. *The Economic Diplomacy of the Suez Crisis.* Chapel Hill: University of North Carolina Press, 1991.

Author Info	"From 1976 to 1983 Dr. Kunz practiced corporate law with the firms of White & Case and Simpson Thacher & Bartlett (Cornell University, J.D. 1976). She left the practice of law and studied diplomatic and economic history at Oxford University (M. Litt. 1986) and Yale University (Ph.D, 1989). From 1988 until 1998 she was Assistant, then Associate Professor of History at Yale University. While at Yale she wrote extensively on twentieth century history, including [this] prize winning book... and *Butter and Guns: The Economic Diplomacy of the Cold War*. From 1998-2001 she taught history and

international relations at Columbia University. In 2001 she and Ann Reese founded the Center for Adoption Policy."
http://www.adoptionpolicy.org/who.html

Bibliography	Yes.
Index	Yes.
Notes	Yes.
Photographs	Yes (B&W).
Appendix	Yes (4).
Tables	No.
Key Words	Presidency, Foreign Relations, Cold War, Middle East
Other Notes	
Annotation	Using British and American archival and financial sources, Kunz undertakes a "systematic treatment of how the American government, with varying degrees of success, used its economic power against Britain, France, Egypt, and Israel" during the Suez crisis of 1956-57. She uses the crisis as a case study "of the utility and limitations of economic diplomacy," arguing that: "Economic diplomacy defined the course of the Suez crisis from beginning to end." The Eisenhower Administration's use of economic pressure "was effective against Britain, ineffectual against Egypt, with the cases of France and Israel falling into the middle." Kunz also argues that the crisis "presents an enlightening tale of governmental errors" and miscalculations, citing, for example, America's withdrawal of its offer to fund the Aswan High Dam, prior to the crisis. Contributes to the discussion of the "special relationship" between American and Britain.

L's

70. Ladino, Robyn Duff. *Desegregating Texas Schools: Eisenhower, Shivers, and the Crisis at Mansfield High*. Austin: University of Texas Press, 1996.

Author Info	From University of Texas Press website: "Robyn Duff Ladino is an independent historian and social scientist with several years of teaching experience. She lives in Los Alamos, New Mexico." http://www.utexas.edu/utpress/books/dufdes.html
Bibliography	Yes.
Index	Yes.
Notes	Yes.
Photographs	B&W Photograph.
Appendix	No.
Tables	No.
Key Words	Presidency, Civil Rights, Domestic Policy
Other Notes	
Annotation	Study of an early school desegregation effort in Mansfield, Texas, using interviews, newspapers, and other archival research. Ladino posits that Mansfield "became a microcosm of the nation's struggle over school

integration" and argues that it could have been "Little Rock," "but its national impact was subdued at the state and national levels by powerful politics." She chronicles Texas governor Shivers' use of the crisis for political gain, and points out that Shivers was a Democrat who supported Republican President Eisenhower. Ladino is critical of Ike, noting that "Eisenhower remained as far removed from the Mansfield situation as he could" citing his strong support of states' rights and federalism. The efforts to desegregate the school at this time were unsuccessful.

71.   Lasby, Clarence G. *Eisenhower's Heart Attack: How Ike Beat Heart Disease and Held on to the Presidency.* Lawrence, Kansas: University Press of Kansas, 1997.

Author Info	Lasby is a professor emeritus at the University of Texas at Austin http://www.utexas.edu/cola/depts/history/faculty/lasbycg
Bibliography	Yes.
Index	Yes.
Notes	Yes.
Photographs	Yes (B &W).
Appendix	No.
Tables	No.
Key Words	Presidency, Personal Life, Media, Politics
Other Notes	
Annotation	Lasby examines Eisenhower's "relationship" with his health, especially his battle with coronary disease, including Ike's focus on preventative medicine and self-reliance. Lasby does not tie particular policy decisions or actions to Eisenhower's disease but does address issues concerning presidential medical care, politics, and presidential press relations. He also examines Ike's mis-diagnosis immediately after his attack, the debates with his physicians concerning a potential second term, and 1950's Americans' experiences with heart disease. Ike emerges as a determined, self-disciplined man. Based on primary sources, including the papers of Dr. Howard McCrum Snyder, Eisenhower's personal and presidential physician, Ike's army cardiologist, Dr. Paul Dudley White, and other papers in the Eisenhower library.

72.   Lesch, David W. *Syria and the United States: Eisenhower's Cold War in the Middle East.* Boulder, CO: Westview Press, 1992.

Author Info	Professor of Middle East History in the Department of History and Coordinator of the Middle East Concentration in the International Studies Program at Trinity University in San Antonio. He received his M.A. and Ph.D. (1991) in History and Middle Eastern Studies from Harvard University.
Bibliography	Yes.
Index	Yes.
Notes	Yes.
Photographs	No.

Appendix	No.
Tables	No.
Key Words	Presidency, Cold War, Middle East, Foreign Relations
Other Notes	Map.
Annotation	Lesch examines the origins and events of the 1957 Syrian Crisis, and broader US-Middle East relations. He argues that the Eisenhower Administration's myopic anti-Communist foreign policies led it to ignore and/or dismiss other important factors in the region, including inter-Middle Eastern politics. He is critical of Ike's handling of Syria, which he labels as deceptive, militaristic "cold-blooded interventionism." He argues that it not only failed, but was counterproductive. Based on U.S. and British sources and Arabic-language newspapers.

73. Lewis, Catherine M. *Don't Ask What I Shot: How President Eisenhower's Love of Golf Helped Shape 1950s America*. New York: McGraw-Hill, 2007.

Author Info	"Dr. Catherine Lewis is an Associate Professor of History and at Kennesaw State University [in Georgia], the Director of the Holocaust Education Program, and the Coordinator of Public History." Bio at: http://www.ksu-amst.com/documents/LEWIS_EB.pdf Website states that she: "joined the KSU faculty in the fall of 2003 and teach[es] and [does] research in a variety of areas: public history, the Holocaust, women's studies, sports history, and American Studies." http://ksuweb.kennesaw.edu/~clewis1/body.htm
Bibliography	No.
Index	Yes.
Notes	Yes.
Photographs	Yes (B&W).
Appendix	No.
Tables	No.
Key Words	Military- WWII, Presidency, Personal Life, Politics
Other Notes	
Annotation	Lewis examines the 1950s through the prism of Ike's "obsession with golf." She finds that he influenced the game, and that the game influenced him and the nation. Golf kept Ike fit, happy, and sane. After his heart attack, his playing gave voters confidence that he could serve another term. He also conducted business on the golf course, including during the Little Rock crisis, and Sputnik. This caused criticism. She finds that Ike's contribution to golf was equal to that of Bobby Jones, Arnold Palmer, and Tiger Woods. Contains golfing vignettes and observations about 1950s America, including Civil Rights issues.

74. Loftus, Geoff. *Lead Like Ike: Ten Business Strategies from the CEO of D-Day*. Nashville, TN: Thomas Nelson Publishers, 2010.

Author Info	A business journalist and corporate communications expert, Loftus has worked

for a number of leading firms, including Deloitte Consulting and News Corp. He is a member of the Writers Guild of America. Information at http://www.geoffloftus.com/about.html

Bibliography	A Brief Bibliographical Note.
Index	No.
Notes	Yes.
Photographs	No.
Appendix	Brief Appendices.
Tables	No.
Key Words	Military—WWII, Leadership
Other Notes	
Annotation	A business journalist draws upon secondary studies (especially those by Stephen Ambrose) to extract ten "strategies" that characterized Eisenhower's leadership in Europe from 1942 to victory against Germany on May 7, 1945. While he remarks on both the negative and positive side of Ike's hypothetical "leadership ledger," Loftus emphasizes the accomplishments that can be traced to staying focused, communicating effectively, avoiding "project creep," being "honest," and similar aspects of Eisenhower's performance in World War II.

M's

75.   Medhurst, Martin J. *Dwight D. Eisenhower: Strategic Communicator*. Westport, CT: Greenwood Press, 1993.

Author Info	Distinguished Professor of Rhetoric and Communication and Professor of Political Science at Baylor University. Published extensively. CV at http://www.baylor.edu/content/services/document.php?id=50268+
Bibliography	Yes.
Index	Yes.
Notes	Yes.
Photographs	B&W Photograph.
Appendix	No.
Tables	No.
Key Words	Army Chief of Staff, Columbia University, Presidency, Speechmaking.
Other Notes	Chronology of Major Speeches.
Annotation	Volume in the Great American Orators series. Part I is a critical analysis of Ike and his speeches in which Medhurst analyzes both the domestic and foreign policy speeches. He divides Part I into examinations of how Ike created a public image, shaped a political stance, and articulated an agenda; Medhurst emphasizes the calculated manner in which Ike communicated foreign and domestic policy positions. He characterizes Ike as a "strategic communicator." Part II contains the full text of eleven of Ike's major speeches, including pre-presidential speeches and speeches made during his presidency.

76. Medhurst, Martin J., ed. *Eisenhower's War of Words: Rhetoric and Leadership.* East Lansing, MI: Michigan State University Press, 1994.

Author Info	See information in Entry #75.
Bibliography	No.
Index	Yes.
Notes	Yes.
Photographs	Yes (B&W).
Appendix	No.
Tables	No.
Key Words	Presidency, Speechmaking
Other Notes	Contributor's bios.
Annotation	Collection of twelve essays, including one essay and an introduction by Medhurst, focusing on Eisenhower's strategic use of rhetoric to wage the Cold War. It is largely organized around significant speeches in Eisenhower's terms as president, made at times, "when rhetorical discourse was brought into play in an effort to effect change or modification in the existing situation." The essays touch upon Little Rock, Sputnik, McCarthyism, and the U-2 incident. First volume in a series on "Rhetoric and Public Affairs".

77. Murray, G. E. Patrick. *Eisenhower Versus Montgomery: The Continuing Debate.* Westport, CN: Praeger, 1996.

Author Info	Professor Emeritus at Valley Forge Military College. Villanova University (B.A., 1969). Kansas State University (M.A., 1972). Temple University (Ph. D, 1991). He published three books on World War II. His research focuses "on the arguments over strategy in command in northwest Europe in 1944-1945." From his online profile at http://college.vfmac.edu/Contact/CollegeFacultyProfiles.aspx
Bibliography	Selected Bibliography.
Index	Yes.
Notes	Yes.
Photographs	B&W Photographs.
Appendix	No.
Tables	No.
Key Words	Military- WWII
Other Notes	Maps.
Annotation	A meticulous examination of one of Eisenhower's most difficult challenges to his WWII leadership of the Allied forces. Based on extensive research in British and American primary materials, Murray's account concludes that Ike's broadfront strategy provided a better chance than Montgomery's single thrust approach to defeat the German forces on the Western Front.

N's

78.   Nash, Philip. *The Other Missiles of October: Eisenhower, Kennedy, and the Jupiters, 1957-1963*. Chapel Hill, NC: University of North Carolina Press, 1997.

Author Info	Assistant Professor of History at Pennsylvania State Shenango. CV available at http://www.personal.psu.edu/pxn4/
Bibliography	Yes.
Index	Yes.
Notes	Yes.
Photographs	Yes (B&W).
Appendix	No.
Tables	Yes.
Key Words	Presidency, Cold War, Foreign Relations, Military Policy, Technology, Leadership
Other Notes	Maps.
Annotation	Nash traces the six-year story of the deployment and removal of the Jupiter Intermediate Ballistic Missiles ("IRBMs") during the Eisenhower and Kennedy Administrations (1957-1963). Nash finds that though both presidents were very dubious of the Jupiter program, both pursued deployment because of issues of credibility—the "credibility of threats" (aimed at the Soviet Union) and the "credibility of commitments" (aimed at our Allies). Nash faults Eisenhower and Kennedy for their failure in leadership during this time and the similar tactics they took in their Jupiter policies: "Both men had feasible options before them that they considered, or could have considered, at the time; both failed to question their assumptions about credibility; and both deployed nuclear missiles that they knew to be provocative, vulnerable, and obsolete." Though the missiles had little military value, Nash says, they were an important political tool during the Cuban Missile Crisis.

79.   Nichols, David A. *A Matter of Justice: Eisenhower and the Beginning of the Civil Rights Revolution*. New York: Simon & Schuster, 2007.

Author Info	"David A. Nichols, a leading expert on the Eisenhower presidency, holds a Ph.D. in history from William and Mary. A former professor and academic dean at Southwestern College." He is also the author of *Lincoln and the Indians*. http://authors.simonandschuster.com/David-A-Nichols/42263792
Bibliography	No.
Index	Yes.
Notes	Yes.
Photographs	Yes (B&W).
Appendix	No.
Tables	No.
Key Words	Presidency, Civil Rights, Domestic Policy
Other Notes	
Annotation	Nichols attempts to put to rest the "myth" that Eisenhower "did nothing" for

Civil Rights during his presidency. He finds multiple reasons for the origin and perpetuation of this "myth", including Eisenhower's unique and complex presidency, the unavailability or neglect of documents, bias, and historical context. Nichols tries to analyze Eisenhower in his own context ("We must try to see the world as the men and women of the early 1950s saw it.") and to assess Ike based on the information he had available at the time and operating under the constraints that bound him. Arguing that Eisenhower was more a man of deeds than words, Nichols highlights Ike's actions in the area of civil rights, noting that he, "desegregated [DC] (including its schools), completed desegregation of the armed forces, appointed progressive federal judges at all levels…, proposed and secured passage of the first civil rights legislation in over eighty years, and took steps to enforce the Supreme Court's school desegregation decision in *Brown v. Board of Education*". With regards to Ike's words, Nichols concedes that "Eisenhower's greatest deficiency as a civil rights leader was his disdain for using the 'bully pulpit' to denounce segregation", but suggests that this rhetorical deficiency has been overblown by historians.

O's

80.   Osgood, Kenneth. *Total Cold War: Eisenhower's Secret Propaganda Battle at Home and Abroad*. Lawrence, KS: University Press of Kansas; 2006.

Author Info	Assistant Professor of History at Florida Atlantic University. http://wise.fau.edu/~kosgood/
Bibliography	Yes.
Index	Yes.
Notes	Yes.
Photographs	Yes B&W.
Appendix	No.
Tables	No.
Key Words	Presidency, Cold War, Foreign Relations, Domestic Policy.
Other Notes	
Annotation	Osgood, "chronicles U.S. psychological warfare programs developed to win the hearts and minds of the free world." He argues that to Americans in the 1950s, the Cold War was a "total war", and that "virtually every aspect of the American way of life… was exposed to scrutiny in this total contest for the hearts and minds of the world's peoples." Osgood divides his book into two parts: Part I examines the "theory and practice of propaganda and psychological warfare." Part II discusses global themes and the campaigns of America's propaganda battle. Osgood has a broad focus, as he argues that America's psychological warfare was directed at the entire free world (he "examined records from roughly three dozen countries"), and he details how the campaign was waged both at home and abroad. He finds that Eisenhower was a key player in utilizing this "fourth weapon", emphasizing "the need for a

powerful and carefully coordinated psychological warfare effort on a national scale, and encourage[ing] all of his advisors to consider psychological factors in the policy-making process."

P's

81.   Pach, Chester J. Jr. and Elmo Richardson. *The Presidency of Dwight D. Eisenhower.* Lawrence, KS: University Press of Kansas, 1991

Author Info	"Chester Pach is a faculty member in the Department of History at Ohio University. He teaches courses in U.S. foreign relations and recent U.S. history. He has an A.B. from Brown University and a Ph.D. from Northwestern University. In 1995, he was a Fulbright Professor … [in] New Zealand. He is director of graduate studies in Ohio's History Department." From http://oak.cats.ohiou.edu/~pach/ Richardson is the author of *Dams, Parks, and Politics: Resource Development and Preservation in the Truman-Eisenhower Era.* (From book).
Bibliography	Bibliographical essay.
Index	Yes.
Notes	Yes.
Photographs	No.
Appendix	No.
Tables	No.
Key Words	Presidency, Domestic Policy, Foreign Relations, Cold War, Politics, Leadership
Other Notes	
Annotation	This is a revised edition of Richardson's 1979 work of the same name; it was re-written by Pach to incorporate and address revisionist scholarship. Pach reviews Ike's two terms as president, examining both foreign and domestic policies. He agrees with revisionists that Ike was "a thoughtful and skillful leader", but finds that, "the Eisenhower presidency was more complex and not as successful as many revisionists have maintained." Pach states that Ike's greatest failures were from "lack of vision." The shortcomings Pach finds with Ike's presidency include his handling of Senator McCarthy, his failure to build a strong GOP, and his failure to "adapt his Cold War principles sufficiently to an increasingly complex world." Part of the American Presidency Series.

82.   Perret, Geoffrey. *Eisenhower.* Holbrook, MA: Adams Media Corporation, 1999.

Author Info	Perret, "served in the U.S. Army from 1958-1961 and attended the University of Southern California, Harvard, and the University of California at Berkeley. His first book was the award-winning *Days of Sadness, Years of Triumph*, his account of America's home front during World War II. He is also the author

of *Ulysses S. Grant*; *Old Soldiers Never Die: The Life of Douglas MacArthur*; and *Winged Victory.*" (From *Eisenhower*).

Bibliography	No.
Index	Yes.
Notes	Yes.
Photographs	Yes (B&W).
Appendix	No.
Tables	No.
Key Words	Early Life, Military- Pre WWII, Military—B/w the Wars, Military- WWII, SACEUR, Columbia University, Presidency, Post-Presidency.
Other Notes	
Annotation	Narrative, readable biography of Eisenhower from birth to death. Perret was inspired to update Ambrose's two-volume biography with primary source materials that had been released and new secondary sources. In addition to the typical highlights of Eisenhower's military and political career, Perret includes examinations of Ike's relationships with Kay Summersby and with General Marshall Montgomery, and his lackluster performance as Columbia University president.

83.   Perry, Mark. *Partners in Command: George Marshall and Dwight Eisenhower in War and Peace*. New York: The Penguin Press, 2007.

Author Info	From book: "Mark Perry is a military, intelligence, and foreign-policy analyst and the codirector of Conflicts Forum, an international policy advocacy organization." He has written six other books on subjects ranging from the Civil War to the Israeli-Palestinian conflict.
Bibliography	Yes.
Index	Yes.
Notes	Yes.
Photographs	Yes (B&W).
Appendix	No.
Tables	No.
Key Words	Military- WWII, Foreign Relations, Presidency
Other Notes	Maps, Chronology
Annotation	Perry examines the careers of and relationship between Eisenhower and Marshall through WWII and the formation of post-war foreign policy, though the majority of the book is focused on the WWII years. He describes how Marshall and Eisenhower worked together to overcome inter-Allied conflict and win the war, and how the superior (Marshall) eventually became the subordinate.

84.   Peterson, Mark A. *Legislating Together: The White House and Capitol Hill from Eisenhower to Reagan*. Cambridge, MA: Harvard University Press, 1990.

Author Info	Professor of Public Policy and Political Science at UCLA School of Public

Affairs. "A specialist on American national institutions and a political scientist, much of Professor Peterson's scholarship focuses on interactions among the Presidency, Congress, and interest groups, evaluating their implications for policy making, both within the general domain of domestic policy and with special attention to health care policy" http://publicaffairs.ucla.edu/mark-peterson

Bibliography	No.
Index	Yes.
Notes	No.
Photographs	No.
Appendix	Yes.
Tables	Yes.
Key Words	Presidency, Politics, Domestic Policy
Other Notes	
Annotation	Peterson, "examines the domestic legislative programs introduced by presidents from Eisenhower to Reagan," to illuminate presidential-congressional relations on legislative issues. He tries to move away from a presidency-centered perspective toward one that is more focused on "tandem institutions". He draws conclusions from analyzing the sample selected *in toto*, but he does find of Eisenhower that Ike was one of the more successful presidents "in getting Congress to move affirmatively on [his] initiatives." He teases out some of the reasons for Eisenhower's success, including his public popularity, the "limited size of his program and the number of his legislative priorities," and the context of his presidency ("serving during a period reasonably favorable to the president's position").

85.   Pickett, William B. *Dwight David Eisenhower and American Power*. The American Biographical History Series, Wheeling, IL: Harlan Davidson, 1995.

Author Info	Professor Emeritus of History at the Rose-Hulman Institute of Technology in Terre Haute, Indiana. CV at http://www.rose-hulman.edu/~pickett/
Bibliography	Bibliographical essay
Index	Yes.
Notes	No.
Photographs	B&W Photo.
Appendix	No.
Tables	No.
Key Words	Early Life, Military- Pre WWII, Military- WWII, Presidency, Post-Presidency
Other Notes	Maps
Annotation	Basing his short biography on primary as well as the abundant secondary studies, Pickett gives his readers a largely positive treatment of Ike as both a soldier and political leader. A well-written, fair-minded book that comments on President Eisenhower's sometimes "questionable operations" in national security, but concludes that on balance his "stewardship of American power" was successful.

86.   Pickett, William B. *Eisenhower Decides to Run: Presidential Politics and Cold War Strategy*. Chicago, IL: Ivan R. Dee, 2000.

Author Info	Professor Emeritus of History at the Rose-Hulman Institute of Technology in Terre Haute, Indiana. CV at http://www.rose-hulman.edu/~pickett/
Bibliography	Yes.
Index	Yes.
Notes	Yes.
Photographs	Yes (B&W).
Appendix	No.
Tables	No.
Key Words	Elections, Presidency
Other Notes	
Annotation	Based on documents in the Eisenhower library, Pickett finds that contrary to popular understanding, Ike wanted to be elected in 1952, and worked behind the scenes to engineer this and a "Draft Ike" movement, well before the 1952 election. Pickett characterizes Ike's decision to become a candidate as "honorable," based on his fear for America because of Communist expansion. Pickett also examines why it was Eisenhower, and not MacArthur who became president, despite both men wanting the presidency. He argues that it was because Ike's approach, "was both appropriate to the situation and in harmony with the outlook of the majority of his countrymen."

87.   Pratico, Dominick. *Eisenhower and Social Security: The Origins of the Disability Program*. San Jose, CA: Writers Club Press, 2001.

Author Info	Dominick Pratico is a novelist and historian who has worked as a Field Representative for the Peekskill Office of the U.S. Social Security Administration. He has also taught in the Lifelong Learning Program at Westchester Community College.
Bibliography	Yes.
Index	No.
Notes	Yes.
Photographs	No.
Appendix	No.
Tables	No.
Key Words	Presidency, Domestic Policy, Politics
Other Notes	
Annotation	The author briefly traces President Eisenhower's successful attempts to amend the Social Security Act to include provision for disabled persons. One chapter is devoted to the original Social Security Act (1935) and the program's evolution to 1953. As the author explains in chapter two, Eisenhower was initially successful despite the opposition of the right-wing of the Republican Party in focusing attention on the need for a rehabilitation program for disabled persons. His interest was in "enhancing, not overhauling, the existing social

insurance programs," while extending coverage to additional workers. To achieve his goal, he promoted the creation of a cabinet-level position: Secretary of Health, Education, and Welfare. The first Secretary, Oveta Culp Hobby, supported the Eisenhower efforts to amend the law. After passage of Ike's amendments, Congress (chapters three and four) further extended Social Security to provide additional coverage to the disabled. Eisenhower was unsuccessful in building a consensus to support medical insurance, and was unable in his second administration to stop the movement to add further refinements and extensions -- that he opposed -- to Social Security.

88.   Pruden, Caroline. *Conditional Partners: Eisenhower, the United Nations, and the Search for a Permanent Peace*. Baton Rouge: Louisiana State University Press, 1998.

Author Info   "Special faculty" in NC State University's History Department. PhD Vanderbilt 1993. http://history.ncsu.edu/faculty/view/caroline_pruden

Bibliography   Yes.

Index   Yes.

Notes   Yes.

Photographs   No.

Appendix   No.

Tables   No.

Key Words   Presidency, Foreign Relations

Other Notes

Annotation   Pruden examines America's policies toward and interactions with the United Nations during the Eisenhower Administration to obtain a broader view and distinct understanding of Eisenhower's foreign policy. She finds that Ike played a large role in shaping policy, but that he and his Administration, "never developed a coherent and clearly articulated long-range strategy toward the United Nations." She concludes the U.S. used the UN "less as an instrument of aggressive foreign policy than a shield… to defend itself against unforeseen events and developments," generally with short-term success. She finds a change in the use of the UN over Eisenhower's two terms, as the Third World became increasingly important. Pruden concludes that: "Ultimately, the Eisenhower administration's use of the United Nations represented, at least potentially, a missed opportunity."

R's

89.   Roadnight, Andrew. *United States Policy Towards Indonesia in the Truman and Eisenhower Years*. New York, New York: Palgrave Macmillan, 2002.

Author Info   "Andrew Roadnight works in Research Support Services at the University of Warwick, where he is the Research & Information Officer. His duties involve supporting major research projects and assisting in the preparation of research-

related policy and strategy. Before joining RSS, in 2003, he was a tax inspector and trade union negotiator in HM Customs & Excise (1974-91) and then a student at Warwick, where he gained a BA (Hons) in Comparative American Studies and a PhD in American Diplomatic History. His publications are *United States Policy Towards Indonesia in the Truman and Eisenhower Years* (Palgrave, 2002) and "Sleeping with the Enemy: Britain, Japanese Troops and the Netherlands East Indies, 1945-1946", *History* (April 2002)."
http://www2.warwick.ac.uk/research/warwickcommission/archive/worldtrade/about/commissioners/roadnight/

Bibliography	Yes.
Index	Yes.
Notes	Yes.
Photographs	No.
Appendix	No.
Tables	No.
Key Words	Presidency, Foreign Relations, Cold War
Other Notes	Map.
Annotation	Third-world nationalism is central to the context in which Roadnight places U.S. policy in the years following World War II. Indonesia -- the world's fifth largest nation -- was sought as an ally due to its abundant resources and strategic position in Southeast Asia. Initially, the American policy was one of benign neglect, but that strategy gave way in the Cold War to active intervention. No longer part of the Dutch empire as of 1949, Indonesia's future became important to the Soviet Union, to the People's Republic of China, and to the United States and its allies. Extensive research in the archival records and secondary materials enables the author to develop a detailed account of the accomplishments and failures of U.S. policies. He gives the Truman program low scores and notes that Eisenhower considered Indonesia more important than his predecessor did to America's global strategy. This did not keep Ike's administration from making mistakes -- each of which Roadnight carefully describes. By 1960, the author concludes, neither diplomacy nor CIA intervention had been successful, leaving the Indonesian problem in the hands of a new administration in 1961.

90.   Roman, Peter J. *Eisenhower and the Missile Gap*. Ithaca, New York: Cornell University Press, 1995.

Author Info	Senior Associate at the Stimson Center. His profile: "Prior to joining the Stimson Center, Dr. Peter Roman was a Senior Fellow at the ANSER Institute for Homeland Security, where he directed the Biological and Agro Anti-Terrorism Partnership Project. He has published widely on homeland and national security issues. Dr. Roman served as a Distinguished Visiting Professor at the National War College in Washington, DC and has taught at the University of Wisconsin-Madison, the University of Alabama, the University of Colorado-Boulder, and Duquesne University. While at Duquesne University, he served as Chairman of the Political Science Department and Co-

Director of the Graduate Center for Social and Public Policy. Dr. Roman earned his MA and PhD at the University of Wisconsin-Madison." http://www.stimson.org/experts/expert.cfm?ID=72

Bibliography	No.
Index	Yes.
Notes	Yes.
Photographs	No.
Appendix	Yes.
Tables	Yes.
Key Words	Presidency, Cold War, Foreign Relations, Space Exploration, Politics, Nuclear, Technology
Other Notes	
Annotation	This fully documented and carefully analyzed account of presidential power and policy finds Eisenhower effective in dealing with the strategic implications of Sputnik (1957) and the "missile gap." Drawing upon extensive internal documentary records as well as secondary materials, Roman applauds Eisenhower for easing the nation through the shift from a position of nuclear superiority to a phase of mutual vulnerability. The author concludes that Ike was far less effective as a political leader in guiding the public debates over national security.

91.   Rosenberg, Victor. *Soviet-American Relations, 1953-1960: Diplomacy and Cultural Exchange During the Eisenhower Presidency*. Jefferson, NC: McFarland & Company, 2005.

Author Info	Book simply mentions that he lives in Cleveland, Ohio.
Bibliography	Yes.
Index	Yes.
Notes	Yes.
Photographs	No.
Appendix	No.
Tables	No.
Key Words	Presidency, Foreign Relations, Cold War
Other Notes	
Annotation	Rosenberg explores social and cultural relations between the U.S. and Soviet Union under Eisenhower and Khrushchev using "eclectic" sources including memoirs and eyewitness accounts of journalists and tourists. The book is organized roughly chronologically and focuses on diplomatic relations between the countries. Rosenberg maintains it was Ike, not Dulles who set America's foreign policy. Also covers such cultural exchanges as American pianist Van Cliburn winning the Tchaikovsky Competition in the Soviet Union, and the Soviet-American chess rivalry. Rosenberg rejects the characterization of Soviet-US relations during the 1950s as a "Thaw" because there was still significant military tension and ideological hostility. Instead, he finds the Soviet Union's "half-offered hand of friendship" during this time to be better characterized as the stopping of a blizzard.

S's

92.   Sander, Alfred Dick. *Eisenhower's Executive Office*. Westport, CT: Greenwood Press, 1999.

Author Info	Sander "is a Professor Emeritus of History from Purdue University. A former analyst at the National Security Agency, he has served as department head and chief academic officer at Purdue, Calumet Campus. Among his earlier publications is *A Staff for the President: The Executive Office, 1921-1952* (Greenwood, 1989)." (From Book). Note: not listed in Purdue's website as of 9/02/10).
Bibliography	Yes.
Index	Yes.
Notes	Yes.
Photographs	No.
Appendix	No.
Tables	No.
Key Words	Presidency, White House, Politics
Other Notes	
Annotation	Sander offers, "an organizational history of the Executive Office of the President from 1953 through 1960 that assesses the effectiveness of Eisenhower's management of his office." Sander discusses the creation and operation of various agencies in the EOP with a heavy focus on the National Security Council and the Operations Coordinating Board. He concludes that, "it seems fair to say that Eisenhower took an Executive Office of the President that was largely in shambles at the end of the Truman administration and turned it into a functioning organization," and that "Eisenhower's only EOP failure was in not utilizing the Bureau of the Budget to its fullest potential".

93.   Saulnier, Raymond J. *Constructive Years: The U.S. Economy Under Eisenhower*. Lanham, MD: University Press of America, Inc., 1991.

Author Info	Economic advisor to Eisenhower and professor of economics at Columbia University and Barnard College. He served on the Council of Economic Advisers for two years and then chaired the Council from 1956-1961. A staunch advocate of fiscal discipline, he was pleased that the government in the 1950s kept inflation under control and reined in federal spending. He died at the age of 100 in 2009. Obituary at http://www.nytimes.com/2009/05/08/business/08saulnier.html. See also *Kent County News*, September 18, 2008.
Bibliography	Note on sources.

Index	Yes.
Notes	Yes.
Photographs	No.
Appendix	No.
Tables	No.
Key Words	Presidency, Economics
Other Notes	
Annotation	The author provides an insider's perspective on the economic policies of the two Eisenhower Administrations. While Saulnier is sensitive to the problems and limitations of the programs of the 1950s, he believes that the middle-way program Eisenhower sought to implement had overwhelmingly positive results and provides some useful lessons for present-day politicians and economic advisors. By eliminating wage and price controls, for instance, the Administration allowed markets to function properly. By keeping taxes on upper-income groups at a very high level and by controlling expenditures, the White House managed to achieve three balanced budgets. Saulnier lists some eleven lessons the history provides us today. He lauds the Eisenhower mixture of pragmatism and ideology and concludes from the vantage point of the early 1990s: "that, in matters basic to the shaping and carrying out of economic policy, 'Ike was right.'"

94.   Showalter, Dennis E. (ed.). *Forging the Shield: Eisenhower and National Security for the 21st Century*. Chicago: Imprint Publications, 2005.

Author Info	From book (contributor bio): "Dennis E. Showalter is Professor of History at Colorado College. He has served as visiting professor at the U.S. Military Academy and the U. S. Air Force Academy. He is Past President of the Society for Military History and joint editor of *War in History*. His most recent books include *The Wars of German Unification* (2004) and *Patton and Rommel: Men of War in the Twentieth Century* (2005)."
Bibliography	No.
Index	Yes.
Notes	Yes (end of each chapter).
Photographs	No.
Appendix	Yes.
Tables	Yes.
Key Words	Presidency, Military Policy, Foreign Relations, Cold War, Politics, Nuclear, Space Exploration, Technology, Leadership
Other Notes	Contributor bios.
Annotation	Collection of essays developed for a 2005 symposium entitled "Eisenhower and National Security for the 21st Century," held at Ft. McNair, Washington, D.C. and co-sponsored by the Dwight D. Eisenhower Memorial Commission and the Industrial College of the Armed Forces at the National Defense University. Contributors include respected Eisenhower scholars and men with first-hand knowledge of the events under discussion. The focus of the volume

is on Eisenhower's role in America's national security, including his foreign, nuclear, and military policies, his contributions to the space program, and his work with federal agencies and military education. The essays also speak to Ike's leadership skills, pragmatism, and character. Appendix contains transcript of a panel and audience discussion from the symposium.

95. Sloan, John W. *Eisenhower and the Management of Prosperity*. Lawrence, KS: University Press of Kansas, 1991.

Author Info	"[P]rofessor of political science at the University of Houston" as of September 2008. From http://www.kansaspress.ku.edu/slofdr.html. He is not listed on the University of Houston's Political Science department website as of September 2010.
Bibliography	Yes.
Index	Yes.
Notes	Yes.
Photographs	Yes (B&W).
Appendix	No.
Tables	Yes.
Key Words	Presidency, Economics, Politics
Other Notes	Figure
Annotation	Sloan evaluates Ike's "macroeconomic policymaking," an area of Ike's presidency he believes has been neglected. He finds that Ike was successful in his economic policies as president, and Ike "played the role of 'manager of prosperity' in a modern, conservative manner." Analyzing multiple factors, including Eisenhower's ideology, advisors, public opinion, and institutions such as the Council of Economic Advisors, Sloan finds that over his two terms, Ike, "avoided both high inflation and high unemployment, while achieving moderate levels of growth and only incremental increases in the national debt." Sloan argues that Ike had more success in his first term than his second, because, "[t]he president of the first half of the 1950s was more in harmony with public opinion than the embittered, pessimistic, and aging man of the second half of the decade." The public and Congress wanted progress and the government to "do more," and Ike's conservatism and prioritization of a balanced budget was not compatible with that desire. This conflict caused Republicans to lose power and Democrats to gain. Sloan also discusses Eisenhower's understanding of the importance of economic prosperity to national security.

96. Smith, Neal. *Mr. Smith Went to Washington: From Eisenhower to Clinton*. Ames: Iowa State University Press, 1996.

Author Info	From book: "Neal Smith was first elected to Congress from the 5th Congressional District in Iowa in 1958. His first term started in January 1959.

After redistricting in 1972, he represented the 4th Congressional District. Mr. Smith was defeated in the 1994 election and left office in January 1995. He now practices law in Des Moines." Longer bio at Iowa State University's alumni association website: http://www.isualum.org/en/awards/distinguished_awards_celebration/honorary_alumni_award/neal_smith_2006.cfm

Bibliography	No.
Index	Yes.
Notes	No.
Photographs	Yes (B&W).
Appendix	No.
Tables	No.
Key Words	Presidency
Other Notes	
Annotation	Memoirs of Neal Smith, Congressman for Iowa from 1959-1995. Book spans from Smith's childhood to the time of his writing. Very little on Ike. Eisenhower was president when Smith came to office, and Smith claims that Ike was less serious about the Presidency than any of the other eight Presidents with whom he worked. He characterizes Ike's two terms as an eight-year "vacation in the White House," though he also states that he "did not know Eisenhower personally" and remembers that Ike had "a sort of intuition about the difference between right and wrong." Smith claims that Eisenhower allowed the "Dewey group" (Thomas Dewey) to run the government. Aside from the U-2 incident, Smith remembers that Ike was generally truthful. Regarding the economy, Smith states: "Eisenhower had inherited the strongest possible growing economy and proceeded to let it run downhill on automatic pilot until it ran out."

97. Smith, Simon C. ed., *Reassessing Suez 1956: New Perspectives on the Crisis and its Aftermath* Burlington, VT: Ashgate, 2008.

Author Info	From book: "Simon C. Smith teaches International History at the University of Hull. He has published five books on different aspects of British imperialism and decolonization, including the Malta volume for the British Documents on the End of Empire series in 2006."
Bibliography	No.
Index	Yes.
Notes	Yes (within each chapter).
Photographs	No.
Appendix	Map.
Tables	No.
Key Words	Presidency, Cold War, Foreign Relations, Middle East
Other Notes	
Annotation	Collection of essays, organized roughly chronologically, selected "to provide fresh perspectives on the [Suez Crisis], its origins and aftermath." The

chapters address multiple countries, including the United States, but Great Britain is most thoroughly examined. Eisenhower's role in the crisis is examined in three chapters: 1) "Supporting the Brave Young King: The Suez Crisis and Eisenhower's New Approach to Jordan, 1953-1958" (by Clea Lutz Bunch); 2) "In Search of 'Some Big, Imaginative Plan': The Eisenhower Administration and American strategy in the Middle East after Suez" (by Richard V. Damms); and 3) "Post-Suez Consequences: Anglo-American Relations in the Middle East from Eisenhower to Nixon" (by Tore T. Peterson).

98.　Snead, David L. *The Gaither Committee, Eisenhower, and the Cold War*. Columbus, OH: Ohio State University Press, 1999.

Author Info	Associate Professor of History and Chair of the Department of History at Liberty University in Lynchburg VA. "Dr. Snead joined the department in 2004 as an associate professor after teaching for the past five years at Texas Tech University. In the fall of 2007 he took over as the Chair of the History Department. He specializes in 20th century American diplomatic and military history." He has also published *An American Soldier in World War I* (2006), and *In Hostile Skies: An American B-24 Pilot in World War II*. From http://www.liberty.edu/index.cfm?PID=7112
Bibliography	Yes.
Index	Yes.
Notes	Yes.
Photographs	B&W Photographs.
Appendix	No.
Tables	No.
Key Words	Presidency, Cold War, Foreign Relations, Military Policy, Politics
Other Notes	
Annotation	Snead examines the origins of the Gaither committee, how and why it reached the conclusions in its report, and how Eisenhower used some of the committee's findings in setting national security policy. In doing so, Snead adds to existing literature on Ike's decision-making process. Snead argues that the Gaither committee, often overshadowed by *Sputnik*, was more important than previous historians have acknowledged, finding that it, "played a pivotal role in the escalation of the Cold War in the late 1950s." Though overall Snead finds it "difficult to criticize the committee too much," he does find two significant short comings: 1) it failed to articulate how or when its recommended increases in U.S. military force levels should be made; and 2) it based its conclusions on assumptions concerning the Soviets' intentions of world domination and did not carefully evaluate these assumptions. Snead finds that Ike took a "hands-off" approach to the Gaither committee; this proved problematic as it allowed the committee to interpret its purpose more broadly than Ike had intended and that he "never fully realized the importance of clearly articulating his views to the committee and, more important, to the

population as a whole." Snead praises Eisenhower, however, in his review and analysis of the committee's report as he, "clearly made decisions based on well-defined principles and after receiving advice from a well-organized decision-making system."

99. Sowell David. *Eisenhower and Golf: A President at Play*. Jefferson, NC: McFarland & Company, Inc., Publishers, 2007.

Author Info	From Book: "Sowell has been a frequent contributor to *Links Magazine* and has written articles for the *USGA's Golf Journal*, *Golf Illustrated*, and *The Green Magazine*. He lives in Taylors, South Carolina."
Bibliography	Yes.
Index	Yes.
Notes	Yes- limited.
Photographs	Yes (B & W).
Appendix	Yes- Selected Golf Correspondence from Ike's White House Mail Room.
Tables	No.
Key Words	Presidency, Personal Life, Military—B/w the Wars, Military- WWII, White House, Post-Presidency
Other Notes	
Annotation	Golf journalist David Sowell describes Ike's love of the game, with a focus on Ike's presidency, during which he played almost 900 rounds. Sowell notes that Eisenhower was never a spectacular golfer, describes his friendship with famous golfers including Bobby Jones and Arnold Palmer, discusses Ike's effect on the popularity of the game, and recounts important events of Ike's presidency as seen from the perspective of the golf course. Limited citations and occasional editorial mistakes.

100. Stans, Maurice H. *One of the Presidents' Men: Twenty Years With Eisenhower and Nixon*. Washington: Brassey's, 1995.

Author Info	Froms book jacket, Stans: "served in the Eisenhower administration as director of the Bureau of the Budget. In Richard Nixon's White House, he was secretary of commerce." His activities as a fund-raiser for the Nixon Administrations resulted in charges that he was involved in the Watergate scandal. He was not, however, convicted of any violations of the law. He died in 1998. http://millercenter.org/academic/americanpresident/nixon/essays/cabinet/640
Bibliography	No.
Index	Yes.
Notes	No.
Photographs	No.
Appendix	No.
Tables	No.
Key Words	Presidency, Economics, Politics

Annotation   In this autobiographical work, Stans, director of the Bureau of the Budget under Eisenhower, recalls his professional life, including his time working under both Eisenhower and Nixon. Three of the seventeen chapters focus on his service under Eisenhower, and Stans describes his work with Ike on matters including the vital and controversial issue of defense spending. Stans was greatly impressed by Eisenhower's decisiveness and his memory. Also includes observations about Ike's relationship with Nixon.

101.   Statler, Kathryn C. and Andrew L. Johns. *The Eisenhower Administration, the Third World, and the Globalization of the Cold War*. Lanham, MD: Rowman & Littlefield Publishers, Inc., 2006.

Author Info   From book: "Kathryn C. Statler (Ph.D., University of California, Santa Barbara, 1999) is associate professor of history at the University of San Diego and an associate at the Joan B. Kroc Institute of Peace and Justice. A specialist in Franco-American relations and the Eisenhower administration, she has published her work in the *Journal of American-East Asian Relations* and as part of the edited volume, *After Stalin's Death: The Cold War as International History 1953-1956* (2005)." See also: http://www.sandiego.edu/cas/history/faculty/biography.php?ID=138
From book: Andrew L. Johns: "(Ph.D., University of California, Santa Barbara, 2000) is assistant professor of history at Brigham Young University and an affiliate of the David M. Kennedy Center for International Studies. His research focuses on U.S. foreign policy and the presidency, and his articles have appeared in [the] *Presidential Studies Quarterly*, the *Journal of American-East Asian Relations*, and the *Michigan Historical Review*." See also: http://fhssfaculty.byu.edu/Faculty/ucsbphd/

Bibliography   Bibliographic Essay.
Index   Yes.
Notes   Yes (at the end of each chapter).
Photographs   No.
Appendix   No.
Tables   No.
Key Words   Presidency, Cold War, Foreign Relations, Vietnam, Middle East
Other Notes
Annotation   Collection of essays, some based on multi-archival and/or international research, addressing the Eisenhower Administration's policies toward the Third World in the context of a globalized Cold War. The authors cover Ike's use of propaganda, covert operations, and aid, important events including the Bandung Conference, and specific locations including Indonesia, South Vietnam, Bolivia, and Israel. The book's conclusion notes that there is a theme of "disconnection" which threads through the essays: "the Eisenhower administration necessarily varied its global responses depending on the regional differences, but it was not able to connect its central containment strategy for protecting the North Atlantic core to its tactical responses to the

challenges to U.S. interests in peripheral areas." Ike recognized the new importance of the African, Asian, Middle Eastern, and South American countries. He and his administration, however, failed to understand fully the historical, cultural, political, and ideological aspects of the areas, and "often found itself at the mercy of events out of its control." Save one, the essays in this volume are revised versions of papers presented at a conference at the University of San Diego in 2003. Part of the Harvard Cold War Studies Book Series.

102.   Stebenne, David L. *Modern Republican: Arthur Larson and the Eisenhower Years.* Bloomington, Indiana: Indiana University Press, 2006.

Author Info	"David Stebenne earned a B.A. from Yale University in 1982, a J.D. and an M.A. in 1986, and a Ph.D. in 1991, all from Columbia University. He is a member of the Maryland bar, and a specialist in modern American political and legal history. He has taught at Ohio State since 1993." Bio at: http://history.osu.edu/people/person.cfm?ID=731
Bibliography	No.
Index	Yes.
Notes	Yes.
Photographs	Yes (B&W).
Appendix	No.
Tables	No.
Key Words	Presidency, Politics
Other Notes	
Annotation	Biography of Arthur Larson, who held three major posts in Ike's Administration: undersecretary of labor (1954-1956), director of the U.S. Information Agency (1956-1957), and chief presidential speechwriter (1957-1958). Ike and Larson had a close relationship, "which Larson likened to that of a farther and son." Focus of the biography is the development of modern conservatism during the Eisenhower era. Stebenne argues that: "Larson's ultimately unsuccessful efforts to prevent the rise of the New Right are especially enlightening, for they help clarify why the party of [Eisenhower] in the 1950s gradually became the party of the more conservative [Reagan] by the 1980s."

T's

103.   Takeyh, Ray. *The Origins of the Eisenhower Doctrine: The US, Britain and Nasser's Egypt, 1953-57.* New York: St. Martin's Press, Inc., 2000.

Author Info   Takeyh is a "senior fellow for Middle Eastern studies at the Council on

Foreign Relations (CFR). His areas of specialization are Iran, the Persian Gulf, and U.S. foreign policy. Dr. Takeyh is also an adjunct professor at the Center for Peace and Security Studies at Georgetown University. He recently held the post of senior adviser to the special adviser for the Gulf and Southwest Asia at the U.S. Department of State... Dr. Takeyh's most recent book is *The Guardians of the Revolution: Iran's Approach to the World* (Oxford University Press, 2009)…" Dr. Takeyh also has published widely. He received his doctorate in modern history from Oxford University. From Council on Foreign Relations bio at http://www.cfr.org/bios/9599/.

Bibliography	Yes.
Index	Yes.
Notes	Yes.
Photographs	No.
Appendix	No.
Tables	No.
Key Words	Presidency, Cold War, Middle East, Foreign Relations
Other Notes	
Annotation	Takeyh explores the complicated relationship between the U.S. and Egypt from 1953-1957. He discusses several complex factors and issues that affected this relationship, most fundamentally, the conflict between America's focus on containing communism by incorporation of Middle Eastern countries in its alliance, and Egypt's focus on its domination of the Middle East, which included a curbing of outside influence. Takeyh also emphasizes the importance of the Eisenhower Doctrine in two respects: 1) it provided "the basis for the rehabilitation of Britain and resumption of close Anglo-American cooperation; and 2) it attempted to "actively bolster the conservative Arab regimes as the foundation of America's influence in the Middle East." Takeyh concludes the Eisenhower Doctrine failed: "Far from achieving stability, the U.S. policy led to a rigid division of the Arab world and greater Russian involvement in a strategically critical region."

104.   Taubman, Philip. *Secret Empire: Eisenhower, the CIA, and the Hidden Story of America's Space Espionage.* New York: Simon & Schuster, 2003.

Author Info	Consulting professor at the Center for International Security and Cooperation at Stanford University. "Before joining CISAC in fall 2008, Mr. Taubman worked at the *New York Times* as a reporter and editor for nearly 30 years, specializing in national security issues, including intelligence and defense policies and operations. At the *Times*, Taubman served as a Washington correspondent, Moscow bureau chief, deputy editorial page editor, Washington bureau chief and associate editor. Taubman also serves as Stanford associate vice president for university affairs, working on special projects for Stanford's president, John Hennessy. Taubman was a history major at Stanford, Class of 1970". From faculty profile page http://cisac.stanford.edu/people/philiptaubman/.

Bibliography	Yes.
Index	Yes.
Notes	Yes.
Photographs	B&W Photographs.
Appendix	No.
Tables	No.
Key Words	Presidency, Cold War, Nuclear, Military Policy, Technology
Other Notes	"Cast of Characters"
Annotation	Former *New York Times* journalist Taubman tells the story of the Eisenhower Administration's partnership with science and technology leaders and the CIA to create reconnaissance planes and satellites. Taubman finds that Eisenhower was a "visionary leader with a high tolerance for risk." He notes that Ike was intelligent and decisive. Many innovations were made in espionagé during this time, but Taubman argues that the reliance on satellites led to a neglect of more traditional forms of espionage (trained spies) and contributed to our unpreparedness on September 11, 2001. Narrative and focus is on the individuals involved.

105. Terzian, Philip. *Architects of Power: Roosevelt, Eisenhower, and the American Century.* New York: Brief Encounters, 2010.

Author Info	From book: Terzian "has been a political and cultural journalist for nearly forty years. He has written and edited for *The New Republic*, the *Los Angeles Times*, *The Wall Street Journal*, *The New Criterion*, and the *Times Literary Supplement*. Since 2005, he has been Literary Editor of *The Weekly Standard*." His website: http://www.philipterzian.com/
Bibliography	Yes.
Index	Yes.
Notes	No.
Photographs	No.
Appendix	No.
Tables	No.
Key Words	Presidency, Cold War, Military Policy, Space Exploration
Other Notes	
Annotation	An experienced journalist has written a series of essays that probe the personalities and foreign policies of two leaders who "guided their country in its methodical embrace of global responsibility." Based on secondary sources, the book is of value more for its excellent prose and provocative insights than its historical depth.

106. Tudda, Chris. *The Truth is Our Weapon: The Rhetorical Diplomacy of Dwight D. Eisenhower and John Foster Dulles.* Baton Rouge: Louisiana State University Press, 2006.

Author Info	Historian in the Office of the Historian at the U.S. Department of State (2003-

present). Visiting/Part time faculty with a focus on U.S. diplomacy at George Washington University. CV at www.gwu.edu/~history/docs/ChrisTuddaCV.doc

Bibliography	Yes.
Index	Yes.
Notes	Yes.
Photographs	No.
Appendix	No.
Tables	No.
Key Words	Presidency, Speechmaking, Media, Cold War, Foreign Relations
Other Notes	
Annotation	After examining Dulles's and Eisenhower's pre-administration experiences, Tudda uses three case studies to explores the relationship between the Eisenhower Administration's public rhetoric and its confidential foreign policy decision-making with regard to Europe. He finds that although Eisenhower and Dulles "confidentially believed that they must reduce the dangers of war and competitively coexist with Moscow," their inflammatory rhetorical diplomacy toward the Soviet Union and its allies increased Cold War tensions and the likelihood of war. He argues that both men realized that the rhetorical strategy was backfiring yet they refused to abandon it: "The administration could not free itself from the never-ending cycle of using threats to achieve diplomatic goals, which in turn impeded the administration's ability to achieve those goals."

V's

107.   van Rijn Guido. *The Truman And Eisenhower Blues: African-American Blues And Gospel Songs, 1945-1960*. New York: Continuum, 2004.

Author Info	van Rijn, "teaches English at Kennemer Lyceum in Overveen, The Netherlands. A freelance writer and blues historian, he has published articles in *Block*, *Blues Unlimited*, *Blues & Rhythm*, *Juke Blues* and *Living Blues*. His Ph.D. dissertation from Leiden University was revised as the award-winning *Roosevelt's Blues: African-American Blues and Gospel Songs on FDR* (1997). [This book was a sequel.] *Kennedy's Blues: African-American Blues and Gospel Songs* on JFK was published in August 2007. *President Johnson's Blues: African American Blues and Gospel Songs* on LBJ, Martin Luther King, Robert Kennedy and Vietnam 1963-1968 was published in 2009. http://home.tiscali.nl/guido/biography.htm
Bibliography	Yes.
Index	Yes.
Notes	Yes.
Photographs	Yes (B&W).

Appendix	No.
Tables	No.
Key Words	Presidency, Civil Rights, Korea
Other Notes	Charts
Annotation	Through an analysis of blues and gospel music, van Rijn "shed[s] new light on the question of how the presidencies of [Truman and Eisenhower] were perceived and experienced by African Americans." Of Eisenhower, he finds that while the African American community was thankful that he ended Korea, they were disappointed in his failure to desegregate the country and improve standards of living. In his second term, "blues and gospel singers ignored Eisenhower in the same way that he ignored the African-American community."

108. Vestal, Theodore M. *The Eisenhower Court and Civil Liberties*. Westport, Conn: Praeger Publishers, 2002.

Author Info	Professor Emeritus of Political Science at Oklahoma State University. "… a member of the faculty… since 1988… Professor Vestal teaches primarily in the field of constitutional law, with an emphasis on civil liberties and civil rights. His research interests include public law, contemporary Ethiopia, and international education…. Vestal earned his B.A. in Government… from the University of North Texas… and his advanced degrees (M.A. and Ph.D.) in political science from Stanford University." From profile at http://fp.okstate.edu/vestal/
Bibliography	Yes.
Index	Yes (Case Index and General Index).
Notes	Yes (at ends of chapters).
Photographs	Yes B&W Photographs.
Appendix	No.
Tables	Yes.
Key Words	Presidency, Civil Rights, Domestic Policy
Other Notes	
Annotation	Examines the civil liberties work of the Supreme Court from 1953-1962, a period of the Warren Court he believes has been understudied and under appreciated. He terms it the "Eisenhower Court" because the period is primarily during Ike's Administration, and Ike's appointees constituted a five-justice majority, including Chief Justice Warren. Eisenhower is not the focus of this book, though Vestal describes the working of the court as similar to what Professor Greenstein termed Ike's "hidden-hand strategy".

W's

109. Wagner, Steven. *Eisenhower Republicanism: Pursuing the Middle Way*. DeKalb, IL: Northern Illinois University Press, 2006.

Author Info	History professor at Missouri Southern State University Bio at: http://www.mssu.edu/socsci/sw.htm PhD from Purdue
Bibliography	Yes.
Index	Yes.
Notes	Yes.
Photographs	No.
Appendix	No.
Tables	No.
Key Words	Presidency, Politics, Domestic Policy, Civil Rights
Other Notes	
Annotation	Wagner examines Eisenhower's political philosophy of the "Middle Way," an ideology that was neither completely conservative nor liberal. He traces Ike's application of the Middle Way through issues including labor, Civil Rights, and health care. Ike's philosophy, which he hoped would change the direction of the Republican party, failed to gain traction despite the former general's popularity with the public because, "more often than not, Eisenhower's legislative proposals were defeated by an unwitting alliance of conservatives, who sought to limit the role of the federal government, and liberals, who wanted the federal government to do more than Eisenhower proposed." He further finds that Ike's other goal, of grooming future Republicans (specifically Nixon) who would come to prominence and pursue the Middle Way, also failed. Ultimately, conservatives came to dominate the Republican party.

110.   Walker, Gregg B. et al, ed. *The Military-Industrial Complex: Eisenhower's Warning Three Decades Later*. New York: Peter Lang Publishing Inc., 1992.

Author Info	Walker "is an associate professor of speech communication and director of the peace studies program at Oregon State University, Corvallis Oregon, USA. His research interests, publications, and papers address international negotiation discourse, argument and persuasion in dispute resolution, and the media and social conflict. Recent writings appear in *Mediation Quarterly*, the *Social Science Journal*, and *The Willamette Journal of the Liberal Arts*, Supplemental Series." (From book) See also http://oregonstate.edu/instruct/comm440-540/biography.htm
Bibliography	References at the end of chapters.
Index	No.
Notes	Citations at the end of chapters.
Photographs	No.
Appendix	Yes.
Tables	Yes.
Key Words	Presidency, Economics, Military Policy
Other Notes	Notes on Contributors, Forward by David Eisenhower.
Annotation	Collection of interdisciplinary essays inspired by the October 1988 conference on the U.S. Military-Industrial Complex and Ike's farewell (held at Oregon

State in Corvallis, Oregon). The book is divided into three sections: Contemporary Perspectives (3 essays), Economic and Historical Perspectives (5 essays), and Rhetorical and Psychological Perspectives (3 essays), and includes an introduction and a conclusion. Though the book is subtitled "Three Decades Later," Eisenhower and his policies are examined, especially in David S. Patterson's chapter entitled: "The Legacy of President Eisenhower's Arms Control Policies."

111.   Warshaw, Shirley A., ed. *The Eisenhower Legacy: Discussions of Presidential Leadership*. Silver Spring, MD: Bartleby Press, 1992.

Author Info	Political science professor at Gettysburg College in PA. "An authority on the American presidency, presidential elections, the president's Cabinet, and organizational decision structures for presidential policy making, Warshaw is a frequent speaker and commentator on network radio, television, and print media on presidential leadership and related topics…. Warshaw has written several books on presidential decision-making and numerous book chapters and articles… She has been a consultant to the White House under three administrations… She earned a bachelor's degree from the University of Pennsylvania, a master's degree from the Wharton School of Business, and a doctorate from Johns Hopkins University." From http://www.gettysburg.edu/podium/faculty_authors/warshaw/index.dot
Bibliography	No.
Index	Yes.
Notes	No.
Photographs	No.
Appendix	No.
Tables	No.
Key Words	Presidency, Civil Rights, Domestic Policy, White House, Foreign Relations, Space Exploration, Media, Leadership
Other Notes	Forward by Gerald R. Ford.
Annotation	This book is the first of two volumes resulting from the Eisenhower Symposium at Gettysburg College from October 10-14, 1990 held in celebration of the 100th anniversary of Ike's birth. The Symposium included members of Eisenhower's cabinet and staff, members of the press, and Eisenhower scholars, including David Eisenhower. This book is focused on Ike's leadership and is divided into chapters based on several topics, including the media, civil rights, and domestic policy. There are transcriptions of speeches and panel discussions on those topics. Editor Warshaw provides introductions to each chapter, broadly outlining the issues raised.

112.   Warshaw, Shirley A., ed. *Reexamining the Eisenhower Presidency*. Westport, Conn: Greenwood Press, 1993.

Author Info	See information in Entry #111.
Bibliography	Bibliographic Essay.
Index	Yes (name index and subject index).
Notes	Yes (at the end of the chapters).
Photographs	No.
Appendix	No.
Tables	No.
Key Words	Columbia University, Presidency, Domestic Policy, Foreign Relations, Politics, White House, Civil Rights, Economics, Middle East, Cold War, Space Exploration
Other Notes	Forward by Louis Galambos.
Annotation	Second of two volumes resulting from the Eisenhower Symposium at Gettysburg College from October 10-14, 1990 held in celebration of the 100th anniversary of Ike's birth. This volume contains a selection of ten essays presented at the Symposium; it "examines how President Eisenhower used a hidden-hand leadership style to direct not only policy development but crisis management." The essays cover Ike's time as president of Columbia University as well as his Presidential Administrations. Most of the essays are centered on domestic policy issues such as Civil Rights, White House staff structure and space policy, but there are also chapters on the Suez and Hungarian crises. From these essays, Ike emerges as "an activist president, totally versed in policy options, and carefully weighing the outcome of each option."

113. Watson, Robert J. *History of the Office of the Secretary of Defense, Vol. 4: Into the Missile Age, 1956-1960.* Washington D.C.: Historical Office, Office of the Secretary of Defense, 1997.

Author Info	From book: "Robert J. Watson graduated from Virginia Polytechnic Institute with a B.S. degree in 1941. Following service in the U.S. Navy during World War II, he obtained M.A. and Ph.D. degrees at the University of Virginia. He worked as a historian with the National Security Agency and with the Joint Chiefs of Staff, serving as chief of the JCS Historical Division from 1977 to 1983. He is the author of *The Joint Chiefs of Staff and National Policy, 1953-1954*, and coauthor (with James F. Schnabel) of *The Joint Chiefs of Staff and the Korean War*."
Bibliography	Yes.
Index	Yes.
Notes	Yes.
Photographs	Yes (B&W).
Appendix	No.
Tables	Yes.
Key Words	Presidency, Military Policy, Foreign Relations, Cold War, Space Exploration, Middle East, Nuclear, Economics, Technology
Other Notes	Maps, Charts.

Annotation   The fourth volume of the History of the Office of the Secretary of Defense focuses on Ike's second term. This massive (over 1,000 pages including notes) official agency history, written by the agency's historian, is arranged both chronologically (first 12 chapters) and topically (chapters 13-21). The final two chapters describe Ike's final year as President and the status of the Office of the Secretary of Defense at the end of 1960. Watson examines economic and military aspects of Ike's New Look policy, the various security crises faced by the three men who served as secretary of defense during this period (Wilson, McElroy, and Gates) including the Suez Crisis, the Hungarian uprising, Lebanon and Taiwan, and technological and military developments such as the space, nuclear, and missile programs. Watson also discuses organizational structures and changes in the OSD. He concludes that during the period under review, "OSD successfully carried out its mission of maintaining the security of the United States."

114.   Weidner, William. *Eisenhower & Montgomery at the Falaise Gap*. Xlibris Corporation, 2010.

Author Info   From Weidner's amazon.com biography: "Mr. Weidner is a military historian who has been studying the Second World War for thirty years… Allied strategy, beginning at the 'Battle of the Falaise Gap,' was determined by political compromise rather than sound military tactics…. Born in Carlisle, Pennsylvania in 1941, William Weidner attended schools in Carlisle and graduated from Carlisle High School in 1959. He attended Dickinson College … and served three years (1963-1966) in the United States Army. He has a Bachelor of Arts Degree from Fort Lewis College in Durango, Colorado and has been employed as a time study engineer, a real estate salesman, and a construction project manager." http://www.amazon.com/William-Weidner/e/B0041A9MGS/ref=ntt_dp_epwbk_0

Bibliography   Yes.
Index   Yes.
Notes   Yes.
Photographs   B&W Photographs.
Appendix   Yes.
Tables   No.
Key Words   Military- WWII
Other Notes   Maps, detailed chronology.
Annotation   The author draws upon careful research in manuscript and secondary materials to draft a tightly focused study of the European campaign mounted by the Allied forces. His history turns on a crucial part of the campaign when there was the potential at the Falaise Gap to encircle a substantial part of the German Army. Weidner concludes that Montgomery stopped the advance at a decisive point in the campaign and thus allowed the German forces to retreat successfully. Eisenhower obfuscated the issue, the author claims, to preserve the alliance with Britain. Later, Eisenhower took direct command of the

ground forces but Weidner says Ike waited too long to corral Montgomery.

115.   Weintraub, Stanley. *15 Stars: Eisenhower, MacArthur, Marshall: Three Generals Who Saved the American Century*. New York: Free Press, 2007.

Author Info	Retired Penn State professor. Served in Korea, has written over 40 books. His original focus was on the Victorian period. PSU bio at http://www.pabook.libraries.psu.edu/palitmap/bios/Weintraub__Stanley.html. Currently an adjunct professor at the University of Delaware in the English department. UD bio at http://www.english.udel.edu/content/index.php?option=com_contact&task=view&contact_id=192&Itemid=698
Bibliography	No.
Index	Yes.
Notes	Only an essay on sources in the back.
Photographs	Yes B&W Photographs.
Appendix	No.
Tables	No.
Key Words	Military- WWII
Other Notes	
Annotation	Weintraub chronicles the lives and careers of three very different men: Eisenhower, MacArthur, and Marshall, in a collective biography, focused largely on WWII, but covering periods both before and after the war. He explains how their lives intersected and were intertwined; they needed each other, he writes, but were never friends: "Colleagues, and on occasion competitors, they had leapfrogged each other, sometimes stonewalled each other, even supported and protected each other, throughout their celebrated careers." Weintraub argues that "[b]ut for the twists of circumstance, all three—[rather than just Ike]—might have occupied the White House." Eisenhower is described as "genial and flexible," and the most gregarious of the three. Ike's relationship with Kay Summersby is discussed.

116.   Wenger, Andreas. *Living with Peril: Eisenhower, Kennedy, and Nuclear Weapons*. Lanham, MD: Rowman & Littlefield Publishers, Inc., 1997.

Author Info	"Professor of International and Swiss Security Policy and Director of the Center for Security Studies. He holds a doctoral degree from the University of Zurich and was a guest scholar at Princeton University (1992-94), Yale University (1998), the Woodrow Wilson Center (2000), and, recently, at the George Washington University (2005).... Wenger was born in 1964 and is a citizen of Thalwil, Zurich, Switzerland. He studied History, Political Science and German Literature at the University of Zurich, where he received his MA in 1991... [H]e wrote his doctoral dissertation [on] the role of nuclear weapons in the Cold War [and] [h]is main research interests are in security and strategic

studies." From http://www.css.ethz.ch/people/stafflist/wengeran

Bibliography	Yes.
Index	Yes.
Notes	Yes.
Photographs	No.
Appendix	No.
Tables	No.
Key Words	Presidency, Cold War, Foreign Relations, Nuclear
Other Notes	
Annotation	An investigation of the political role of nuclear weapons that examines how the Eisenhower and Kennedy Administrations learned to live with the reality of the Soviet Union possessing weapons capable of destroying America. He divides the period under question (1953-1963) into three parts: 1) Eisenhower and the period of America's "overwhelming nuclear superiority"; 2) Eisenhower during an "evolving mutual vulnerability"; and 3) Kennedy's Administration and a period of "perceived mutual vulnerability." Wenger's focus is on the evolution of political thinking, and he finds that the presidents ultimately "adapted United States policy to evolving mutual nuclear vulnerability in ways that contributed to the avoidance of war." He finds that the process was a long one, both men made mistakes, and that it was not inevitable that international stability would be achieved.

117. Whiting, Charles. *American Deserter: General Eisenhower and the Execution of Eddie Slovik*. J Whiting Books, 2005 and York, England: Eskdale Publishing, 2005.

Author Info	"Born in the Bootham area of York, England, he was a pupil at the prestigious Nunthorpe Grammar School, leaving at the age of 16 to join the British Army by lying about his age. Keen to be in on the wartime action, Whiting was attached to the 52nd Reconnaissance Regiment and by the age of 18 saw duty as a sergeant in France, Holland, Belgium and Germany in the latter stages of World War II. While still a soldier, he observed conflicts between the highest-ranking British and American generals, [conflicts] he would write about extensively." An author of fiction and history…. Whiting… died on July 24 2007". From his website http://www.charleswhiting.net/
Bibliography	Yes (brief).
Index	Yes.
Notes	Yes (brief).
Photographs	Yes (B&W).
Appendix	No.
Tables	No.
Key Words	Military- WWII
Other Notes	
Annotation	The author discusses a particular event, the execution of Eddie Slovik, an ex-con who deserted his unit in combat in the European campaign and was shot on orders signed by General Eisenhower. In an account marred by numerous typos and mistakes, the author contends that Slovik's execution was part of "a

calculated plan" which he attempts to trace to Eisenhower and assorted other U.S. military leaders. Slovik apparently wrote his own explanation of what he was doing: "...I'll run away again if I have to go out their [sic]." Whiting looks to the Battle of the Bulge and the German attempts to kill Eisenhower as part of the context for Slovik's execution.

118.   Wicker, Tom. *Dwight D. Eisenhower*. New York: Times Books, 2002.

Author Info	"For more than thirty years, Tom Wicker covered American politics at *The New York Times* where he began writing the *Times*'s "In the Nation" column. He is the author of numerous books, including *One of Us: Richard Nixon and the American Dream* and *JFK* and *LBJ*, as well as several novels." (From book)
Bibliography	Selected bibliography.
Index	Yes.
Notes	Yes.
Photographs	No.
Appendix	No.
Tables	No.
Key Words	Presidency
Other Notes	"Milestones" section (chronology).
Annotation	Short biography of Eisenhower by journalist and author, Wicker, focusing almost exclusively on his time as president. Wicker includes personal anecdotes and concludes that "For my part, from memory and research, I believe that Dwight D. Eisenhower was a great man—but not quite a great president." His reasons include his contention that Ike prevented war but failed to make peace, and that Ike's civil rights record was weak. Part of The American Presidents series, the aim of which is "to present the grand panorama of our chief executives in volumes compact enough for the busy reader, lucid enough for the student, authoritative enough for the scholar."

119.   Williamson, Daniel C. *Separate Agendas: Churchill, Eisenhower, and Anglo-American Relations, 1953-1955*. Lanham, MD: Lexington Books, 2006.

Author Info	Associate Professor of History at the University of Hartford.
Bibliography	Yes.
Index	Yes.
Notes	Yes.
Photographs	No.
Appendix	No.
Tables	No.
Key Words	Presidency, Foreign Relations, Cold War, Middle East
Other Notes	
Annotation	Williamson examines four case studies to assess British-US relations between 1953 and 1955. Britain and the U.S. had differing foreign policy goals at this

time: Britain sought to hold onto its eroding power, and America sought to stop the spread of Communism. Williamson analyzes four diplomatic controversies arising from those conflicting goals (East-West Summit, arms supply to Iraq, Buraimi Oasis, and the first Offshore Islands Crisis) to determine what level of success Britain had in retaining its position as an independent global power. He finds that in the years before Suez, Britain did retain power, as evidenced by its ability to "pursue foreign policy goals that were at odds with those of its gargantuan American ally." Great Britain did not subordinate its aims of continued global power to America's aims of containment, and the U.S. valued Britain's alliance too much to force the issue and potentially lose the ally. Williamson explores the important roles Churchill and Eisenhower played in Anglo-American relations at this time.

120.   Winand, Pascaline. *Eisenhower, Kennedy, and the United States of Europe.* New York: St. Martin's Press, 1993.

Author Info	"[P]rofessor and Director of the Monash European and EU Centre at Monash University [in Victoria, Australia]. She was born in Brussels, Belgium and holds degrees in Germanic studies, political science, international relations and diplomatic history from the *Université libre de Bruxelles* (BA in Germanic Studies and PhD in Political Science), Yale University (MA in International Relations) and Purdue University (MA in Diplomatic History)." Winand is also the co-author and co-editor of four volumes and of numerous articles and chapters, "chiefly on the external relations of the European Union (EU). She is editor of the series 'European Policy'http://www.monash.edu.au/europecentre/about/winand.html
Bibliography	Yes.
Index	Yes.
Notes	Yes.
Photographs	No.
Appendix	No.
Tables	No.
Key Words	Presidency, Foreign Relations
Other Notes	
Annotation	Winand engages in a "study of the American administration's attitudes towards the unification of Europe, and the continuous dialogue between American supporters and opponents of European integration, and their European counterparts". She believes this study "will help contribute to a better understanding of how patient and determined individuals bring about such changes." She focuses on the Eisenhower and Kennedy Administrations, but also discusses the Johnson years and discusses issues and events including the European Defense Community, the Free Trade Area negotiations, and the Organization for Economic Cooperation and Development. Her perspective on Ike is basically favorable to his policies and leadership. Based on secondary and primary sources, including interviews. Jean Monnet features prominently.

121.   Wukovits, John. *Eisenhower: A Biography*. New York: Palgrave Macmillan, 2006.

Author Info	From his bio in Macmillan press: "John Wukovits is the author of *Pacific Alamo* and *Devotion to Duty*. His writings have appeared in numerous publications including *The Washington Post* and the *Chicago Tribune*." http://us.macmillan.com/author/johnwukovits Bio on his website at: http://www.johnwukovits.com/john_wukovits/About_the_Author.html
Bibliography	Yes.
Index	Yes.
Notes	Yes.
Photographs	Yes (B&W).
Appendix	No.
Tables	No.
Key Words	Early Life, Military- Pre WWII, Military—B/w the Wars, Military- WWII, Presidency.
Other Notes	
Annotation	An experienced military historian describes Eisenhower's career as a soldier. The book, in the Great Generals Series, is based upon a careful mining of secondary studies and published documents. The author occasionally looks over his shoulder to recent events, but for the most part, he keeps his focus on what he sees as a remarkably successful military career. Wukovits is critical of Eisenhower's early timidity but concludes that the career was overwhelmingly successful.

Y's

122.   Yaqub, Salim. *Containing Arab Nationalism: The Eisenhower Doctrine and the Middle East*. Chapel Hill, NC: The University of North Carolina Press, 2004.

Author Info	"Salim Yaqub is an Associate Professor of History at the University of California at Santa Barbara. He received his B.A. from the Academy of Art College and an M.A. at San Francisco State University, continuing on to Yale University, where he earned an M. Phil and a Ph.D. in American History." He specializes in the history of American foreign relations, 20th century American policial history, and modern Middle Eastern history since 1945. "His dissertation [on which this book is based] earned him the John Addison Porter Prize and the George Washington Egleston Prize from Yale University." Profile from http://www.teach12.com:80/tgc/professors/professor_detail.aspx?pid=268 See also: http://www.history.ucsb.edu/people/person.php?account_id=56&first_name=Salim&last_name=Yaqub
Bibliography	Yes.

Index	Yes.
Notes	Yes.
Photographs	Yes (B&W).
Appendix	No.
Tables	No.
Key Words	Presidency, Middle East, Cold War, Foreign Relations
Other Notes	Maps, Cartoons.
Annotation	Yaqub provides his readers a fully researched and documented account of U.S. relations with the Middle East between the Suez War of 1956 and the end of the second Eisenhower Administration. Eisenhower's attempt to fill the vacuum left by British withdrawal from the region placed America in opposition to the pan-Arab policies of Egypt's president Gamal Abdel Nasser. This "was not a conflict over values; it was a contest of interests…," with the United States seeking always to prevent the extension of Soviet power. Arab nationalism was incidental to the United States and of central importance to Nasser and his allies. Eisenhower's policies were more cautious than those of his successors, Yaqub concludes, and America was unable to achieve the anti-communist coalition it sought during these tense years of the Cold War.

Article Annotations

A's

123.   Abbott, Philip. "Eisenhower, King Utopus, and the Fifties Decade in America."
       Presidential Studies Quarterly 32, no. 1 (Mar, 2002): 7-29.

Author Info   Professor of political science at Wayne State University (Detroit). Research
                  interests include the American presidency and American political thought and
                  culture. He also published *Exceptional American: Newness and American
                  Identity* (1999). Profile at http://www.clas.wayne.edu/faculty/abbott
Bibliography References.
Index   No.
Notes   Footnotes and References.
Photographs   No.
Appendix   No.
Tables   No.
Key Words   Presidency
Other Notes
Annotation   Examines assessments of Eisenhower's presidency from the 1950s through the
                  1990s as being intimately tied to each scholar's and political actor's
                  utopian/dystopian characterizations of the 1950s.

124.   Adamson, Michael R. "Delusions of Development: The Eisenhower Administration and
       the Foreign Aid Program in Vietnam, 1955-1960." *Journal of American-East Asian
       Relations* 5, no. 2 (Summer 1996): 157-182.

Author Info   Adjunct Professor, Department of History, California State University,
                  Sonoma, CA. Ph.D. in History, University of California, Santa Barbara, CA
                  (2000). Resume at
                  http://www.coastalresearchcenter.ucsb.edu/cmi/VitaAdamson.html
Bibliography No.
Index   No.
Notes   Endnotes (76).
Photographs   No.
Appendix   No.
Tables   No.
Key Words   Presidency, Economics, Cold War, Foreign Relations
Other Notes
Annotation   Using documents from the Foreign Relations of the United States series,
                  including those penned by Ambassador Elbridge Durbrow, Adamson argues
                  that the Eisenhower Administration's reliance on the approach of MIT
                  economists, who held that economic aid and technical assistance to less

developed nations would promote rapid economic growth, failed in South Vietnam because the critical factor in foreign aid programs is not the intent of the donor country but the actions of the government receiving the funds. The Eisenhower Administration provided the aid in an attempt to shore up the Diem government as a bulwark against Communism, but the aid resulted in no economic development and served only to provide Diem with the funds to remain in power and exacerbate the misery and poverty of the Vietnamese people.

125. Allen, Craig. "Eisenhower's Congressional Defeat of 1956: Limitations of Television and the GOP." *Presidential Studies Quarterly* 22, no. 1 (Winter, 1992): 57-71.

Author Info	Associate professor at the Walter Cronkite School of Journalism and Mass Communication at Arizona State University. His two books include *News Is People: The Rise of Local TV News* (2001) and *Eisenhower and the Mass Media* (1993). Teaches classes on reporting, communication, and media. *Eisenhower and the Mass Media* is based on Allen's dissertation, "Peace, Prosperity and Prime Time TV: Eisenhower, Stevenson and the TV Politics of 1956 (Ohio U, 1989).
Bibliography	No.
Index	No.
Notes	Footnotes.
Photographs	No.
Appendix	No.
Tables	No.
Key Words	Presidency, Media, Politics, Elections
Other Notes	
Annotation	Using party records and materials in the Eisenhower Library, and recollections of key participants, Allen traces the Republican TV strategy for the 1956 Congressional elections and shows that party strategists miscalculated that Eisenhower's popularity could be transferred to other Republicans through television. This revealed some of the limitations of the new medium as a political tool.

126. Allen, Craig. "News Conferences on TV: Ike-Age Politics Revisited." *Journalism Quarterly* 70, no. 1 (Spring 1993): 13-25.

Author Info	See information in Entry #125.
Bibliography	No.
Index	No.
Notes	Endnotes (52).
Photographs	No.
Appendix	No.
Tables	No.

Key Words	Presidency, Media, Politics
Other Notes	
Annotation	Notes that although the first TV news conferences were a great advancement in media history and a breakthrough in electronic journalism, it was Eisenhower, not the television industry, who shaped them, using them to bypass journalists and speak directly to the American people.

127.   Ambrose, Stephen E. "Eisenhower." *Miller Center Journal* 4, (January 1997): 11-21.

Author Info	Well-known Eisenhower historian. Ambrose was the Associate Editor of the Eisenhower Papers. He taught at Johns Hopkins University and University of New Orleans. For a time America's most popular biographer and historian, Ambrose's reputation sagged late in his life: there were persistent reports of plagiarism, falsification, and inaccuracies regarding his work. Ambrose died in 2002.
Bibliography	No.
Index	No.
Notes	No.
Photographs	No.
Appendix	No.
Tables	No.
Key Words	Early Life, Military- Pre WWII, Military- WWII, Presidency, Post-Presidency
Other Notes	The Miller Center on Public Affairs at the University of Virginia. See http://millercenter.org/about
Annotation	Print of Ambrose's speech given in a forum of the Miller Center on Public Affairs at the University of Virginia on March 30, 1996 entitled "Eisenhower". Speech weaves together various anecdotes about Eisenhower in an attempt to reveal his character. Ambrose emphasizes Eisenhower's respect for his peers, his honesty, his regard for the rule of law, his religious beliefs, and his humility.

128.   Ambrose, Stephen E. "Eisenhower's Legacy." *Prologue* 22 (Fall 1990): 227-236. (Reprinted in vol. 26, (Special 25th Anniversary Issue 1994): 160-167).

Author Info	See information in Entry #127.
Bibliography	No.
Index	No.
Notes	No.
Photographs	Yes (10).
Appendix	No.
Tables	No.
Key Words	Military- WWII, Presidency
Other Notes	
Annotation	In this glowing essay, Ambrose lists Eisenhower's legacies, including

"freedom", abhorrence of war, respect for the Constitution and executive privilege. He discusses telephone conversation tape recording precedents, admonitions against covering up when one is caught, a more active CIA and FBI, the importance of foreign aid and a balanced budget, good stewardship of public lands, a foreign policy of containment and peace keeping, and constrained defense spending aimed at sufficiency, not superiority.

129.   Ambrose, Stephen E. "U.S. Foreign Policy in the 1950s" *Contemporary Austrian Studies* 3, (January 1995): 12-23.

Author Info	See information in Entry #127.
Bibliography	No.
Index	No.
Notes	Footnotes (20).
Photographs	No.
Appendix	No.
Tables	No.
Key Words	Foreign Relations, Presidency, Cold War
Other Notes	
Annotation	Broad, brief overview of Eisenhower's foreign policy in the 1950s with a particular focus on Central Europe, especially Germany and Austria. Special attention is paid to Eisenhower's achievement in avoiding war, the creation of a free Austria, and the alliance forged b/w West Germany and America.

130.   Andrew, John, III. "Cracks in the Consensus: The Rockefeller Brothers Fund Special Studies Project and Eisenhower's America." *Presidential Studies Quarterly* 28, no. 3 (Summer 1998): 535-552.

Author Info	Andrews died in approx 2000. His book, *Power to Destroy -- The Political Uses of the IRS from Kennedy to Nixon*, was published posthumously in 2002. He received his Ph.D. from University of Texas, Austin and was a professor of history at Franklin and Marshall College. Other books he authored: *The Other Side of the Sixties: Young Americans for Freedom* and the *Rise of Conservative Politics and Lyndon Johnson and the Great Society*.
Bibliography	No
Index	No
Notes	Footnotes
Photographs	No
Appendix	No
Tables	No
Key Words	Presidency, Politics.
Other Notes	
Annotation	The Special Studies Project of the Rockefeller Brother's Fund produced six panel reports between 1958 and 1960. The panel reports attempted to provide

an agenda for the future, were critical of the Eisenhower administration, influenced Republican and Democrat platforms for the 1960 election, and offered a glimpse into the thinking of the American elites who wrote them. Andrew argues that despite this, they fell short of stimulating broad critical thinking. Based on material from the Rockefeller Archive Center.

B's

131. Bacevich, A. J. "The Paradox of Professionalism: Eisenhower, Ridgway, and the Challenge to Civilian Control, 1953-1955." *The Journal of Military History* Vol. 61, No. 2 (Apr., 1997), pp. 303-333.

Author Info	Boston University Professor of International Relations (Was at Hopkins). Profile at http://www.bu.edu/ir/faculty/alphabetical/bacevich/
Bibliography	No.
Index	No.
Notes	Footnotes.
Photographs	No.
Appendix	No.
Tables	No.
Key Words	Presidency; Military Policy, Cold War
Other Notes	
Annotation	Using the Ridgway Papers in the U.S. Army Military History Institute, Bacevich traces Chief of Staff General Matthew B. Ridgway's challenges to President Eisenhower's national security policies, especially the President's declared strategy of massive retaliation, which Ridgway believed threatened military professionalism.

132. Baucom, Donald R. "Eisenhower and Ballistic Missile Defense The Formative Years, 1944-1961." *Air Power History* 51, no. 4 (Winter 2004): 4-17.

Author Info	Donald Baucom is the historian of the Ballistic Missile Defense Organization, popularly known as "Star Wars." He is a graduate of the Air Force Academy and served as a commissioned officer for twenty-eight years. He has taught history and strategy at the Academy and the Air War College and has directed the Air Power Research Institute at Maxwell AFB, Alabama. Dr. Baucom was editor of the *Air University Review*, currently the *Airpower Journal*. He is the author of The Origins of SDI, 1944–1983, which won the Organization of American Historians' Leopold Prize in History. (From http://www.airforcehistory.hq.af.mil/Publications/fulltext/golden/14.pdf) See also https://casweb.ou.edu/home/news/events/event_daa10.html)
Bibliography	No.

Index	No.
Notes	Footnotes (78).
Photographs	Yes (4).
Appendix	No.
Tables	No.
Key Words	Military- WWII, Army Chief of Staff, Presidency, Nuclear, Cold War, Military Policy, Technology
Other Notes	
Annotation	Traces the development of America's Ballistic Missile Defense (BMD) program from 1944-1961. Germany's WWII long-range ballistic missile made a strong impression on Eisenhower, but he was skeptical of the feasibility of BMD. His failure to provide strong presidential support for BMD left the program to languish until his creation of the Advanced Research Projects Agency (1958), which centralized management of BMD research.

133.   Benson, Maxine. "Dwight D. Eisenhower and the West." *Journal of the West* 34, no. 2 (April 1995): 58-65.

Author Info	Former state historian at the Colorado Historical Society, has written extensively on her native state. She is author of *Mountain Naturalist* and coauthor of *A Colorado History*. Ph.D. from University of Colorado Boulder.
Bibliography	No.
Index	No.
Notes	Endnotes (48).
Photographs	Yes (5).
Appendix	No.
Tables	No.
Key Words	Early Life, Military- WWII, Presidency, Family, Personal Life
Other Notes	
Annotation	Describes the influence of three western states— Texas (where he was born) Kansas (where he was raised), and Colorado (his wife's home)—on Eisenhower. She finds that the West impacted Eisenhower in many ways including: providing him with a "a code of behavior," a love of western lore, and a respect for, and consideration of, the people in small towns of the western United States.

134.   Bergman, Gerald. "The Influence of Religion on President Eisenhower's Upbringing." *Journal of American & Comparative Cultures* 23, no. 4 (Winter 2000): 89-107.

Author Info	Has nine academic degrees, (none of which are in history). His focus is on science and he says he's been discriminated against because of his beliefs in creation science. Adjunct associate professor at Medical University of Ohio and an instructor in the Division of Arts & Sciences at Northwest State Community College in Ohio. He teaches biochemistry, biology, chemistry and

physics. He has many publications in a variety of scientific and popular journals, plus books. From http://creationwiki.org/Jerry_Bergman Also wrote article on the Jehovah's Witnesses' influence on Eisenhower.

Bibliography	No.
Index	No.
Notes	Endnotes and references.
Photographs	No.
Appendix	No.
Tables	No.
Key Words	Early Life, Military- WWII, Presidency, Family, Religion
Other Notes	Author conflates Eisenhower's respect for his mother w/ respect for her particular brand of religion. He was clearly religious, but he also clearly steered away from Watchtower. As did his father and all of his brothers. See also Bergman's 1998 article, item # 135 below.
Annotation	Relying mainly on secondary sources and church publications, scientist author examines the religious life of the Eisenhower family, with a particular focus on Dwight and his mother, Ida. He concludes that early Watchtower, or Jehovah's Witnesses, teachings influenced Eisenhower and affected his work in the military and as President. This is true, the author writes, despite the facts that Dwight Eisenhower was never formally involved with Watchtower, tried to conceal his Watchtower background, and did not accept many of Watchtower's teachings.

135. Bergman, Jerry. "Steeped in Religion: President Eisenhower and the Influence of the Jehovah's Witnesses." *Kansas History* 21, no. 3 (September 1998): 148-167.

Author Info	Same as Gerald but he is listed in this article as "Jerry". See information in Entry #134.
Bibliography	No.
Index	No.
Notes	Footnotes (76).
Photographs	Yes (9).
Appendix	No.
Tables	No.
Key Words	Early Life, Military- WWII, Presidency, Family, Religion
Other Notes	Text is substantially similar to the 2000 article. Entire chunks are verbatim and others are only slightly altered. Structure is very similar. The one major difference in the text is that the 2000 article is more critical of the claim that Ida wrote to a young private in the army about converting. This 1998 article accepts this as true, and the 2000 concedes that it was only "alleged."
Annotation	See the previous article entry as the articles are essentially the same.

136. Beschloss, Michael R. "A Tale of Two Presidents." *Wilson Quarterly* 24, no. 1 (Winter 2000): 60-70.

Author Info	Michael Beschloss has been called "the nation's leading Presidential historian" by *Newsweek*. He has written eight books on American presidents and is NBC News Presidential Historian, as well as contributor to PBS's The NewsHour with Jim Lehrer. (From Simon and Schuster website).
Bibliography	No.
Index	No.
Notes	No.
Photographs	Yes (1).
Appendix	No.
Tables	No.
Key Words	Presidency
Other Notes	Two cartoons.
Annotation	Compares the strengths and weaknesses of the presidencies of Eisenhower and John F. Kennedy, which Beschloss characterizes as very different. He finds that Eisenhower had enormous public popularity and was more intelligent than people believed at the time, but that he was not a good orator and had a difficult time achieving his goals with Congress. Also posits that Eisenhower lacked the ambitions and skills necessary in a president, and Beschloss gives him "demerits" for McCarthy, civil rights, and his attempt at "modern Republicanism." Notes, however, that he was "magnificently suited to the 1950s." Article adapted from an essay Beschloss wrote for *Power and Presidency*, ed. Robert A. Wilson (PublicAffairs: 1999).

137. Bielakowski, Alexander M. "Eisenhower: The First NATO SACEUR." *War & Society* 22, no. 2 (October 2004): 95-108.

Author Info	Bielakowski was at the University of Findlay in Ohio. Then was at the Command and General Staff college until at least 2008.
Bibliography	No.
Index	No.
Notes	Footnotes (69).
Photographs	No.
Appendix	No.
Tables	No.
Key Words	NATO, Cold War, SACEUR
Other Notes	
Annotation	In his 17 months as the first NATO Supreme Allied Commander, Europe (SACEUR), Eisenhower was largely successful in changing European and North American public opinion to support NATO and make NATO into a legitimate military force. Author argues that Eisenhower was uniquely suited to this task because of his experience in WWII, his organizational skills, and his popularity and credibility at home and in Western Europe.

138.   Biles, Roger. "Public Housing Policy in the Eisenhower Administration." *Mid America*
        81, no. 1 (Winter 1999): 5-25.

Author Info	Professor of History at Illinois State University, is the author of *Richard J. Daley: Politics, Race, and the Governing of Chicago* and *Crusading Liberal: Paul H. Douglas of Illinois*. Was previously a professor of history at East Carolina University.
Bibliography	No.
Index	No.
Notes	Footnotes (34).
Photographs	No.
Appendix	No.
Tables	No.
Key Words	Presidency, Domestic Policy, Economics
Other Notes	
Annotation	Traces the evolution of Eisenhower's stance on public housing through his two terms as president. When he assumed the office, he had little knowledge of issues concerning public housing, but was leery of it because of his discomfort with the federal government's involvement in the private housing market and because of the expenditures required. Over the course of his presidency, and on the advice of his appointed advisors, he limited, but did not terminate, the construction of low-cost housing. Biles finds that by the end of his second term, Eisenhower actively opposed public housing.

139.   Birkner, Michael J. "Eisenhower and the Red Menace." *Prologue* 33, no. 3 (September
        2001): 196-205.

Author Info	Senior professor at Gettysburg College: "scholarship has focused on aspects of 19th- and 20th-century America: political, urban, oral and biographical history. He has most recently written about the presidency of Dwight D. Eisenhower, with special interest in the role of his Chief of Staff Sherman Adams. He has also written a book on James Buchanan, the only Pennsylvania-born American president, and an award-winning book titled *A Country Place No More: The Transformation of Bergenfield, N.J., 1894-1994*, which traced the development of that town from small community to a major suburb of New York City. Birkner received his bachelor's degree from Gettysburg College and his master's degree and doctorate from the University of Virginia in American history with a specialization in Jacksonian politics." From profile at http://www.gettysburg.edu/podium/faculty_authors/birkner/index.dot
Bibliography	No.
Index	No.
Notes	Endnotes (44).
Photographs	Yes (9).
Appendix	No.
Tables	No.

Key Words   Presidency, Cold War, Politics
Other Notes   Illustrations.
Annotation   Examines Eisenhower's strategies for dealing with Joseph McCarthy's red scare. Finds that we will never really know if Eisenhower's indirect tactics, such as his speeches regarding his Administration's efforts to assure that there were no communists in the executive branch, asserting executive privilege on White House documents to keep them out of McCarthy's hands, and disagreeing with McCarthy's methods in speeches without ever naming McCarthy directly, were the best method of combating the "demagogue" McCarthy. He does find, however, that Eisenhower's methods "seem defensible" due to the "complexion of Congress" and American's fear of communism. Article was originally delivered as a paper on September 30, 2000 at a symposium sponsored by the Herbert Hoover Library entitled "The Culture of Conspiracy."

140.   Bikner, Michael J. "'He's My Man': Sherman Adams and New Hampshire's Role in the 'Draft Eisenhower' Movement." *Historical New Hampshire* 58, no. 1 (February 2003): 5-25.

Author Info   See information in Entry #139.
Bibliography   No.
Index   No.
Notes   Endnotes (57).
Photographs   Yes (7).
Appendix   No.
Tables   No.
Key Words   Presidency, Elections, Politics
Other Notes   Cartoons (3)
Annotation   Details New Hampshire Governor Sherman Adams' campaigning efforts for Eisenhower in his state's primary. Adams latched onto Eisenhower's presidential possibilities as an effort to pull himself out of New Hampshire, where he lacked political prospects. The success of his "Draft Eisenhower" campaign, so called because it was unclear at that point if Eisenhower would run, or if he was even a Republican, earned him Eisenhower's gratitude when he returned to America from Europe, where he had been during Adams' work for his primary campaign. Adams later went on to become the White House Chief of Staff under Eisenhower.

141.   Bischof, Günter. "The Collapse of Liberation Rhetoric: The Eisenhower Administration and the 1956 Hungarian Crisis." *Hungarian Studies Review* 20, no. 1 (Spring 2006): 51-63. The year of publication for this article may have been 1993.

Author Info   Günter Bischof is the chair and Marshall Plan professor of history and the director of CenterAustria at the University of New Orleans. He has been teaching American and European Diplomatic History at the University of New Orleans since 1989 and is the recipient of the junior and senior research awards of the UNO Alumni Foundation; he was Executive Director of CenterAustria since its founding in 1997 and then director since 2000. He is the author of "Austria in the First Cold War, 1945/55: The Leverage of the Weak" (1999), the co-editor... of "Contemporary Austrian Studies" (16 vols), and co-editor of a dozen other books and numerous articles on World War II, the Cold War, and contemporary Austrian history.... Bischof is an alumnus of both the University of Innsbruck and the University of New Orleans and holds a Ph.D. in American history from Harvard University (1989).

Bibliography	Selected bibliography.
Index	No.
Notes	Internal citations.
Photographs	No.
Appendix	No.
Tables	No.
Key Words	Presidency, Foreign Relations, Cold War
Other Notes	
Annotation	Bischof examines the disconnect between Eisenhower's liberation rhetoric and his failure to intercede in the 1956 Hungarian revolt specifically and in Eastern European liberation movements generally. He examines both the domestic and international contexts of Eisenhower's policies and finds that: "The price of an escalation of conflict towards nuclear war was deemed too dangerous" and thus "no direct interventions were launched in the Soviet sphere of influence." Eisenhower toned down his "empty liberation rhetoric" after the Hungarian crisis, and it was the Hungarian rebels, encouraged by American propaganda, who suffered most.

142.   Blumenson, Martin. "Eisenhower Then and Now: Fireside Reflections." *Parameters: US Army War College* 21, no. 2 (June 1991): 22-34.

Author Info	Died in 2005. *Washington Post* obituary: a leading historian of World War II who wrote the Army's official account of the D-Day invasion and was perhaps the foremost authority on the life of Gen. George S. Patton Jr. Spent more than 20 years as an official historian of the Army, compiling authoritative accounts of the European theater of World War II. http://www.washingtonpost.com/wp-dyn/articles/A59628-2005Apr16.html
Bibliography	Very brief bibliographical note at the end of the article.
Index	No.
Notes	No.
Photographs	No.
Appendix	No.
Tables	No.
Key Words	Military- WWII
Other Notes	

Annotation   Notes that some flaws in Eisenhower's WWII performance have been noticed recently by historians. Agrees with Ike's grandson David's assessment that called Ike's "decisions in northwest Europe political in the main rather than military." Although Ike excelled at coalition building, his style of command was too hands-off, perhaps due to inexperience in the battlefield. Also discusses Ike's military contemporaries and their opinions of Ike, including Montgomery and Patton.

143. Borhi, László. "Rollback, Liberation, Containment, or Inaction?: U.S. Policy and Eastern Europe in the 1950s." *Journal of Cold War Studies* 1, no. 3 (Fall 1999): 67-110.

Author Info   From article: László Borhi "is the holder of the Ranki György Hungarian Chair in the Department of Central Eurasian Studies at the University of Indiana at Bloomington, and a research fellow at the Institute of History of the Hungarian Academy of Sciences." His field of research is great power diplomacy and Eastern Europe after 1938. Indiana University profile at http://www.indiana.edu/~ceus/faculty/borhi.shtml

Bibliography   No.
Index   No.
Notes   Footnotes (199).
Photographs   No.
Appendix   No.
Tables   No.
Key Words   Presidency, Military Policy, Cold War, Foreign Relations
Other Notes
Annotation   Borhi examines the ineffective U.S. response to the Hungarian Crisis of 1956 and America's policies toward Hungry leading up to it to show that the American policy of aggressive "rollback" of communism was gradually abandoned during the Eisenhower Administration in favor of avoiding war and improving Soviet-American relations.

144. Borzutzky, Silvia and David Berger. "Dammed If You Do, Dammed If You Don't: The Eisenhower Administration and the Aswan Dam." *Middle East Journal* 64, no. 1 (Winter 2010): 84-102.

Author Info   Silvia Borzutzky is Teaching Professor of Political Science and International Relations at Carnegie Mellon. Dr. Borzutzky holds a Law Degree from the University of Chile, and an M.A. and a Ph.D. in Political Science from the University of Pittsburgh. Her focus is on Latin America. David Berger is listed in the article as having a Masters in Public Policy and Management from the Heinz College at Carnegie Mellon. Studied Arabic. Currently independent researcher, interests include the media, organized cognition, and political behavior in international relations.

Bibliography   No.

Index	No.
Notes	Footnotes (62).
Photographs	No.
Appendix	No.
Tables	No.
Key Words	Presidency, Middle East, Foreign Relations
Other Notes	Eisenhower is in this article, but he's not the focus.
Annotation	Using a conceptual framework derived from the work of Richard Cottam and Richard Herrmann, the authors examine the U.S.'s decision to not fund the Aswan Dam. They conclude that American decision-maker's unconscious adoption of schema—a set of preconceived perceptions—led them to interpret Egypt and 'Abd al-Nasser's actions in a way which contradicted U.S. interests.

145. Bose, Meena. "Words as Signals: Drafting Cold War Rhetoric in the Eisenhower and Kennedy Administrations." *Congress & the Presidency* 25, no. 1 (Spring 1998): 23-42.

Author Info	Professor of Political Science at Hofstra University. Author of is a contributor to the tenth edition of the American Government: Institutions and Policies textbook. Her current research focuses on the changing role of the United Nations in American foreign policy... She taught for six years at the United States Military Academy at West Point... She earned her undergraduate degree in international politics from Penn State University (1990), and she received her master's (1992) and doctoral (1996) degrees in politics from Princeton University. Hofstra University profile at http://www.hofstra.edu/academics/Colleges/HCLAS/PRSSTY/prssty_chair.html
Bibliography	Selected Bibliography.
Index	No.
Notes	Yes (57).
Photographs	No.
Appendix	No.
Tables	No.
Key Words	Presidency, Speechmaking, Foreign Relations, Cold War
Other Notes	
Annotation	Bose compares and contrasts the drafting processes and ultimate wordings of the inaugural addresses and state of the union messages of Eisenhower and Kennedy. She also examines the intentional and unintentional messages the speeches sent to the Soviet Union. She concludes that while Alexander L. George's "multiple advocacy" theory for foreign policy decision making can be successfully applied to presidential speechwriting, its utilization can result in speeches with less rhetorical appeal.

146. Boyle, Peter G. "Eisenhower." *Historian* no. 43 (September 1994): 9-11.

Author Info	Boyle was a senior Lecturer in U.S. History at the University of Nottingham. He has written multiple books on Eisenhower.
Bibliography	No.
Index	No.
Notes	Endnotes.
Photographs	Yes (1).
Appendix	No.
Tables	No
Key Words	Presidency
Other Notes	
Annotation	Concise historiographical essay tracing the evolution of Eisenhower's reputation from the time of his presidency (great popular support, but poor reputation among intellectuals), to his immediate post-presidency (nadir of his reputation), to the revisionist view beginning in the early 1970s (holding that the intellectuals of Eisenhower's time were wrong and that he was an effective leader), to the post-revisionist view of the 1990s (revisionist view with major qualifications).

147. Branigar, Thomas. "No Villains- No Heroes: The David Eisenhower-Milton Good Controversy." *Kansas History* 15, no. 3 (September 1992): 168-179.

Author Info	"Active genealogist and is assisting the Dickinson County Historical Society in collecting information on early pioneers of Abilene… employed at the Eisenhower Library". Quote from article.
Bibliography	No.
Index	No.
Notes	Footnotes (48).
Photographs	Yes (10).
Appendix	No.
Tables	No.
Key Words	Early Life, Family
Other Notes	
Annotation	Article concerns Dwight Eisenhower's father, David, and his failed general store business venture with Milton D. Good. Author "attempts to set the record straight" on the matter, as historians have taken as true Eisenhower family lore on the circumstances surrounding and following the failure of the business. Using local newspapers and state and county records, Branigar finds that the truth is less dramatic than the family lore and that Eisenhower and Good were neither hero nor villain, but simply two men with very different personalities whose business venture was unsuccessful. He does, however, find that the David Eisenhower had a vindictive streak and a violent temper.

148. Brinkley, Douglas. "Eisenhower the Dove." *American Heritage* 52, no. 6 (September 2001): 58-65.

Author Info	"Dr. Brinkley currently serves as director of the Theodore Roosevelt Center for American Civilization and professor of history at Tulane University. He completed his bachelor's degree at Ohio State University and received his doctorate in U.S. Diplomatic History from Georgetown University in 1989. While a professor at Hofstra University, Dr. Brinkley spearheaded the American Odyssey course, in which he took students on numerous cross-country treks where they visited historic sites and met seminal figures in politics and literature. Dr. Brinkley's 1994 book, *The Majic Bus: An American Odyssey* chronicles his first experience teaching this innovative on-the-road class which became the progenitor of C-SPAN's Yellow School Bus. Four of Dr. Brinkley's biographies have been selected as *New York Times* "Notable Books of the Year". … Three of his recent publications have become *New York Times* best-sellers: In May 2006, Dr. Brinkley published *The Great Deluge: Hurricane Katrina, New Orleans, and the Mississippi Gulf Coast*". http://www.theodorerooseveltcenter.org/Symposia_2006.asp He is currently a Professor of history at Rice University. See http://history.rice.edu/content.aspx?id=388
Bibliography	No.
Index	No.
Notes	No.
Photographs	Yes (6).
Appendix	No.
Tables	No.
Key Words	Presidency, Speechmaking, Foreign Relations, Military Policy
Other Notes	
Annotation	Author finds echoes of George Washington's farewell address in President Eisenhower's parting words to the American people. Eisenhower's admonitions against the military-industrial complex and abhorrence for war were largely underappreciated during his presidency, but would find resonance with the 1960s anti-war movements.

149. Brinkley, Douglas. "The United States in the Truman and Eisenhower Years." *European Contributions to American Studies* 42, (January 1999): 15-29.

Author Info	See information in Entry #148.
Bibliography	No.
Index	No.
Notes	No—the only footnote indicates that "Sources and notes may be found in Douglas Brinkley, *American Heritage History of the United States* (New York: Viking Press, 1998).
Photographs	No.
Appendix	No.
Tables	No.
Key Words	Presidency, Foreign Relations, Domestic Policy, Civil Rights, Cold War

Other Notes
Annotation   Overview of America's domestic and foreign affairs during Truman's and
                  Eisenhower's administrations. Issues addressed include Civil Rights, the
                  Korean War, and McCarthyism. Brinkley states that "the agenda for the rest
                  of the century was being laid out" between 1945 and 1955.

150. Broadwater, Jeff. "President Eisenhower and the Historians: Is the General in Retreat?"
      Canadian Review of American Studies 22, no. 1 (June 1991): 47-60.

Author Info   Associate professor of history at Barton College (North Carolina). Holds a
                  Ph.D. from Vanderbilt University. His main teaching and research interests
                  are early American history and the history of the South. His most recent
                  book, *George Mason, Forgotten Founder*, was published by the University of
                  North Carolina Press in 2006. http://www2.barton.edu/cgi-
                  bin/MySQLdb?FILE=/academics/faculty/list.html&currentprogram=1009
Bibliography No.
Index   No.
Notes   Yes (56).
Photographs   No.
Appendix   No.
Tables   No.
Key Words   Presidency
Other Notes
Annotation   Broadwater goes deeper than simple presidential rankings, tracing the
                  evolution of the historiography of Eisenhower's presidency. He finds that
                  writers never quite agreed about the peaks or valleys of his reputation as
                  found in presidential polls. He concludes that: "As the passions of postwar
                  politics cool and memories dim, Eisenhower's reputation is likely to settle
                  somewhere between the old, critical caricature and the most extreme
                  revisionist paean."

151. Brogi, Alessandro. "Ike and Italy: The Eisenhower Administration and Italy's 'Neo-
      Atlanticist' Agenda." *Journal of Cold War Studies* 4, no. 3 (Summer 2002): 5-35.

Author Info   University of Arkansas--Assistant Professor. B.A. Universita degli Studi di
                  Firenze, Italy, 1987; M.A. Ohio University, 1992; Ph.D. Universita degli Studi
                  di Firenze, Italy, 1993; Ph.D. Ohio University, 1998.
                  http://history.uark.edu/cvs/brogi.pdf
Bibliography No.
Index   No.
Notes   Footnotes (61).
Photographs   No.
Appendix   No.
Tables   No.

Key Words	Presidency, Foreign Relations, Cold War
Other Notes	
Annotation	Focus of article is more on Italy than Ike. Brogi argues that: "Despite the Italian government's care for appearances, its preoccupation with domestic concerns, and its staunch loyalty to American leadership, Italy has not been as fatalistically submissive as often portrayed" in the 1950s. The author analyzes the successes and failures of Italy's "Neo Atlanticism" foreign policy and concludes that it ultimately helped the country improve its position within the Western Alliance, despite some evident failures. He also examines how the United States was affected by and used Italy's foreign policy to confirm that it tolerated its ally countries' autonomous initiatives.

152. Bromley, D. Allan. "Science and Technology: from Eisenhower to Bush." *Presidential Studies Quarterly* 21, no. 2 (1991): 243-250.

Author Info	"D. Allan Bromley, [was] a Yale University professor, nuclear physicist and architect of national science policy during the administration of President George H. W. Bush". He Died in 2005. Obituary at http://www.nytimes.com/2005/02/13/obituaries/13bromley.html He "was the Assistant to the President for Science and Technology and Director of the Office of Science and Technology Policy in the Executive Office of the President from 1989–1993… Prior to his government service, Dr. Bromley… founded and was Director of [Yale's] A.W. Wright Nuclear Structure Laboratory…. He [carried] out pioneering studies on both the structure and dynamics of nuclei and is considered the father of modern heavy ion science.". http://www.aip.org/history/historymatters/bromley.htm
Bibliography	No.
Index	No.
Notes	No.
Photographs	No.
Appendix	No.
Tables	No.
Key Words	Presidency, Technology
Other Notes	
Annotation	Then Assistant to the President for Science and Technology, Bromley reflects on Eisenhower's creation of that position and establishment of the President's Science Advisory Committee. Bromley traces the evolution and devolution of both positions from Eisenhower's Administrations to Bush's Administration.

153. Brown, Roger G. and Carolyn R. Thompson. "Management of Political Functions in the Eisenhower White House: An Organizational Perspective." *Presidential Studies Quarterly* 24, no. 2 (Spring 1994): 299-307.

Author Info	In the article both are listed as being at the University of North Carolina

Charlotte in Political Science Department. On the Center for the Study of the Presidency and Congress, Brown is listed as Chancellor, University of Tennessee-Chattanooga. She was also at UNC Pembroke (2005-2006).

Bibliography	No.
Index	No.
Notes	Footnotes (39).
Illustrations	No.
Photographs	No.
Appendix	No.
Tables	No.
Key Words	Presidency, Politics, White House
Other Notes	
Annotation	Using some established concepts of organization theory, the authors examine the "evolution of the White House as a complex, goal-directed collection of offices and bureaus." They show a shift during Eisenhower's administration from party professionals coordinating and managing political functions to the increasingly differentiated and specialized White House staff.

154. Brownell, Herbert. "Eisenhower's Civil Rights Program: A Personal Assessment." *Presidential Studies Quarterly* 21, no. 2 (Spring 1991): 235-242.

Author Info	"Herbert Brownell Jr. was attorney general under President Eisenhower from January 21, 1953, to October 23, 1957. Brownell recieved [sic] his B.A. from the University of Nebraska in 1924 and earned a law degree from Yale in 1927.... After playing an important part in securing delegates for Eisenhower's nomination in the 1952 national convention and then during the presidential campaign, Brownell became attorney general. He often advised Eisenhower on civil rights matters. He also helped to expedite the electrocution of Ethel and Julius Rosenberg, who were sentenced to death for passing secret files about the atomic bomb to the Soviet Union. He also enshrined the practice of allowing the American Bar Association to vet judicial appointments. Finally, Brownell was instrumental in advising Eisenhower to send federal troops to enforce the desegregation of Central High School in Little Rock, Arkansas. After resigning in 1957, he rejoined his old law firm as a senior partner until 1977 and then until 1989 as counsel. He died in 1996." From the Miller Center. http://millercenter.org/academic/americanpresident/eisenhower/essays/cabinet/583
Bibliography	No.
Index	No.
Notes	No.
Photographs	No.
Appendix	No.
Tables	No.
Key Words	Presidency; Civil Rights, Domestic Policy

Other Notes
Annotation   Former Attorney General of the United States under Eisenhower (1953 to 1957) Herbert Brownell recalls Civil Rights issues during his time in office; he discusses the desegregation of Washington D.C. and the armed forces and *Brown v. Board of Education.* Brownell concludes that Eisenhower's decisive actions in Little Rock crushed the "Southern Manifesto"—the pledge of Southern politicians to nullify *Brown v. Board of Education* and the new federal policy on school desegregation.

155. Burr, William. "Avoiding the Slippery Slope: The Eisenhower Administration and the Berlin Crisis, November 1958 - January 1959." *Diplomatic History* 18, no. 2 (Spring 1994): 177-205.

Author Info   "Senior Analyst, directs the Archive's nuclear history documentation project. He edited two of the Archive's document collections: The Berlin Crisis, 1958-1962 and U.S. Nuclear History: Nuclear Arms and Politics in the Missile Age, 1955-1968. He received his Ph.D. in history from Northern Illinois University, was formerly a visiting assistant professor at Washington College, and has taught at the Catholic University of America, George Mason and American universities. In 1998 The New Press published his critically-acclaimed document reader, The Kissinger Transcripts: The Top-Secret Talks with Beijing & Moscow." http://www.gwu.edu/~nsarchiv/nsa/arc_staff.html

The Archive is "[a]n independent non-governmental research institute and library located at The George Washington University, the Archive collects and publishes declassified documents obtained through the Freedom of Information Act." http://www.gwu.edu/~nsarchiv/nsa/the_archive.html

Bibliography   No.
Index   No.
Notes   Footnotes (91).
Photographs   No.
Appendix   No.
Tables   No.
Key Words   Presidency, Foreign Relations, Cold War
Other Notes
Annotation   Using then-newly declassified documents, Burr re-examined the Berlin Crisis and found that the Eisenhower Administration was willing to threaten or use force rather than recognize the government of East Germany, even if it risked general war. The Administration believed that America's nuclear superiority would cause the Soviets to abandon their position. The British and French objected to such a plan as too militarily and politically risky. Ultimately, the Administration decided that an Allied consensus on the matter was of paramount importance and adopted a more moderate approach to the Berlin Crisis.

C's

156.   Carletta, David M. "'Those White Guys are Working For Me': Dizzy Gillespie, Jazz, and
the Cultural Politics of the Cold War During the Eisenhower Administration."
International Social Science Review 82, no. 3/4 (June 2007): 115-134.

Author Info	Article notes that he is "a Ph.D. Candidate in History at the College of Social Science, Michigan State University in East Lansing, Michigan".
Bibliography	No.
Index	No.
Notes	Endnotes (89).
Photographs	No.
Appendix	No.
Tables	No.
Key Words	Presidency, Cold War, Foreign Relations, Civil Rights
Other Notes	
Annotation	Explores how various players and groups involved in America's jazz musicians' goodwill tours abroad each tried to advance their own agendas. The U.S. government sent the musicians abroad as propaganda to demonstrate that America was not culturally bereft and sent African Americans specifically to downplay charges of domestic racism. In turn, the tours helped jazz musicians and supporters by creating an international following and by aiding the musical form's transition to a respected part of America's culture. Also addresses Eisenhower's belief in the importance of cultural diplomacy.

157.   Carroll, Robert C. "The Making of a Leader: Dwight D. Eisenhower." *Military Review*
89, no. 1 (Jan- Feb 2009): 77-85.

Author Info	U.S. Army, retired. Author's father worked for Eisenhower and he has personal recollections of him. Is a "consultant in leadership development and corporate cultural change" (from article). He has a BS from U.S. Military Academy; MA from Northwestern, and MPA from Auburn University.
Bibliography	No.
Index	No.
Notes	No citations.
Photographs	Yes (4).
Appendix	No.
Tables	No.
Key Words	Early Life, Military- Pre WWII, Military- WWII, Leadership
Other Notes	
Annotation	Biographical essay that traces Eisenhower's early life through his military career in WWII. Author's focus is on the development of Eisenhower's leadership capabilities during his Army career. Includes the author's first-hand

recollections of Eisenhower.

158.   Carter, Donald Alan. "Eisenhower Versus the Generals." *The Journal of Military History*, 71, No. 4 (Oct., 2007): 1169-1199.

Author Info	Bio from article notes that he received his doctorate in history from Ohio State University in 1987. While serving as a field artillery officer in the U.S. Army, he also taught military history at West Point and the U.S. Army Field Artillery School. He was employed as an historian at the U.S. Army Center of Military History.
Bibliography	No.
Index	No.
Notes	Footnotes (117).
Photographs	No.
Appendix	No.
Tables	No.
Key Words	Presidency, Military Policy, Cold War
Other Notes	
Annotation	Though the Air Force and the Navy generally accepted Eisenhower's New Look strategic policy, which emphasized nuclear weapons and economic strength over a traditional large standing military, Army officers disagreed with the underlying premise of the policy-- that any conflict with the Soviet Union would be a nuclear one-- and believed that it threatened the very existence of the Army. Carter argues that while the Army officers agreed with the concept of civilian control of the armed forces, they strenuously objected when Eisenhower suggested that they had provided their unqualified support for the New Look policy and budget, when they had in fact made recommendations against both. Eisenhower's reorganizations of the Department of Defense (1953 and 1958) insulated him from the objections of military officers to his policy, but deprived Kennedy of unfiltered military advice that could have assisted him in making military and strategic decisions.

159.   Catsam, Derek. "The Civil Rights Movement and the Presidency in the Hot Years of the Cold War: A Historical and Historiographical Assessment." *History Compass* 6, no. 1 (January 2008): 314-344.

Author Info	Assistant professor of history at University of Texas of the Permian Basin
Bibliography	Selected bibliography.
Index	No.
Notes	Endnotes (129).
Photographs	No.
Appendix	No.
Tables	No.
Key Words	Presidency, Civil Rights, Cold War, Domestic Policy

Other Notes

Annotation   Provides an overview history and historiography of the four Cold War
                      Presidents—Truman, Eisenhower, Kennedy, and Johnson—and their actions
                      and inactions in the area of Civil Rights. Catsam finds Eisenhower to be the
                      least engaged of the four presidents on Civil Rights issues. He also finds him
                      to be the President who had the greatest ability to do more for Civil Rights than
                      he did, because of the Constitutional protections stemming from *Brown v.
                      Board of Education* and because of his popularity and ability to marshal
                      Republican support.

160.   Chang, Su-Ya. "Unleashing Chiang Kai-Shek? Eisenhower and the Policy of Indecision
       Toward Taiwan, 1953." *Bulletin of the Institute of Modern History, Academia Sinica
       (Zhongyang Yanjiuyuan Xiandaishi Yanjiusuo Jikan)* 20, (January 1991): 369-401.

Author Info
Bibliography   No.
Index   No.
Notes   Yes (96).
Photographs   No.
Appendix   No.
Tables   No.
Key Words   Presidency, Foreign Relations, Cold War
Other Notes
Annotation   Despite Nationalists' expectations to the contrary, the Eisenhower
                      Administration's actions towards Taiwan in 1953 were not drastically different
                      from those of the Truman Administration. Although committed to anti-
                      communism and desirous to see the Nationalists re-conquer communist
                      mainland China, the Eisenhower Administration's policies were "ambiguous."
                      The "wishfulness" of the Administration, the author says, was undercut by
                      timidity, inaction, arrogance, and pragmatism. An earlier version of the article
                      was presented at the Gettysburg College Eisenhower Symposium in October
                      1990.

161.   Charnock, Emily Jane, James A. McCann, and Kathryn Dunn Tenpas. "Presidential
       Travel From Eisenhower to George W. Bush: An 'Electoral College' Strategy." *Political
       Science Quarterly* 124, no. 2 (Summer 2009). : 323-339.

Author Info   Charnock: as of 2009, doctoral candidate at the University of Virginia.
                      McCann: Political Science professor at Purdue University. CV at
                      http://www.cla.purdue.edu/polsci/docs/mccann.pdf. Tenpas: Brookings
                      Institute expert. Studies the U.S. presidency and has written extensively
                      about presidential campaigns; White House operations; presidential polling
                      and political consultants; and President Bush's faith-based initiative. She has
                      also advised the White House on administration transitions.

Bibliography	No.
Index	No.
Notes	Footnotes (23).
Photographs	No.
Appendix	Yes. Appendices A and B.
Tables	Yes (1).
Key Words	Presidency, Elections, Politics
Other Notes	3 Figures.
Annotation	Authors examine first-term presidential travel from Eisenhower to G. W. Bush and find an apparently determined travel strategy that takes into consideration the electoral college and reelection concerns. Authors statistically analyze factors including state-level political competition, the number of electoral votes cast by a state, and the passage of time in the president's first term, and conclude that generally speaking, more recent presidents have utilized first term domestic travel as a re-election tool more often than earlier presidents examined. Revised version of an article that was presented at the American Political Science Association's annual meeting in 2006.

162.   Chernus, Ira. "Eisenhower's Ideology in World War II." *Armed Forces and Society* 23, no. 4 (Summer 1997): 595-613.

Author Info	Professor of Religious Studies, University of Colorado, Boulder. http://spot.colorado.edu/~chernus/. Research focuses on the discourse of peace, war, foreign policy, and nationalism in the United States, especially during the cold war and the nuclear age, and how that discourse has affected our public culture and life up to the present. Completed a large project on President Dwight D. Eisenhower and his impact on our discourse. Three books came out of that project. See entries 28, 29, and 30, above.
Bibliography	No.
Index	No.
Notes	Endnotes (33).
Photographs	No.
Appendix	No.
Tables	No.
Key Words	Military- WWII
Other Notes	
Annotation	Chernus attempts to uncover the fundamental ideology General Eisenhower carried throughout the war as a General and into the Presidency. He argues that it was a moral dualism between the forces of the "disorderly selfish" and the "orderly selfless". This tension between selfishness and selflessness was not only between the Axis and the Allies, but within them as well—military and civilian. Voluntary self-restraint and obedience to duty (selflessness) was the way by which the war would be won, as well as the ultimate virtue to attain.

163.   Chernus, Ira. "Operation Candor: Fear, Faith, and Flexibility." *Diplomatic History* 29, no. 5 (November 2005): 779-809.

Author Info	See information in Entry #162.
Bibliography	No.
Index	No.
Notes	Footnotes (78).
Photographs	No.
Appendix	No.
Tables	No.
Key Words	Presidency, Foreign Relations, Cold War, Religion, Leadership
Other Notes	
Annotation	Chernus explores the Eisenhower Administration's 1953 Operation Candor as "a fascinating case study in the dialectical interplay of policy, power, discourse, and ideology." He notes that Eisenhower and his Administration understood the power of words and ideas and used carefully constructed rhetoric to manage the emotions of the American people in the nuclear age. Eisenhower framed issues, events, and ideas in a way meant to keep Americans in an emotional state between complacency and hysteria that would create a population willing to sacrifice and endure for the long haul of the Cold War.

164.   Cizel, Annick. "The Eisenhower Administration and Africa: Racial Integration and the United States Foreign Service." *Annales du Monde Anglophone* no. 1 (1995): 21-38.

Author Info	Annick Cizel is "an Associate Professor of American history at Université Sorbonne nouvelle (Paris 3). A specialist of US Cold War policies in the developing world, she is currently finishing the revision of her Ph.D. entitled « African and Middle-Eastern Policies in the Making : The United States and Ethiopia (1953-1958) » for publication in 2006." http://transatlantica.revues.org/583. See aslo http://www.univ-paris3.fr/10103/0/fiche___annuaireksup/&RH=ACCUEIL
Bibliography	No.
Index	No.
Notes	Endnotes (87).
Photographs	No.
Appendix	No.
Tables	No.
Key Words	Presidency, Civil Rights, Foreign Relations, Domestic Policy, Cold War
Other Notes	
Annotation	Cizel examines how the Soviet Union's focus on racial inequality in America and the formation of newly-independent African countries forced the Eisenhower Administration to make changes in its racial policies, including integrating the U.S. foreign service. Policy changes made, such as sending Black American Ambassadors to African countries, however, "appeared to be

blatantly opportunistic, not to say outwardly hypocritical" when compared to the continued discrimination at home.

165.   Clayman, Steven E. and John Heritage. "Questioning Presidents: Journalistic Deference and Adversarialness in the Press Conferences of U.S. Presidents Eisenhower and Reagan." *Journal of Communication* 52, no. 4 (Dec, 2002): 749-775.

Author Info	Clayman is a professor of sociology at UCLA. "My research lies at the intersection of language, interaction, and mass communication. I apply the methods of conversation analysis to forms of broadcast talk such as news interviews and presidential news conferences." From his webpage: http://www.sscnet.ucla.edu/soc/faculty/clayman/Site/Home.html Heritage is also a professor in the sociology department at UCLA. From his faculty webpage: "My research focuses on the sphere of social organization that Erving Goffman calls the "interaction order". This involves looking at social interaction from the point of view of how it is constructed, the social, cultural and psychological factors that impact its implementation, and its impact on social outcomes, including the distribution of goods and services and the (re-production of social structure." http://www.soc.ucla.edu/people/faculty?lid=825
Bibliography	References listed.
Index	No.
Notes	Endnotes (11).
Photographs	No.
Appendix	No.
Tables	Yes (11).
Key Words	Presidency, Media
Other Notes	
Annotation	The authors develop a quantitative system for "analyzing the questions that journalists ask public figures in broadcast news interviews and press conferences," and then use that system to analyze and compare the press conferences of Eisenhower and Reagan. Their findings "suggest that journalists have become much less deferential and more aggressive in their treatment of the U.S. president."

166.   Coleman, David G. "Eisenhower and the Berlin Problem, 1953-1954." *Journal of Cold War Studies* 2, no. 1 (Winter 2000): 3-34.

Author Info	"David Coleman is an Associate Professor who specializes on nuclear and defense policy, U.S.-European relations, and Cold War history. He is Director of the Presidential Recordings Program, heading up the John F. Kennedy project." Coleman joined the Miller Center in the fall of 1999 after completing his Ph.D. at the University of Queensland, Australia. From http://millercenter.org/about/staff/coleman CV at http://millercenter.org/about/staff/cvs/coleman

Bibliography	No.
Index	No.
Notes	Footnotes (109).
Illustrations	No.
Photographs	No.
Appendix	No.
Tables	No.
Key Words	Presidency, Cold War, Foreign Relations
Other Notes	
Annotation	Argues that events of 1953-1954, specifically the 1953 East German uprising, significantly influenced Eisenhower's policy toward Germany. By early 1954, America had decided that: 1) it would "stay in West Berlin even at the risk of general war"; and thus 2) the U.S. would "use West Berlin as the 'free world's outpost' against the Soviet bloc." These decisions to make Berlin a priority laid the foundations for the 1958-1962 Berlin Crisis. An earlier version of this essay was presented in 1999 at the annual conference of the Society of Historians and American Foreign Relations at Princeton University.

167. Collier, Ken. "Eisenhower and Congress: The Autopilot Presidency." *Presidential Studies Quarterly* 24, no. 2 (Spring 1994): 309-325.

Author Info	Associate Professor at Stephen F. Austin State University (Texas). CV at http://www.kencollier.org/CollierVitae.pdf. Teaches classes on politics, the presidency, and Eisenhower. Two books in print. Ph.D. is in Government. He wrote this article when he was an Assistant Professor of Political Science at the University of Kansas.
Bibliography	No.
Index	No.
Notes	Footnotes (57) and References (5).
Photographs	No.
Appendix	No.
Tables	No.
Key Words	Presidency, Politics, White House, Leadership
Other Notes	
Annotation	While offering an alternative to Fred Greenstein's (1982) "hidden hand" characterization of Eisenhower's leadership, Collier argues that in Ike's relations with Congress, his leadership style could be described as an "autopilot" approach. Eisenhower created a mechanism for maintaining friendly relations with Congress that consisted mainly of decentralization of legislative responsibility within the executive branch. This allowed him to concentrate on foreign affairs.

168. Conley, Richard S. and Richard M. Yon. "The 'Hidden Hand' and White House Roll-Call Predictions: Legislative Liaison in the Eisenhower White House, 83d-84th Congresses." *Presidential Studies Quarterly* 37, no. 2 (June 2007): 291-312.

Author Info	"Richard S. Conley is Associate Professor of Political Science [at the University of Florida]. He holds a Ph.D. from the University of Maryland and an M.A. from McGill University in Montréal, Québec, Canada. His research interests focus on the presidency, Congress, executive-legislative relations, and comparative executives." From http://www.polisci.ufl.edu/people/faculty/conleyr.shtml Richard M. Yon completed his Master's degree in political science at Florida Atlantic University in 2004. As of 2007, he was a doctoral student at the University of Florida. Listed as an "Editorial Assistant" at James Madison University's "White House Studies" (http://www.jmu.edu/whstudies/board.htm).
Bibliography	References listed at end.
Index	No.
Notes	Endnotes and internal citations.
Photographs	No.
Appendix	Yes (1).
Tables	Tables (2).
Key Words	Presidency, Politics
Other Notes	
Annotation	Research note which accesses the accuracy of Eisenhower's staff in forecasting presidential legislative support in the House of Representatives by examining the headcount data assembled by Eisenhower's Legislative Liaison Unit (LLU), following the midterm elections of 1954. The authors developed a model to account for the successes and failures of the LLU and found that "the least accurate forecasts of individual members' positions are best explained by constituency factors, partisan politicking, and disunity in the Republican House Conference." The article also shows the limits of Eisenhower's hidden-hand style of legislative leadership, including his reluctance to "go public". Revised version of a paper delivered at the Southern Political Science Association's 2006 annual meeting.

169. Cook, Kevin L. "Ike's Road Trip." *MHQ: Quarterly Journal of Military History* 13, no. 3 (Spring 2001): 68-74.

Author Info	Author is a "retired librarian living in Oklahoma." From article.
Bibliography	No.
Index	No.
Notes	No.
Photographs	Yes (13).
Appendix	No.
Tables	No.

Key Words   Military—B/w the Wars; Transportation

Other Notes

Annotation   The article describes the arduous 1919 journey of the U.S. Army's First Transcontinental Motor Convoy from D.C. to San Francisco. Eisenhower, a Lieutenant Colonel at the time, joined the convoy in Frederick, MD and his experiences on the trip influenced his support as President for the Federal-Aid Highway Act of 1956.

170.   Cornfield, Michael. "The 'First Rough Draft'? Reflections on Presidential Politics, Journalism and History." *Film & History* 21, no. 2/3 (May/September 1991): 77-82.

Author Info   "Michael Cornfield is a political scientist who studies… campaign politics, public discourse, and the Internet. He is the author of two books: *Politics Moves Online: Campaigning and the Internet* (The Century Foundation, 2004) and The *Civic Web: Online Politics and Democratic Values*, co-edited with David M. Anderson (Rowman & Littlefield, 2003)… As adjunct professor at the Graduate School of Political Management (GSPM) of the George Washington University, he has taught the core course on strategy and message development since 1994…. Cornfield received a Bachelor of Arts from Pomona College and Doctor of Philosophy from Harvard University."
http://www.knightdigitalmediacenter.org/speakers/name/michael_cornfield/

Bibliography   No.

Index   No.

Notes   Endnotes (9).

Photographs   No.

Appendix   No.

Tables   No.

Key Words   Presidency, Media

Other Notes   Article opens by stating that: "I've been asked to talk about how media historians can make better use of declassified documents…".

Annotation   Using Eisenhower's interactions with the press during the Quemoy-Matsu crisis of 1954-1955, Cornfield challenges Phil Graham's famous quote that journalism is "the first rough draft of history" and finds it to not be an accurate characterization of the news. In this case, presidential rhetoric and purposeful evasion greatly influenced reporting, and we could only discover that after documents became declassified and Eisenhower divulged further information. Thus: "Journalism, history, and… political rhetoric should be viewed as distinctive discourses, each of which generates public narratives and related information at a constant rate."

171.   Cuddy, Edward. "Vietnam: Mr. Johnson's War - Or Mr. Eisenhower's?" *Review of Politics* 65, no. 4 (Autumn 2003): 351-374.

Author Info   J. Edward Cuddy: Professor Emeritus (also listed under Adjunct/part time/or visiting) Professor of History at Daemen College in Amherst NY; B.A., St. Bernard's College; M.A., Catholic University of America; Ph.D., University at Buffalo.

Bibliography	No.
Index	No.
Notes	Endnotes.
Photographs	No.
Appendix	No.
Tables	No.
Key Words	Presidency, Vietnam, Foreign Relations, Cold War
Other Notes	
Annotation	Revisionist argument, positing that the "main burden of responsibility" for America's entanglement in Vietnam falls on President Eisenhower rather than on President Johnson. Cuddy cites several of Eisenhower's policies and actions, including his disregard of the Geneva Accords, SEATO, a State Department purge of Asian experts, and the general politics of anticommunism to show that he played a major role, both during and after his presidency, in committing the U.S. to the support of South Vietnam.

D's

172.   Damms, Richard V. "Containing the Military-Industrial-Congressional Complex: President Eisenhower's Science Advisers and the Case of the Nuclear-Powered Aircraft." *Essays in Economic & Business History* 14, (March 1996): 279-289.

Author Info	Associate Professor of American history at Mississippi State University. He has published articles on science and national security in the Eisenhower era and recently published "In Search of some big, imaginative plan: the Eisenhower Administration and American Strategy in the Middle East after Suez," in Simon C. Smith, ed., *Reassessing Suez 1956* (Ashgate, 2008). He has recently presented papers at international conferences in the United Kingdom and Ireland. http://www.msstate.edu/dept/history/rdamms.htm
Bibliography	No.
Index	No.
Notes	Endnotes (37).
Photographs	No.
Appendix	No.
Tables	No.
Key Words	Presidency, Military Policy, Nuclear, Technology
Other Notes	
Annotation	Examines Eisenhower's use of independent science advisors, including James R. Killian, Jr. and the President's Science Advisory Committee, to evaluate the merits of the Aircraft Nuclear Propulsion (ANP) program. Although the "Military-Industrial-Congressional Complex" pushed for the ANP project in

the wake of Sputnik, the science advisory system allowed Eisenhower to make informed decisions about the feasibility and cost of the project and ultimately to resist the pressure to support it.

173.   Damms, Richard V. "James Killian, the Technological Capabilities Panel, and the Emergence of President Eisenhower's 'Scientific-Technological Elite'." *Diplomatic History* 24, no. 1 (Winter 2000): 57-78.

Author Info	See information in Entry #172.
Bibliography	No.
Index	No.
Notes	Footnotes (62).
Photographs	No.
Appendix	No.
Tables	No.
Key Words	Presidency, Military Policy, Technology
Other Notes	
Annotation	Details Eisenhower's integration of science and technology into national security policy through an examination of the work of James R. Killian, Jr. and the Technological Capabilities Panel. Eisenhower hoped that science and technology would provide cost control measures, reduce interservice rivalries, and temper the growth of the military-industrial complex. Ironically, however, some of these problems were exacerbated by the technological solutions Eisenhower approved, and the author finds that Eisenhower, "did more than any previous peacetime president to integrate science into the national security state and foster the growth of the very military-industrial complex and the scientific-technological elite against which he railed." Earlier version of this paper had been presented at the annual meeting of the Society for Historians of American Foreign Relations in Virginia in 1993.

174.   Dockrill, Saki. "Cooperation and Suspicion: The United States' Alliance Diplomacy for the Security of Western Europe, 1953-54." *Diplomacy & Statecraft* 5, no. 1 (March 1994): 138-182.

Author Info	"Saki Dockrill was an historian who blended strategy, defence policy, international relations and cultural themes. Her analysis focused primarily on the Pacific War, 1941-45, the Cold War, and relations between the West and the Pacific Rim." Taught at Kings College London. "Her authoritative study, *Eisenhower's New Look National Security Policy, 1953-1961* (1996), placed this controversial policy in a broad context and offered a sustained defence of her hero, Dwight D. Eisenhower." She also, "served as founding editor of the journal, *Cold War History*, and then sat on its editorial board, while in 1997-2004 she presided over 21 volumes as general editor of Palgrave Macmillan's Cold War History series." Dockrill died in 2009. Her obituary is at

http://www.timesonline.co.uk/tol/comment/obituaries/article6817516.ece

Bibliography	No.
Index	No.
Notes	Endnotes (177).
Photographs	No.
Appendix	No.
Tables	No.
Key Words	Presidency, Foreign Relations, Military Policy
Other Notes	
Annotation	Analyzes western European security affairs, including the interrelated factors of Eisenhower's attempted implementation of his New Look policy, EDC negotiations, and the nuclearization of NATO. Dockrill argues that NATO's agreement on MC 48 applied only part of the New Look policy to Europe. By the end of 1954, "the Eisenhower administration had achieved some of its NATO goals… [but] it had been an uphill struggle even to advance this far." Further, one of the central tenets of the policy was the reduction of troops, and though there was some reduction in overall numbers, the number of divisions in Europe remained the same. She concludes that "[t]he core of the difficulty of maintaining a collective security system in western Europe lay in the divergent approaches of the United State and her allies to this issue." The United States wanted to return home and serve as a temporary mentor for western Europe, and western Europe did not believe it could be secure without an American military presence.

175.   Dockrill, Saki. "Eisenhower's New Look: A Maximum Deterrent at a Bearable Cost? A Reappraisal." *Storia delle Relazioni Internazionali* 13, no. 1 (January 1998): 11-25.

Author Info	See information in Entry #174.
Bibliography	No.
Index	No.
Notes	Footnotes (55).
Photographs	No.
Appendix	No.
Tables	No.
Key Words	Presidency, Nuclear, Cold War, Foreign Relations, Military Policy
Other Notes	
Annotation	Evaluates Eisenhower's New Look strategy and determines that it suffered from several flaws. These included: an underestimation of the importance of the presence of American troops overseas; the incorrect assumption that nuclear weapons would be more economical than ground troops and conventional weapons; and a failure to fully integrate European allies into the New Look policies.

176. Daniel, Douglass K. "They Liked Ike: Pro-Eisenhower Publishers and His Decision to Run for President." *Journalism & Mass Communication Quarterly* 77, no. 2 (Summer 2000): 393-404.

Author Info	Douglass K. Daniel is a writer and editor for the Associated Press' Washington Bureau. Article notes that he was "an assistant professor at the E.W. Scripps School of Journalism at Ohio University," but the school does not now list him on their website.
Bibliography	No.
Index	No.
Notes	Endnotes (62).
Photographs	No.
Appendix	No.
Tables	No.
Key Words	Elections, Presidency, Media
Other Notes	
Annotation	Using correspondence in the Eisenhower Library, Daniel examines how a segment of the mainstream media press supported the Eisenhower political campaign and may have influenced his decision to run. Publishers and reporters offered help by providing "campaign advice, analysis, and research, all of it behind the scenes and away from the judgment of readers." Daniel believes that they might have supported Ike because they already had a long association with him from his position as a General in WWII, they honestly believed he was the best candidate for the presidency, and/or they wanted to cultivate a personal relationship with him because of the influence he would have as President.

177. Duchin, Brian R. "The 'Agonizing Reappraisal': Eisenhower, Dulles, and the European Defense Community." *Diplomatic History* 16, no. 2 (April 1992): 201-221.

Author Info	Tacoma Community College history Professor. B.A., M.A., University of Washington; Ph.D., University of Texas. Article notes he was at Williams College as an assistant professor of history.
Bibliography	No.
Index	No.
Notes	Footnotes (54).
Photographs	No.
Appendix	No.
Tables	No.
Key Words	Presidency, Foreign Relations, Cold War
Other Notes	
Annotation	Chronicles Dulles's and Eisenhower's efforts to make Western European countries, especially France, ratify the European Defense Community (EDC). Although Dulles threatened failure to ratify the EDC would compel the United States to perform an "agonizing reappraisal" of America's commitment to

Europe's defense, the threat was a hollow one and never seriously considered. The U.S. efforts ultimately failed and the EDC was never ratified. Instead, European countries adopted a NATO/Brussels alternative, which fulfilled Washington's crucial objectives of incorporating Western Germany into the community of western nations. This fostered the political and military reunification of Europe.

178.　Duchin, Brian R. "'The Most Spectacular Legislative Battle of That Year:' President Eisenhower and the 1958 Reorganization of the Department of Defense." *Presidential Studies Quarterly* 24, no. 2 (Spring 1994): 243-262.

Author Info	See information in Entry #177.
Bibliography	No.
Index	No.
Notes	Footnotes.
Photographs	No.
Appendix	No.
Tables	No.
Key Words	Presidency, Politics, Cold War, Military Policy
Other Notes	
Annotation	Duchin traces the "spectacular" battle between President Eisenhower and Congress over the control of America's military establishment. Eisenhower believed that the exigencies of the Cold War required that the executive branch have centralized and streamlined decision-making powers. Congress believed that the vigor with which he pursued executive power demonstrated the need for executive-legislative balance and tried to re-brand his plan as something un-American. Ultimately, the Defense Reorganization Act (1958) was a limited presidential victory.

E's

179.　Eliades, George C. "Once More unto the Breach: Eisenhower, Dulles, and Public Opinion During the Offshore Islands Crisis of 1958." *Journal of American-East Asian Relations* 2, no. 4 (Winter 1993): 343-367.

Author Info	A Harvard undergraduate and graduate student. Wrote his Ph.D. dissertation on the U.S. decision-making in Laos (1999).
Bibliography	No.
Index	No.
Notes	Footnotes (68).
Photographs	No.
Appendix	No.

Tables	No.
Key Words	Presidency, Foreign Relations, Cold War
Other Notes	
Annotation	Analyzing the Offshore Islands Crisis of 1958 with then newly declassified documents, Eliades argues that public opinion influenced Eisenhower's foreign policy more than revisionist historians have acknowledged. Eisenhower was constrained by two factors during the crisis: 1) his "opposition to appeasement" and thus his refusal to abandon Chaing Kai-shek under Communist pressure; and 2) America's public opinion, which was decidedly against fighting merely for the "insignificant real estate" of the Offshore Islands.

180. Evans, Tony. "Hegemony, Domestic Politics, and the Project of Universal Human Rights." *Diplomacy & Statecraft* 6, no. 3 (September 1995): 616-644.

Author Info	Professor of Global Politics at the University of Southampton, UK. http://www.southampton.ac.uk/socsci/staff/profile.php?name=TonyEvans
Bibliography	No.
Index	No.
Notes	Endnotes (72).
Photographs	No.
Appendix	No.
Tables	No.
Key Words	Presidency, Bricker Amendment, Domestic Policy, Foreign Relations, Civil Rights
Other Notes	
Annotation	Evans examines the role of America in efforts to create a human rights regime after World War II. He argues that while during the war the U.S. had stressed the importance of creating such a regime, when the time came to take action, domestic actors in the U.S. "began to question the challenge that a human rights regime would present to existing political and social practices and beliefs," including southern states' racist policies and U.S. immigration laws. The specter of the Bricker Amendment, which would have severely limited a President's ability to make treaties, forced Eisenhower to announce that America would not enter a human rights regime, but would work for human rights in its own ways. This compromise "meant that the USA withheld the necessary hegemonic authority to establish a human rights regime that went beyond the weakest declarations of intent" and weakened America's moral authority in the world. Essay is a shortened version of an argument the author made in his book, *US Hegemony and the Project of Universal Human Rights* (Basingstoke: St. Martin's Press, 1995).

181. Ewald, William Bragg Jr. "Ike's First Move." *New York Times Magazine* (November 14, 1993): 57.

Author Info	"William Bragg Ewald, Jr. has written eight books, including a biography of former President Eisenhower. He served as a member of the White House staff during the Eisenhower administration and assisted the President in writing his two volumes of White House memoirs. Dr. Ewald received his doctorate from Harvard University. He is also the author of two books on eighteenth-century English literature." http://www.buzzle.com/editorials/9-21-2005-77265.asp
Bibliography	No.
Index	No.
Notes	No.
Photographs	Yes (2).
Appendix	No.
Tables	No.
Key Words	SACEUR, Presidency, Elections
Other Notes	
Annotation	Bragg prints, for the first time, an October 14, 1951 letter from Ike to Senator Jim Duff of Pennsylvania regarding his agreement to accept the Republican nomination for President in 1952, if the party chose him.

F's

182. Foot, Rosemary. "The Eisenhower Administration's Fear of Empowering the Chinese." *Political Science Quarterly* 111, no. 3 (Autumn 1996): 505-521.

Author Info	"Professor of International Relations, and the John Swire Senior Research Fellow at St Antony's College, Oxford University. She has been a Fellow of the College since 1990, and was Senior Tutor from 2003-2005." Profile at http://www.sant.ox.ac.uk/people/foot.html
Bibliography	No.
Index	No.
Notes	Endnotes (47).
Photographs	No.
Appendix	No.
Tables	No.
Key Words	Presidency, Cold War, Foreign Relations
Other Notes	
Annotation	Foot argues that while there are multiple factors explaining the Eisenhower Administration's harsh policies towards China, one reason deserves more attention than it has received. She posits that the Administration, specifically Dulles, feared that if their policies towards China were less forceful, they would serve to empower the Chinese and the U.S. would correspondingly lose prestige, control, and power in Asia.

183. Førland, Tor Egil. "Eisenhower, Export Controls, and the Parochialism of Historians of American Foreign Relations." *Newsletter of the Society for Historians of American Foreign Relations* 24, no. 4 (September 1993): 4-17.

Author Info	Professor at the University of Oslo.
	http://www.hf.uio.no/iakh/personer/vit/teforlan/index.html
Bibliography	No.
Index	No.
Notes	Footnotes (25).
Photographs	No.
Appendix	No.
Tables	No.
Key Words	Presidency, Foreign Relations, Politics, Cold War
Other Notes	
Annotation	The article is a response to Spaulding's "'A Gradual and Moderate Relaxation': Eisenhower and the Revision of American Export Control Policy, 1953-1955." *Diplomatic History* 17, no. 2 (April 1993): 223-249. Førland dismisses Spaulding's conclusions, which credit Eisenhower with relaxing Western export controls, as "methodologically [and empirically] flawed, based solely on *FRUS*, and without due regard for recent nuances in Eisenhower revisionism". He accuses Spaulding of historical parochialism and cites his failure to examine non-U.S. sources. Førland argues that Eisenhower does not deserve all of the credit for the relaxation of controls, and that Britain and external circumstances (including the death of Stalin and the Korean armistice) deserve far more attention than they were given by Spaulding. Førland argues that the British "short list" arose independently from America, and was not triggered by Eisenhower's new export control policy.

184. Førland, Tor Egil. "Eisenhower, Export Controls, and the Perils of Diplomatic History: A Reply to Spaulding." *Newsletter of the Society for Historians of American Foreign Relations* 25, no. 3 (June 1994): 9-22.

Author Info	See information in Entry #183.
Bibliography	No.
Index	No.
Notes	Footnotes (27).
Photographs	No.
Appendix	No.
Tables	No.
Key Words	Presidency, Foreign Relations, Politics, Cold War
Other Notes	
Annotation	Furthering a debate with Spaulding, Førland responds to Spaulding's

"Eisenhower and Export Controls Revisited: A Reply to Førland." *Newsletter of the Society for Historians of American Foreign Relations* 25, no. 1 (January 1994): 9-16. He reaffirms his argument with Spaulding as being about: 1) "President Eisenhower's role in the process leading to the reduction of CoCom's export control lists in summer 1954"; and 2) "[h]ow far was the British idea of replacing CoCom's three export control lists with one 'short list' independent of the 'new look' in U.S. embargo policy?" Førland argues that Spaulding's argument fails for several reasons, including: "It is not supported by the evidence but undermined by records- foreign and domestic- that Spaulding has ignored...". Førland argues, "the U.S. vs. U.K. dichotomy is crucial to understanding what was going on from summer 1953 to summer 1954."

185.   Førland, Tor Egil. "'Selling Firearms to the Indians': Eisenhower's Export Control Policy, 1953-54." *Diplomatic History* 15, no. 2 (April 1991): 221-244.

Author Info	See information in Entry #183.
Bibliography	No.
Index	No.
Notes	Footnotes (62).
Photographs	No.
Appendix	No.
Tables	No.
Key Words	Presidency, Foreign Relations, Politics, Cold War
Other Notes	
Annotation	Post-revisionist examination of the 1953-54 export control debate. Eisenhower was unable to liberalize export controls on trade with the Soviet bloc, thereby easing conflict between America and its European allies, because of personal and institutional reasons. Personally, he did not want to jeopardize his relationship with Congress over the issue. Institutionally, he was hindered by the bureaucracy, and though he made some advances in formulating policy, he lost control over the process to his subordinates at the policy implementation stage.

186.   Forsberg, Aaron. "Eisenhower and Japanese Economic Recovery: The Politics of Integration with the Western Trading Bloc, 1952-1955." *Journal of American-East Asian Relations* 5, no. 1 (Spring 1996): 57-75.

Author Info	Published, *America and the Japanese Miracle: The Cold War Context of Japan's Postwar Economic Revival* (University of North Carolina Press, 2000). "A former history teacher at the University of Maryland's Asian Division in Tokyo, Forsberg is now a legal translator with White & Case LLP in Tokyo. He is working on a new book introducing recent changes in Japan." http://www.whitman.edu/magazine/july2000/collection.html

Bibliography	No.
Index	No.
Notes	Footnotes (73).
Photographs	No.
Appendix	No.
Tables	No.
Key Words	Presidency, Foreign Relations, Economics, Cold War
Other Notes	
Annotation	Argues that the Eisenhower Administration's effort to integrate Japan into the Western trading bloc was a qualified success. Strategically, Eisenhower was successful as, "American assistance promoted Japanese revival and bound Japan more closely to the West." This was important as the U.S. wanted to avoid Japan becoming dependent on China and other Communist countries for trade. Economically, however, "progress toward trade liberalization was slow, and the precise contours of the new order fell far short of the multilateral economic integration which... the Truman and Eisenhower administrations initially desired." The limited nature of Japan's integration was partially due to the resistance of populations at home and abroad.

187. Foyle, Douglas C. "Public Opinion and Foreign Policy: Elite Beliefs as a Mediating Variable." *International Studies Quarterly* 41, no. 1 (March 1997): 141-169.

Author Info	Professor at Wesleyan University. "His teaching and research specializations include U.S. Foreign Policy, international security, and the influence of public opinion and elections on foreign policy. He completed his A.B. in political science at Stanford University and his M.A. and Ph.D. in political science with specialties in the fields of international relations and international security at Duke University. In addition to other articles and book chapters, his book *Counting the Public In: Presidents, Public Opinion, and Foreign Policy* (Columbia University Press, 1999) considers the role that public opinion has on American foreign policy decision making." From http://dfoyle.web.wesleyan.edu/
Bibliography	List of References.
Index	No.
Notes	Internal citations, footnotes (12).
Photographs	No.
Appendix	No.
Tables	Yes (1).
Key Words	Presidency, Foreign Relations
Other Notes	
Annotation	Foyle argues that "how decision makers perceive and react to public opinion depends upon their views of the proper relationship between public opinion and foreign policy choices." The author performs a qualitative content analysis of Eisenhower's and Dulles' public opinion beliefs, concluding that though they were both "pragmatists," Dulles was "more accepting of public input on

broad policy objectives than Eisenhower." He compares his predictions of their behavior to their actual reactions to the September 1954 Chinese offshore island crisis, and finds that "[d]ifferences in the timing of Eisenhower's and Dullus's concern with public opinion appear attributable to nuances in their public opinion beliefs within the overall pragmatist construct." A previous draft of this article had been presented at the Annual Meeting of the International Studies Association in 1995.

188.   Fraser, Cary. "Crossing the Color Line in Little Rock: The Eisenhower Administration and the Dilemma of Race for U.S. Foreign Policy." *Diplomatic History* 24, no. 2 (Spring 2000): 233-264.

Author Info	Fraser teaches African American history in the 20th century and the history of American foreign policy at Pennsylvania State University. http://history.psu.edu/faculty/fraserCary.php
Bibliography	No.
Index	No.
Notes	Endnotes (106).
Photographs	No.
Appendix	No.
Tables	No.
Key Words	Presidency, Civil Rights, Foreign Relations, Domestic Policy
Other Notes	Illustrations.
Annotation	Essay highlights the importance of Little Rock to American foreign relations. The domestic issue received international attention, especially in Africa and in the Communist nations, and generated debate on America's credibility in its global affairs. Author notes Eisenhower's ambivalence concerning the desegregation of schools in Little Rock and issues of race in foreign policy.

189.   Friman, H. Richard. "The Eisenhower Administration and the Demise of GATT: Dancing with Pandora." *American Journal of Economics and Sociology* 53, no. 3 (Jul, 1994): 257-272.

Author Info	Professor for International Studies and Professor of Political Science at Marquette University (Wisconsin). Ph.D, Cornell University, 1987.
Bibliography	No.
Index	No.
Notes	Footnotes, endnotes, and references.
Photographs	No.
Appendix	No.
Tables	No.
Key Words	Presidency, Economics, Foreign Relations
Other Notes	
Annotation	Author finds fault with the Eisenhower administration's trade policy choices, which he says created unnecessary conflict between domestic and international

pressures in international trade. The Administration's introduction of voluntary export restraints ("VER") on Japan's export of textiles to the U.S. legitimized VER as a method to resolve trade disputes, thereby weakening the influence of GATT.

G's

190. Gaskin, Thomas M. "Senator Lyndon B. Johnson, the Eisenhower Administration and U.S. Foreign Policy, 1957-60." *Presidential Studies Quarterly* 24, no. 2 (Spring 1994): 341-361.

Author Info	Full time faculty member of Everett Community College in the History Department. B.A., University of California, Berkeley; M.A., University of California, Los Angeles; Ph.D., University of Washington
Bibliography	No.
Index	No.
Notes	Endnotes (70).
Photographs	No.
Appendix	No.
Tables	No.
Key Words	Presidency, Foreign Relations, Politics
Other Notes	
Annotation	Author details Johnson's efforts to distinguish himself in the area of foreign policy from 1957-1960, in an attempt to become a presidential candidate. Also, Gaskin describes Eisenhower's and his Administration's reactions to Johnson's efforts. Events highlighted include the debate over sanctions against Israel, Johnson's missile and satellite hearings post-Sputnik, and Johnson's publicized meetings with Mexican leaders. Gaskin finds that surprisingly, some members of Eisenhower's Administration gave active support to Johnson's foreign policy activities.

191. Goar, Dudley C. "A Chance for Peace? The Eisenhower Administration and the Soviet Peace Offensive of 1953." *Mid America* 76, no. 3 (Fall 1994): 241-278.

Author Info	Dudley C. Goar is an attorney.
Bibliography	No.
Index	No.
Notes	Footnote (129).
Photographs	No.
Appendix	No.
Tables	No.
Key Words	Presidency, Cold War, Foreign Relations, Speechmaking

Annotation   Article explores the Eisenhower Administration's reaction to the 1953 Soviet Peace offensive following Stalin's death. Goar argues that the Administration did not capitalize on the possibilities posed by the peace offensive "because it had no strategy to handle a lull in the cold war." The Administration did not believe that the Soviet's gestures towards reconciliation were genuine. They viewed these gestures "through the prism of the administration's own priorities," which included the EDC ratification and West German integration. The "peace offensive was seen as part of a comprehensive strategy to disrupt these priorities." Further, peace negotiations threatened Eisenhower's New Look policy because if the threat from the Soviet Union seemed to be waning, European allies could be less likely to assume the financial burdens of security, and Congress and the American people could demand greater defense budget cuts.

192.   Goldhamer, Joan D. "General Eisenhower in Academe: A Clash of Perspectives and a Study Suppressed." *Journal of the History of the Behavioral Sciences* 33, no. 3 (Summer 1997): 241-259.

Author Info   The author took graduate courses in sociology at Columbia, which she remembers with little fondness. "Columbia was horrible…[W]e went on strike even because the professors paid no attention—no mind to the graduate students….never a kind word—it was rough…. I suppose that there are people who had wonderful experiences at Columbia; I just hated it, and most of my friends did, too." From http://www.outofthequestion.org/Women-of-the-Film/Joan-Doris-Goldhamer.aspx.

Bibliography   No.
Index   No.
Notes   Endnotes (86).
Photographs   No.
Appendix   No.
Tables   No.
Key Words   Columbia University, Elections
Other Notes
Annotation   A first-hand account, supported by citations to primary sources, including *The Eisenhower Diaries* and documents from the Eisenhower Library in Kansas, of a suppressed 1949 analysis of Eisenhower's incoming mail sent by the public urging his presidential candidacy in 1948. The study was undertaken by Columbia University's Bureau of Applied Social Research, and the author was a research assistant. She describes the study and its termination, concluding that it was suppressed as a result of "a subculture parallax"—the confrontation of Eisenhower's military subculture and the Bureau's academic subculture.

193.	Grant, Philip A. Jr. "The Presidential Election of 1952 in Tennessee." *West Tennessee Historical Society Papers* 48, (January 1994): 73-80.

Author Info	History professor at Pace University.
Bibliography	No.
Index	No.
Notes	Footnotes (80).
Photographs	No.
Appendix	No.
Tables	Yes (4).
Key Words	Presidency, Elections, Politics
Other Notes	
Annotation	Grant explores the narrow margin of victory of Eisenhower over Stevenson in Tennessee in the 1952 presidential election. He provides an overview of the campaigns and finds three reasons for Eisenhower's narrow success in Tennessee: 1) the "failure of Stevenson and the Democrats to retain the normally Democratic vote in Tennessee's principal urban centers"; 2) Ike's great success in East Tennessee; and 3) "The remarkable similarity between Tennessee and the surrounding states of Virginia, Kentucky, and North Carolina." Ike's success in Tennessee was "an integral part of a nationwide trend" that ended Democratic rule of the White House.

194.	Greenberg, Paul. "Eisenhower Draws the Racial Battle Lines with Orval Faubus." *The Journal of Blacks in Higher Education*, 18 (Winter, 1997-1998): 120-121.

Author Info	The editorial page editor of the *Arkansas Democrat-Gazette*; he has won the Pulitzer Prize for editorial writing.
Bibliography	No.
Index	No.
Notes	No.
Photographs	Yes (1).
Appendix	No.
Tables	No.
Key Words	Presidency, Civil Rights, Domestic Policy
Other Notes	One cartoon.
Annotation	At the fortieth anniversary of the Little Rock crisis, the editorial page editor of the *Arkansas Democrat-Gazette* writes a short, unreferenced essay about Arkansas Governor Orval Faubus' motivations at Little Rock.

195.	Greenstein, Fred I. "Colin Powell's *American Journey* and the Eisenhower Precedent: A Review Essay." *Political Science Quarterly* 110, no. 4 (1995): 625-629.

Author Info	Fred I. Greenstein is Professor of Politics Emeritus at Princeton University. He has written several books about the office of the presidency and presidents,

including an important study of Eisenhower (*The Hidden-Hand Presidency: Eisenhower as Leader* (1982)).

Bibliography	No.
Index	No.
Notes	No.
Photographs	No.
Appendix	No.
Tables	No.
Key Words	Presidency
Other Notes	
Annotation	In this review of Colin Powell's autobiography, Greenstein compares Powell to Eisenhower to determine what light Eisenhower's experience could shed on Powell as a potential presidential candidate. Greenstein notes many similarities between the two men, including their backgrounds from peripheral groups of American society, their educational and military experiences, and their popularity and political appeal. Greenstein argues that like Ike, "Powell would exercise a moderating influence on the Republican party."

196. Greenstein, Fred I. "Pursuing Eisenhower's Hidden Hand in the Princeton Archives." *Princeton University Library Chronicle* 67, no. 1 (Fall 2005): 114-124.

Author Info	See information in Entry #195.
Bibliography	No.
Index	No.
Notes	Footnotes (11).
Photographs	Yes (2).
Appendix	No.
Tables	No.
Key Words	Presidency
Other Notes	
Annotation	Greenstein summarizes the thesis of his book, *The Hidden-Hand Presidency: Eisenhower as Leader* (1982), and explains how the archives at Princeton were helpful to his research. The most important resources for his research at Princeton were the John Foster Dulles papers and the papers of *New York Times* Washington bureau head Arthur Krock.

197. Greenstein, Fred I. "Taking Account of Individuals in International Political Psychology: Eisenhower, Kennedy and Indochina." *Political Psychology* 15, no. 1 (Mar, 1994): 61-74.

Author Info	See information in Entry #195.
Bibliography	References.
Index	No.
Notes	Internal citations.
Photographs	No.

Appendix	No.
Tables	No.
Key Words	Presidency, Foreign Relations
Other Notes	
Annotation	Greenstein makes a case for the merger of the individual-level analysis work done by Alexander George with George's later system-level analysis. To do so, he uses the example of Eisenhower's meeting with Kennedy in 1961 and notes that the participants at that meeting came away with different understandings of Eisenhower's stance on military intervention in Indochina. Greenstein characterizes this as "a historical episode of misperception on the part of policy makers which cannot be adequately understood without analyzing the particular personal qualities of the individuals who figured in the episode."

198. Greenstein, Fred. "The Hidden-Hand Presidency: Eisenhower as Leader, a 1994 Perspective." *Presidential Studies Quarterly* 24, no. 2 (Spring 1994): 233-241.

Author Info	See information in Entry #195.
Bibliography	No.
Index	No.
Notes	Footnotes (22).
Photographs	No.
Appendix	No.
Tables	No.
Key Words	Presidency, Leadership
Other Notes	
Annotation	Greenstein, author of the influential *The Hidden-Hand Presidency: Eisenhower as Leader* (1982), reacts to then-recent scholarship and notes that the rationality and self-confidence integral to Ike's leadership style could also be detrimental.

199. Greenstein, Fred I. "The President Who Led by Seeming Not to: A Centennial View of Dwight Eisenhower. *The Antioch Review*, 49, no. 1 (Winter, 1991): 39-44.

Author Info	See information in Entry #195.
Bibliography	No.
Index	No.
Notes	No.
Photographs	No.
Appendix	No.
Tables	No.
Key Words	Presidency, Leadership
Other Notes	
Annotation	In this short essay, Greenstein gives a succinct overview of Eisenhower's

leadership tactics and limitations. Greenstein cites Ike's effective hidden-hand leadership, his adept use of language, his selective delegation of authority, and his congenial public manner. He also, however, notes that Ike did not always act on his insights and that his confidence and rationality could actually hamper his effectiveness.

200.   Greenstein, Fred I. and Richard H. Immerman. "Effective National Security Advising: Recovering the Eisenhower Legacy," *Political Science Quarterly*, Vol. 115, No. 3 (Autumn, 2000), pp. 335-345.

Author Info	On Greenstein: see information in Entry #195.
	Richard H. Immerman (Ph.D., Boston College)—Edward J. Buthusiem Family Distinguished Faculty Fellow and Department Chair at Temple University; Director of the Center for the Study of Force and Diplomacy.
Bibliography	No.
Index	No.
Notes	Endnotes (22).
Photographs	No.
Appendix	No.
Tables	No.
Key Words	Presidency, Military Policy, Politics
Other Notes	
Annotation	The authors outline the features of Eisenhower's national security advisory system and analyze its performance. They note that Eisenhower's NSC system was a policy-planning process, not a decision-making process, and conclude that while it did not guarantee successful national security actions, it did increase the likelihood that those actions were well-informed and rigorously analyzed.

201.   Greenstein, Fred I., and Immerman, Richard H. "What Did Eisenhower Tell Kennedy about Indochina? The Politics of Misperception." *The Journal of American History* 79, no. 2 (Sept, 1992): 568-587.

Author Info	On Greenstein: see information in Entry #195; on Immerman: see information in Entry #200.
Bibliography	No.
Index	No.
Notes	Footnotes (39).
Photographs	Yes (4).
Appendix	No.
Tables	No.
Key Words	Presidency, Vietnam, Foreign Relations, Cold War
Other Notes	
Annotation	Explores "Eisenhower's stance on American military intervention in Southeast

Asia in the period before the Johnson administration transformed the United States advisory presence in Vietnam into a military intervention." Authors focus on Eisenhower and Kennedy's January 19, 1961 meeting and the conflicting recollections and records of the meeting's participants as to what Eisenhower said in regards to military intervention in Laos. Although we will never know exactly what Eisenhower said, or meant, the authors determined that "at a minimum, Eisenhower had not made an unambiguous recommendation to intervene" as had been suggested by some of the meeting participants. This meeting "provides unusually vivid evidence of the ubiquity of misperception and miscommunication in human affairs". America's involvement in Vietnam was not inevitable, but was the result of decisions made by particular individuals in particular historical circumstances.

202. Griffin, Charles J. G. "New Light on Eisenhower's Farewell Address." *Presidential Studies Quarterly* 22, no. 3 (Summer, 1992): 469-479.

Author Info	An associate professor and head of Communication Studies, Theater, and Dance at Kansas State University.
Bibliography	No.
Index	No.
Notes	Footnotes (33).
Photographs	No.
Appendix	No.
Tables	No.
Key Words	Presidency, Speechmaking, Politics
Other Notes	
Annotation	Using the then newly-available oral history of an Eisenhower staff speechwriter, along with the recollections of the president's head speechwriter, Griffin examines the drafting of Eisenhower's farewell address with special attention to the famous admonition against the "military industrial complex." His conclusions illuminate Eisenhower's speechwriting methodologies as well as Eisenhower's reasons for including the "military industrial complex" warning. Griffin argues that Eisenhower embraced the warning, which originated with his speechwriters, because it "would convey his legitimate concerns about an expanding defense establishment and score a tactical blow against his political adversaries, even as it enhanced his ethos as a statesman 'above politics'."

203. Guth, David W. "Ike's Red Scare: The Harry Dexter White Crisis." *American Journalism* 13, no. 2 (Spring 1996): 157-175.

Author Info	Teaches public relations at the University of Kansas' school of journalism. http://www.journalism.ku.edu/faculty/people/guth.shtml
Bibliography	No.

Index	No.
Notes	Footnotes (72).
Photographs	No.
Appendix	No.
Tables	No.
Key Words	Presidency, Media
Other Notes	
Annotation	Guth argues that because of the volatility of the crisis and the importance Eisenhower placed on language and public relations, the Harry Dexter White (spy) crisis accelerated the evolution of presidential news conferences from a "reporters-only affair" to complete direct attribution in which the President spoke to the American people.

H's

204. Haight, David. "Ike and his Spies in the Sky." *Prologue* 41, no. 4 (Winter 2009): 14-22.

Author Info	Archivist at the Eisenhower library for 37 years. Retired in 2008, but still volunteers there.
Bibliography	No.
Index	No.
Notes	Essay—Notes on Sources.
Photographs	Yes (10).
Appendix	No.
Tables	No.
Key Words	Presidency, Cold War, Military Policy, Technology
Other Notes	
Annotation	Using records, some then newly declassified, from the Eisenhower Library, archivist Haight chronicles Eisenhower's efforts to balance his desire for reliable intelligence concerning the Soviet Union's military activities against the risks involved in obtaining such information. Also traces Eisenhower's efforts to mitigate that risk and the technological evolution of overflight reconnaissance.

205. Hale, Frederick. "Challenging the Swedish Social Welfare State: The Case of Dwight David Eisenhower." *Swedish-American Historical Quarterly* 54, no. 1 (January 2003): 55-71.

Author Info	As of 2003, he held "a number of advanced degrees, including doctorates from Johns Hopkins and the University of South Africa, and he has published extensively in the areas of Scandinavian and Scandinavian-American history,

literature, and theology… He lives part of each year in Scandinavia and currently is a Senior Research Fellow at the University of Stellenbosch, South Africa. [From article]

Bibliography	No.
Index	No.
Notes	Endnotes (33).
Photographs	No.
Appendix	No.
Tables	No.
Key Words	Presidency, Politics, Foreign Relations
Other Notes	
Annotation	Hale details a little remembered incident in which Eisenhower, during an event to support Nixon's presidential run, made an oblique remark concerning Sweden that negatively characterized their welfare state as "'the experiment of almost complete paternalism'[that] had resulted in a supposedly skyrocketing rate of suicide and 'more than twice our drunkenness'." He also implied that the Swedes were sexually promiscuous. Ike's remarks "temporarily strained relations between Sweden and the United States several years before American policies in Southeast Asia brought them to their nadir." Ike later apologized in Sweden, and the incident "proved to be a short-lived rhetorical teapot tempest" but Hale states that it is important "because it highlights the failure inherent in a high-ranking and extremely prominent American echoing a stereotypical judgment about Swedish society without first acquiring first-hand knowledge of Sweden or, for that matter, adequately considering related social realities in his own country."

206. Hall, R. Cargill. "Denied Territory: Eisenhower's Policy of Peacetime Aerial Overflight." *Air Power History* 56, no. 4 (Winter 2009): 4-9.

Author Info	"R. Cargill Hall, Historian Emeritus, National Reconnaissance Office, has held a variety of posts in the U.S. Air Force History Program. He served as a historian at Headquarters Strategic Air Command and as NASA historian at Caltech's Jet Propulsion Laboratory. Hall is the author of Lunar Impact: A History of Project Ranger and is the editor of Case Studies in Strategic Bombardment; The U.S. Air Force in Space; and Early Cold War Overflights, 1950-1956." His recent work includes "Clandestine Victory: Eisenhower and Overhead Reconnaissance in the Cold War," which appears in Dennis E. Showalter, ed., *Forging the Shield: Eisenhower and National Security for the 21st Century* (2005). http://www.marshall.org/experts.php?id=147
Bibliography	No.
Index	No.
Notes	Endnotes (7).
Photographs	Yes (3).
Appendix	No.
Tables	No.

Key Words   Presidency, Military Policy, Technology
Other Notes
Annotation   An overview of Eisenhower's clandestine, peacetime, high-altitude overflights
                  to gather data in the Soviet Union. Article emphasizes the secrecy of the
                  program.

207.   Hall, R. Cargill. "The Eisenhower Administration and the Cold War: Framing American
       Astronautics to Serve National Security." *Prologue* 27, no. 1 (Spring 1995): 58-72.

Author Info   See information in Entry #206.
Bibliography No.
Index   No.
Notes   Endnotes (45).
Photographs   Yes (12).
Appendix   No.
Tables   No.
Key Words   Presidency, Cold War, Space Exploration, Military Policy, Technology
Other Notes
Annotation   Hall discusses how Eisenhower framed astronautics national policy and
                  structured the organizations to guide such policy in ways best suited to serve
                  national security concerns. For example, Eisenhower framed astronautics under
                  three wings: "civil space science and applications, Department of Defense
                  military support missions… and reconnaissance satellites." Eisenhower and
                  his Administration's pursuit of the new technology, "contributed enormously
                  to the nation's security and the maintenance of a delicate peace with the Soviet
                  Union".

208.   Hall, R. Cargill. "Sputnik, Eisenhower, and the Formation of the United States Space
       Program." *Quest: History of Spaceflight* 14, no. 4 (October 2007): 32-39.

Author Info   See information in Entry #206.
Bibliography No.
Index   No.
Notes   Endnotes (28).
Photographs   Yes (13).
Appendix   No.
Tables   No.
Key Words   Presidency, Cold War, Space Exploration, Military Policy, Technology
Other Notes
Annotation   Details the evolution of America's space program and policies over the course
                  of Eisenhower's Presidency. When Eisenhower entered the office, there was a
                  dearth of reliable intelligence on Communist activities. Eisenhower's interest
                  in surveillance satellites and need for information led to a revolution in
                  American intelligence and civilian space policy. Hall explains that by the end

of his two terms, Eisenhower had "authorized a variety of spaceflight projects, established a core national space policy, organized the space program of the United States in a structure that has endured, and, with reconnaissance satellites, solved America's Cold War intelligence problem."

209.   Hahn, Peter L. "Securing the Middle East: The Eisenhower Doctrine of 1957."
        Presidential Studies Quarterly 36, no. 1 (Mar, 2006): 38-47.

Author Info	Professor at Ohio State, specializing in United States diplomatic history in the Middle East since 1940. For further information, see Book Entry #52.
Bibliography	No.
Index	No.
Notes	Footnotes (29).
Photographs	No.
Appendix	No.
Tables	No.
Key Words	Presidency, Foreign Relations, Military Policy, Middle East, Cold War
Other Notes	
Annotation	Examines the origins of, Middle East reaction to, and three applications of the Eisenhower Doctrine of 1957. The Doctrine was a "declaration that the United States would use economic aid, military aid, and armed forces to stop the spread of communism" in the Middle East. Eisenhower believed such a commitment was necessary to fill the vacuum created when Britain and France became discredited in the region after the Suez-Sinai War of 1956-1957. The Middle East nations had a wide variety of reactions to the Doctrine, but overall, Eisenhower "found it difficult to convince the Arab states or Israel of its purpose or usefulness." Although it was never formally invoked, Eisenhower applied the doctrine in 1957-1958 three times (in Jordan, Syria, and Lebanon). The Doctrine faded in importance after 1958 but had a long legacy that included the U.S. assuming responsibilities in the Middle East and a precedent of using military force to stop the spread of communism.

210.   Harris, Douglas B. "Dwight Eisenhower and the New Deal: The Politics of Preemption."
        Presidential Studies Quarterly 27, no. 2 (Spring, 1997): 333-342.

Author Info	Associate Professor at Loyola University of Maryland in the Department of Political Science. Ph.D. from Johns Hopkins University. http://www.loyola.edu/academics/politicalscience/faculty/index.html
Bibliography	No.
Index	No.
Notes	Endnotes (54).
Photographs	No.
Appendix	No.
Tables	No.

Key Words   Presidency, Politics, Domestic Policy
Other Notes
Annotation   Using Stephen Skowronek's typology of presidential politics, Harris argues that Eisenhower was the most successful of the "preemptive presidents," defined as those "opposed to resilient regimes, but in the difficult position of searching for reconstructive opportunities where reconstruction is neither warranted by mandate nor sufficiently supported by segments of society." Eisenhower "privately held antipathy toward the New Deal" but nonetheless supported and upheld some of the New Deal policies because of the strength and popularity of those programs. He did, however, attempt to preempt the aspects of the New Deal which he believed to be the most dangerous for America: what he perceived as the New Deal's "trends toward federal centralization, socialism, and paternalism." Harris suggests that future preemptive presidents would be wise to consider Ike's successes which "highlight the necessity of being sensitive to the strength of the existing regime, being careful in selecting one's policy battles, and going at a pace appropriate to one's mandate in light of the strength of the regime."

211.   Hart, John. "Eisenhower & the Swelling of the Presidency," *Polity*, Vol. 24, No. 4 (Summer, 1992), pp. 673-691.

Author Info   Professor at the Australian National University. Interests: Government and politics in the United States; American presidency; American elections; British politics and comparative executive government.
http://politicsir.cass.anu.edu.au/people/academic-staff/john-hart

Bibliography	No.
Index	No.
Notes	Footnotes (46).
Photographs	No.
Appendix	No.
Tables	No.
Key Words	Presidency, White House
Other Notes	

Annotation   Argues that "Eisenhower carries rather more responsibility for the expansion of the presidential staff system than has generally been recognized by the post-Watergate critics of the swelling of the presidency and by Eisenhower revisionists whose focus on leadership style and skill has, perhaps, obscured the longer-term institutional relevance of staffing developments during the Eisenhower period." Hart uses several different sets of statistics to show high levels of growth in White House staff during Eisenhower's Administration. He also examines the source of salaries for the White House staff under Eisenhower, including the Special Projects Fund, "an important source of 'the swelling of the presidency.'"

212. Hartung, William D. "Eisenhower's Warning: the Military-Industrial Complex Forty Years Later," *World Policy Journal*, 18, no. 1 (Spring, 2001): 39-44.

Author Info	"William D. Hartung is Director of the Arms and Security Initiative at the New America Foundation. The project serves as a resource for journalists, policymakers, and citizen's organizations on the issues of weapons proliferation, the economics of military spending, and alternative approaches to national security strategy." http://newamerica.net/user/22
Bibliography	No.
Index	No.
Notes	Footnotes (11).
Photographs	No.
Appendix	No.
Tables	No.
Key Words	Presidency, Speechmaking
Other Notes	
Annotation	Hartung takes a fresh look at Eisenhower's farewell address warning to analyze the present and ponder the future of the military-industrial complex. Focus is more on the then-current state of military spending than Ike's warning.

213. Heller, Francis H. "The Eisenhower White House." *Presidential Studies Quarterly* 23, no. 3 (1993): 509-517.

Author Info	Was Roy A. Roberts Professor of Law and Political Science at the University of Kansas and vice president of the Harry S. Truman Library Institute.
Bibliography	No.
Index	No.
Notes	Endnotes (36).
Photographs	No.
Appendix	No.
Tables	No.
Key Words	Presidency, White House
Other Notes	
Annotation	Heller argues that the "modern Presidency came into being during the Eisenhower years" and points to Eisenhower's experience with managing large-scale operations and his familiarity with the military's staff organization as the two most significant factors in Eisenhower's success in formalizing the procedures and structures of the executive office. White House innovations instituted by Eisenhower included organizational changes, stricter staff controls, and systematic follow-ups. Slightly different version of a paper Heller presented in October, 1990 at the conference on "Ike's America" at the University of Kansas.

214.   Hoff, Samuel B. "The President's Removal Power: Eisenhower and the War Claims Commission Controversy." *Congress & the Presidency* 18, no. 1 (Spring 1991): 37-54.

Author Info	Law Studies Director, Professor at Delaware State University.
Bibliography	List of sources.
Index	No.
Notes	Internal citations.
Photographs	No.
Appendix	No.
Tables	No.
Key Words	Presidency, Politics, Domestic Policy
Other Notes	
Annotation	Details Eisenhower's dismissal of members of the War Claims Commission and the questionable legality of his actions in doing so; this ultimately led to what Hoff characterizes as "one of the most influential court rulings on the parameters of presidential removal power in American history." In the case brought by one of the commissioners the Supreme Court ruled for the commissioner, finding Eisenhower's removal improper. Article also addresses Eisenhower's personal role in the events, but leaves unresolved whether or not Eisenhower was involved in the removal decision on a first-hand basis.

215.   Hopkins, Robert S., III. "An Expanded Understanding of Eisenhower, American Policy and Overflights." *Intelligence and National Security* 11, no. 2 (Apr, 1996): 332-344.

Author Info	MPH, Ph.D., was a qualified facilitator for LifeWings, providing CRM-based training to physicians, nurses and other health care professionals throughout the United States. Dr. Hopkins flew combat reconnaissance missions during Operation DESERT STORM and was an Air Force pilot and aircraft commander. After his military service Hopkins taught history at Creighton University in Omaha, Nebraska. Hopkins is a graduate of the University of North Carolina-Chapel Hill, with a Master of Public Health degree and also has earned a Doctor of Philosophy degree in history from the University of Virginia. (From LifeWings website)
Bibliography	No.
Index	No.
Notes	Endnotes (44).
Photographs	No.
Appendix	No.
Tables	No.
Key Words	Presidency, Cold War, Military Policy, Technology
Other Notes	
Annotation	Examines the previously underexplored military overflight program under President Eisenhower. Though historians have examined Eisenhower's *civilian* overflight program, the military's aerial intelligence reconnaissance program was more extensive than previously thought. Further, Eisenhower

approached military overflight differently than he did civilian overflight: he did not control it as strictly, giving the Air Force wide discretion, and was influenced by military concerns, as well as political, when approving missions.

216. Hoxie, R. Gordon. "Eisenhower and 'My Scientists'." *National Forum* 71, no. 4 (Fall 1990): 9-12.

Author Info   Hoxie was dean of the College of Liberal Arts and Sciences of Long Island University, and in 1964 he was appointed as chancellor. After 1968, he and others founded the Center for the Study of the Presidency, a scholarly forum which publishes Presidential Studies Quarterly as a resource for scholars. He died in 2002. From *NY Times* Obituary at http://www.nytimes.com/2002/10/30/nyregion/r-gordon-hoxie-83-chancellor-of-long-island-university-in-60-s.html

Bibliography   No.
Index   No.
Notes   No.
Photographs   No.
Appendix   No.
Tables   No.
Key Words   Presidency, Technology
Other Notes
Annotation   In this short article, Hoxie describes the "unique relationship" between Eisenhower and the men he called "my scientists," describing it as "a shining hour in the history of the Presidency and of science and technology." Eisenhower created the Office of Special Assistant to the President for Science and Technology and the President's Science Advisory Committee, which Hoxie says, Ike considered crucial in advising him on matters related to science and advanced technology.

I's

217. Ingimundarson, Valur. "Containing the Offensive: The 'Chief of the Cold War' and the Eisenhower Administration's German Policy." *Presidential Studies Quarterly* 27, no. 3 (Summer 1997): 480-495.

Author Info   "Dr. Valur Ingimundarson is Associate Professor of History and Chairman of the History Department at the University of Iceland. He received his Ph.D. from Columbia University [and] has written extensively on US-European political and security relations, NATO, US-UK relations with Iceland, and post-war developments and peacekeeping operations in the Balkans." Bio at http://www.rusi.org/about/staff/associates/ref:A40B10A0F4BDF2/

Bibliography   No.

Index	No.
Notes	Footnotes (91).
Photographs	No.
Appendix	No.
Tables	No.
Key Words	Presidency, Foreign Relations, Cold War
Other Notes	
Annotation	Article focuses on "Chief of the Cold War," C. D. Jackson, Eisenhower's special assistant for psychological warfare during his first year in office. Jackson's offensive Cold War strategy was entertained by Eisenhower and Dulles, but ultimately turned down as too costly or risky and at odds with Eisenhower's defensive, containment strategy.

218. Ingimundarson, Valur. "The Eisenhower Administration, the Adenauer Government, and the Political Uses of the East German Uprising in 1953." *Diplomatic History* 20, no. 3 (Summer 1996): 381-409.

Author Info	See information in Entry #217.
Bibliography	No.
Index	No.
Notes	Footnotes (56).
Photographs	No.
Appendix	No.
Tables	No.
Key Words	Presidency, Cold War, Military Policy
Other Notes	
Annotation	Essay focuses on two central elements of the United States and West German reaction to the 1953 East German uprising: 1) the proposed four-power meeting with the Soviets; and 2) the food relief plan for East Germany. Ingimundarson also examines the cold war implications of these actions. The meeting proposal "enabled the West to wrest the initiative on the German question from the Soviets," a development which was positive for America's propaganda war, and contributed to Adenauer's reelection success. On the American side, the food relief plan was motivated more by propaganda than by humanitarian concerns, and was more successful in its initial stages than historians have previously believed. The program was ultimately undermined, however, by disagreements within the Eisenhower administration and among the U.S. Allies over cold war strategy.

219. Irish, Kerry E. "Apt Pupil: Dwight Eisenhower and the 1930 Industrial Mobilization Plan." *The Journal of Military History*, 70, No. 1 (Jan., 2006): 31-61.

Author Info	Irish has written previous articles on Eisenhower and is a professor of history at George Fox University. The program is described

inhttp://www.georgefox.edu/academics/undergrad/departments/history/index.html

Bibliography	No.
Index	No.
Notes	Endnotes (165).
Photographs	No.
Appendix	No.
Tables	No.
Key Words	Military- Pre WWII, Military Policy
Other Notes	
Annotation	Argues that historians have been remiss in passing over the period of Eisenhower's work as a staff officer in the War Department in the early 1930s, during which time he wrote America's first detailed industrial mobilization plan. Though it was never implemented in Eisenhower's original form, it served to ready the public for Army industrial planning for war and prepared the Army to accept a civilian-led centralized planning agency as integral to war mobilization. This period and the drafting process were also important to Eisenhower personally as it resulted in significant contacts and friendships, including that with MacArthur, and gave him valuable political and military experience and insight.

220. Irish, Kerry E. "Dwight Eisenhower and Douglas MacArthur in the Philippines: There Must Be a Day of Reckoning." *Journal of Military History* 74, no. 2 (2010): 439-473.

Author Info	See information in Entry #219.
Bibliography	No.
Index	No.
Notes	Footnotes (182).
Photographs	Yes (2).
Appendix	No.
Tables	No.
Key Words	Military—B/w the Wars
Other Notes	
Annotation	During the inter-war years when Eisenhower worked under MacArthur in the Philippines (1935-1939), each man developed a deeply negative impression of the other. Eisenhower's main disagreements with MacArthur were strategic and professional: 1) how best to build the Filipino Army in the midst of budgetary constraints; and 2) the type of leadership style and professional standards that a United States Army General should exhibit.

221. Irish, Kerry E. "Hometown Support in the Midst of War: Dwight Eisenhower's Wartime Correspondence with Abilene Friends." *Kansas History* 25, no. 1 (Spring 2002): 14-37.

Author Info	See information in Entry #219.

Bibliography	No.
Index	No.
Notes	Endnotes (82).
Photographs	Yes—14.
Appendix	No.
Tables	No.
Key Words	Military- WWII
Other Notes	
Annotation	Drawing on letters between Eisenhower and friends and family back home in Kansas, Irish argues that Eisenhower's correspondence with the men and women of his hometown was sincere, sustained him during WWII, and was not a nuisance to him. Author posits that the hero worship Eisenhower's letters incited in Abilene was only a secondary purpose in his correspondence and can only be inferred, not proven. Includes many excerpts from the letters.

J's

222.   Jackson, Ian. "'The Limits of International Leadership': The Eisenhower Administration, East-West Trade and the Cold War, 1953-54." *Diplomacy & Statecraft* 11, no. 3 (November 2000): 113-138.

Author Info	A faculty member at De Montfort University (DMU), Leicester, UK.
Bibliography	No.
Index	No.
Notes	Endnotes (67).
Photographs	No.
Appendix	No.
Tables	No.
Key Words	Presidency, Cold War, Foreign Relations
Other Notes	
Annotation	Jackson suggests that historians have had too narrow a focus in their examination of the liberalization of East-West trade controls in August 1954. He argues that in focusing on Eisenhower, historians have neglected the crucial role played by Winston Churchill. Though Eisenhower played a significant role in relaxing American embargo policy, he was hindered by the Defense and Commerce Departments, which were staunchly opposed to trade liberalization. Britain and Churchill provided the "main impetus behind the revisions." Churchill's desire to reduce the list of embargoed goods radically forced the hand of American diplomats to compromise in order to maintain good relations with London in the multilateral export control regime (CoCom).

223.   Jackson, Michael Gordon. "Beyond Brinkmanship: Eisenhower, Nuclear War Fighting, and Korea, 1953-1968." *Presidential Studies Quarterly* 35, no. 1 (Mar, 2005): 52-75.

Author Info   A lecturer in political science at Brown University and other colleges and universities in New England. Scholarly Resources Librarian. He wrote his Brandeis dissertation on "Thinking about Armageddon: Eisenhower and the Use of Atomic Weapons, 1945-1969," (1991).

Bibliography	No.
Index	No.
Notes	Endnotes (41); References.
Photographs	No.
Appendix	No.
Tables	No.
Key Words	Presidency, Korea, Nuclear, Foreign Relations, Post-Presidency
Other Notes	

Annotation   Author offers a self-described post-revisionist reading of debates within the Eisenhower Administration and Eisenhower's statements during the fighting on the Korean peninsula (1953-1960) and the 1968 Pueblo Crisis to argue that Eisenhower "was much more committed to the *necessity*, if not the *desirability*, of nuclear war fighting than most have been willing to accept." (emphasis in original).

224.   Jacobs, Matt. "Unforeseen Consequences: The Eisenhower Administration and Fidel Castro's Revolutionary Nationalism in Cuba, 1959-1961." *Journal of the North Carolina Association of Historians* 17, (April 2009): 53-80.

Author Info   Was graduate student at the University of North Carolina at Wilmington when this was written.

Bibliography	No.
Index	No.
Notes	Footnotes (71).
Photographs	No.
Appendix	No.
Tables	No.
Key Words	Presidency, Foreign Relations, Cold War
Other Notes	

Annotation   Chronicles the deterioration of U.S.-Cuban relations. Fidel Castro's Cuban revolution caused the Soviet Union and America to change their policies toward Cuba and bring the country into the center of the cold war conflict. Eisenhower and his Administration were opposed to Castro not because he was a communist, but "rather a fervent revolutionary nationalist whose desire to establish a revolutionary character among Cubans did not fall in line with what the United States had envisioned for Cuba." The Soviet Union was intrigued by a country so close to the U.S. which so actively opposed America, and Castro sought assistance for his country from the Soviets.

225.   Jacobs, Seth. "'A Monumental Struggle of Good Versus Evil': American Crusaders in Vietnam and Iraq." *New England Journal of History* 64, no. 1 (Fall 2007): 214-232.

Author Info   Associate professor at Boston College. "Jacobs is a political and cultural historian of the United States in the twentieth century, especially the period since World War II, and his research interests focus on the connection between U.S. domestic culture and foreign policy... In 2002, the Society for Historians of American Foreign Relations (SHAFR) honored him with its Stuart Bernath Prize for the best article published in the field of diplomatic history. He won SHAFR's Bernath Book Prize in 2006." http://www.bc.edu/schools/cas/history/faculty/alphabetical/jacobs_seth.html

Bibliography   No.
Index   No.
Notes   Endnotes (58).
Photographs   No.
Appendix   No.
Tables   No.
Key Words   Presidency, Vietnam, Religion
Other Notes
Annotation   Focus more on Dulles than Eisenhower. Compares the Eisenhower Administration's policies and actions involving Vietnam with George W. Bush's policies and actions toward Iraq. Both presidents appointed very religious men to their Administrations and their work in Vietnam and Iraq were characterized as "crusades". Jacobs finds that the "problem with viewing geopolitical conflicts in terms of a religious crusade—as the Eisenhower administration demonstrated in Vietnam, and as the Bush administration [was then] currently proving in Iraq—is that it tends to produce mind-lock, an inability to reexamine premises, admit errors, and, if necessary, change courses."

226.   Jacobs, Travis Beal. "Eisenhower, the American Assembly, and 1952." *Presidential Studies Quarterly* 22, no. 3 (Summer, 1992): 455-468.

Author Info   Middlebury College Fletcher D. Proctor Professor Emeritus of American History. Son of a Dean at Columbia, who was a contemporary there with Ike.
Bibliography   No.
Index   No.
Notes   Footnotes.
Photographs   No.
Appendix   No.
Tables   No.
Key Words   Elections, Columbia University, Politics
Other Notes
Annotation   Highlights the role of Columbia University on Eisenhower's journey to the White House. The presidency of the University, and especially his efforts launching the American Assembly, provided him with valuable political

experience. It also allowed him to create a vast network of support. His experiences at Columbia, however, generated sharp academic opposition to his candidacy.

K's

227.   Kahn, Michael A. "Shattering the Myth About President Eisenhower's Supreme Court Appointments." *Presidential Studies Quarterly* 22, no. 1 (Winter 1992): 47-56.

Author Info	Senior Counsel at Crowell Moring Law firm in San Francisco. Political Science MA from Stanford. Has published other articles on appointments of Supreme Court justices. Bio at http://www.crowell.com/Professionals/Michael-Kahn
Bibliography	No.
Index	No.
Notes	Footnotes (47).
Photographs	No.
Appendix	No.
Tables	No.
Key Words	Presidency, Civil Rights
Other Notes	
Annotation	Relying primarily on *Eisenhower's Mandate for Change* and secondary sources, attorney Kahn argues against the theory that Eisenhower was surprised by the Civil Rights decisions of his Supreme Court appointments. Examining each of the five appointments in turn, he posits that Eisenhower "clearly and undeniably attempted to influence the Supreme Court in the direction of entrenching *Brown v. Board of Education* and enforcing its terms." Kahn also compares Eisenhower and his appointees with Bush and Souter during Souter's appointment proceedings and argues that Bush lacked the strength of character and commitment to judicial precedent of Eisenhower and five of his appointees.

228.   Kengor, Paul. "Comparing Presidents Reagan and Eisenhower." *Presidential Studies Quarterly* 28, no. 2 (Spring 1998): 366-393.

Author Info	"Dr. Paul Kengor is professor of political science at Grove City College, a four-year, private Christian liberal arts college in Grove City, Pennsylvania... He is executive director of the Center for Vision & Values, a Grove City College think-tank/policy center. He is also a visiting fellow at the Hoover Institution on War, Revolution, and Peace at Stanford University." http://www.visandvals.org/Paul_Kengor,_Ph_D_.php
Bibliography	No.

Index	No.
Notes	Footnotes (122).
Photographs	No.
Appendix	No.
Tables	Yes (1).
Key Words	Presidency
Other Notes	
Annotation	Relying mainly on secondary sources, Kengor compares the presidencies of Reagan and Eisenhower and concludes that they had both similarities and differences, with interesting parallels. The most interesting parallel Kengor finds is that while both were underestimated by academia and the media, they both enjoyed high public approval ratings.

229. Khrushchev, Sergei. "The Cold War Through the Looking Glass." *American Heritage* 50, no. 6 (October 1999): 34-50.

Author Info	Author is the son of Soviet Premier Nikita Khrushchev. He is a senior fellow at the Watson Institute for International Studies at Brown University. http://www.watsoninstitute.org/contacts_detail.cfm?id=26
Bibliography	No.
Index	No.
Notes	No.
Photographs	Yes (7).
Appendix	No.
Tables	No.
Key Words	Presidency, Cold War, Foreign Relations
Other Notes	
Annotation	In this article, Khrushchev provides anecdotes regarding what the Cold War was like from the Soviet perspective. Includes some brief observations regarding the relationship between Nikita Khrushchev and Eisenhower, which Sergei Khrushchev says began tentatively; nevertheless, he notes, their relationship built a foundation for Khrushchev's interactions with future U.S. presidents.

230. King, James D., and James W. Riddlespeger, Jr. "Presidential Leadership of Congressional Civil Rights Voting: The Cases of Eisenhower and Johnson." *Policy Studies Journal* 21, no. 3 (September 1993): 544-555.

Author Info	King is a professor of Political Science at University of Wyoming: "Jim King joined the UW political science faculty in 1992 and previously taught at the University of Memphis… During election years he is frequently interviewed by national and state media outlets about Wyoming politics." http://www.uwyo.edu/pols/people/king.html

Riddlespeger: is a professor of Political Science at Texas Christian University. http://www.pol.tcu.edu/faculty_staff/riddlesperger.htm

Bibliography	References.
Index	No.
Notes	Endnotes (5).
Photographs	No.
Appendix	Appendix of data sources.
Tables	Yes (2).
Key Words	Presidency, Elections, Politics.
Other Notes	
Annotation	Noting that Eisenhower and Johnson had very different styles of leadership and served in very different political climates, the authors statistically examined how each succeeded in passing landmark Civil Rights legislation. They determined that neither leadership style nor political context could alone account for these successes, but that it was a factor of the symbiotic combination of the two.

231. Kingseed, Cole C. "Dark Days of White Knights." *Military Review* 73, no. 1 (January 1993): 67-75.

Author Info	"Colonel Cole C. Kingseed, United States Army (Retired), is a thirty-year infantry veteran who commanded at the platoon, company, and battalion level. A graduate of the University of Dayton (OH) in 1971, he served in a variety of military assignments, culminating in his tenure as full professor of history and chief of military history at the U S Military Academy at West Point. Colonel Kingseed holds a Ph.D. from Ohio State University and a Master of Arts in National Security and Strategic Studies from the U.S. Naval War College. Kingseed… authored… *Eisenhower and the Suez Crisis of 1956*." See Book Entry #64. http://www.battlefieldleadership.com/bios/colonel-cole-c-kingseed-u-s-army-retired
Bibliography	No.
Index	No.
Notes	Endnotes (33).
Photographs	Yes (3).
Appendix	No.
Tables	No.
Key Words	Military- Pre WWII, Military—B/w the Wars
Other Notes	
Annotation	Author examines the difficulties in the pre-WWII careers of MacArthur, Eisenhower, and Patton and considers how each man dealt with the obstacles he faced. Eisenhower's difficult relationship with a superior, Major General Frank L. Sheets, and an Inspector General investigation into alleged improprieties are discussed. Kingseed notes that in the interwar years, the three men pursued their professional development (especially Eisenhower), read military history extensively, and possessed the ability to make quick, correct

decisions.

232. Kingseed, Cole C. "Eisenhower's Prewar Anonymity: Myth or Reality?" *Parameters: US Army War College* 21, no. 3 (Autumn 1991): 87-98.

Author Info	See information in Entry #231.
Bibliography	No.
Index	No.
Notes	Endnotes (98).
Photographs	Yes (1).
Appendix	No.
Tables	No.
Key Words	Military- Pre WWII, Military—B/w the Wars
Other Notes	
Annotation	Kingseed argues that although Eisenhower might not have been a recognizable name to civilians before the Texas-Louisiana maneuvers of 1941, he was "widely respected within the Army as a brilliant staff officer whose extraordinary skills made him virtually indispensible to some of the most distinguished soldiers and statesmen of his generation." Kingseed cites Eisenhower's numerous pre-WWII accomplishments including earning the Distinguished Service Medal for his command of Camp Colt, graduating first in his class at the Command and General Staff School, commanding over 10,000 men within the first three years of graduating from West Point, and earning superior ratings and commendations from Pershing, MacArthur, and Krueger. The author disproves the idea that but for World War II, Ike would have lived an obscure life.

233. Kingseed, Cole C. "'Ike' Takes Charge." *Military Review* 72, no. 6 (June 1992): 73-76.

Author Info	See information in Entry #231.
Bibliography	No.
Index	No.
Notes	Endnotes (13).
Photographs	Yes (2).
Appendix	No.
Tables	No.
Key Words	Military- WWII
Other Notes	Includes chronology of major military events in June 1942.
Annotation	Briefly describes Marshall's grooming of Eisenhower and Ike's assignment as commanding general, European Theater of Operations.

234. Kingseed, Cole C. "The Juggler and the Supreme Commander." *Military Review* 76, no. 6 (November 1996): 77-82.

Author Info	See information in Entry #231.
Bibliography	No.
Index	No.
Notes	Yes (21).
Photographs	No.
Appendix	No.
Tables	No.
Key Words	Military- WWII
Other Notes	
Annotation	Revisionist interpretation of Roosevelt's decision to appoint Eisenhower, rather than Marshall, as commander of Operation Overlord. Kingseed argues that Roosevelt's decision was based more in politics than in military strategy. Both men were capable of commanding the operation, but: "In the end, Marshall's political credits simply outweighed his military merits." Roosevelt wanted Marshall in Washington DC to continue serving as his most trusted military adviser.

235. Kingseed, Cole C. "Victory in Europe." *Military Review* 75, no. 3 (May 1995): 92-94.

Author Info	See information in Entry #231.
Bibliography	No.
Index	No.
Notes	Endnotes (14).
Photographs	Yes (2).
Appendix	No.
Tables	No.
Key Words	Military- WWII
Other Notes	
Annotation	Briefly chronicles the last months of the war in Europe, ending with V-E Day. Includes a brief discussion of Eisenhower's controversial decision to let the Soviets take Berlin.

236. Korda, Michael. "Ike at D-Day." *Smithsonian* 38, no. 9 (December 2007): 48-58.

Author Info	"Michael Korda is the former editor in chief of Simon & Schuster and is the author of many books, most recently *With Wings Like Eagles: A History of the Battle of Britain*. He served in the Royal Air Force". (From HarperCollins website http://www.harpercollins.com/author/microsite/About.aspx?authorid=15370)
Bibliography	No.
Index	No.
Notes	No.
Photographs	Yes (15).

Appendix	No.
Tables	No.
Key Words	Military- WWII
Other Notes	
Annotation	Describes Eisenhower's decision to land troops in Normandy on June 6. Korda discusses factors Eisenhower had to consider, including the weather and doubts of air marshals about nighttime, large-scale parachute and glider operations. Excerpt from Korda's *Ike: An American Hero* (2007), Entry #68.

237. Krebs, Ronald R. "Liberation à la Finland: Reexamining Eisenhower Administration Objectives in Eastern Europe." *Journal of Strategic Studies* Vol. 20 Issue 3 (Sep. 1997): 1-26.

Author Info	Associate professor of political science at the University of Minnesota. "Professor Ron Krebs (Ph.D., Columbia University, 2003) conducts research at the juncture of international relations and comparative politics, with a particular interest in the origins and consequences of international conflict and military service. His recently published book, Fighting for Rights: Military Service and the Politics of Citizenship (Cornell University Press, 2006), explores the conditions under which and the mechanisms through which military participation policies shape contestation over citizenship rights…. He is also the author of a historical monograph, *Dueling Visions: U.S. Strategy Toward Eastern Europe Under Eisenhower* (Texas A & M University Press, 2001)." http://www.polisci.umn.edu/~ronkrebs/ See Entry #66.
Bibliography	No.
Index	No.
Notes	Endnotes (52).
Photographs	No.
Appendix	No.
Tables	No.
Key Words	Presidency, Cold War, Foreign Relations
Other Notes	
Annotation	Krebs examines the Eisenhower Administration's policies towards Eastern Europe and finds that the Administration, particularly Dulles, used the Finnish model to define the American vision for Eastern Europe. The Finnish model was a balanced one in which a country had an independent domestic policy, but a foreign policy tied to the Soviet Union. Though not ideal, this model would help achieve several U.S. objectives: "domestic autonomy for the Eastern European satellites, possibly with popularly elected governments; retreat of Soviet military forces to within Soviet borders; and containment of German aggressive potential."

L's

238.	LaFantasie, Glenn. "Monty and Ike Take Gettysburg." *MHQ: The Quarterly Journal of Military History*, vol. 8 (Autumn 1995): 67-73.

Author Info	Professor of Civil War History at Western Kentucky University. Scholarly interests: Civil War social, political, and military history, with a particular focus on Gettysburg and Abraham Lincoln; slavery and antislavery; Southern cultural history; the legacy of the American Revolution. Publications: *Twilight at Little Round Top* (2005), *Gettysburg Requiem: The Life and Lost Causes of Confederate Colonel William C. Oates* (2006), *Gettysburg Heroes: Perfect Soldiers, Hallowed Ground* (forthcoming, 2008). From http://www.wku.edu/IA/bucks/lafantasie.html
Bibliography	No.
Index	No.
Notes	No.
Photographs	Yes (3).
Appendix	No.
Tables	No.
Key Words	Presidency, Politics
Other Notes	
Annotation	Details the visit of British General Bernard Law Montgomery and Eisenhower to the Civil War battle site of Gettysburg and the press's coverage of their tour. Comments made during the visit to Gettysburg, mainly by Montgomery, were critical of Generals Lee's and Meade's actions and strategies during the battle, and caused great public outcry in America and abroad, turning the visit into a political liability for Eisenhower. The Gettysburg tour also further soured the relationship between Montgomery and Eisenhower.

239.	Launius, Roger D. "Eisenhower, Sputnik, and the Creation of NASA." *Prologue* 28, no. 2 (Summer 1996): 126-143.

Author Info	Curator at the National Air and Space Museum (http://www.si.edu/ofg/Staffhp/launiusr.htm)
Bibliography	No.
Index	No.
Notes	Endnotes (71).
Photographs	Yes (16).
Appendix	No.
Tables	No.
Key Words	Presidency, Space Exploration, Politics, Technology, Domestic Policy
Other Notes	
Annotation	Launius examines the origins of NASA and finds that though Eisenhower believed that such a separate federal agency was unnecessarily costly, he was forced to create one by pressure exerted from multiple interest groups, including scientists, politicians, business groups, and space flight enthusiasts

following the launch of the Soviet satellites. The agency he created, and the man he chose to run it, however, served to place limits on the size, scope, and cost of the endeavor. Thus, "NASA's creation and initial modest space exploration agenda was the product of the interchange between Eisenhower's vision of government mission and organization and a loosely defined set of interest groups that pressed for exceptionally aggressive action in the immediate post-Sputnik era."

240.   Larres, Klaus. "Eisenhower and the First Forty Days after Stalin's Death: The Incompatibility of Détente and Political Warfare." *Diplomacy and Statecraft* 6, no. 2 (July, 1995): 431-469.

Author Info	Professor in History and International Affairs at the University of Ulster. http://www.ulster.ac.uk/staff/k.larres.html
Bibliography	No.
Index	No.
Notes	Footnotes (158).
Photographs	No.
Appendix	No.
Tables	No.
Key Words	Presidency, Foreign Relations, Cold War, Speechmaking
Other Notes	
Annotation	Larres finds that Eisenhower was personally responsible for "the initial and the final substance, tone, and underlying aims of the 'Chance for Peace' speech" and that the speech was not intended to bring about an end to the Cold War, but was an attempt to score a propaganda victory over the new leaders of the Soviet Union after Stalin's death. Eisenhower was initially influenced by C. D. Jackson and his own Cold Warrior hawkishness and wanted to make the speech a psychological warfare offensive. The popularity of the Soviet Union's peace offensive, and to some extent Dulles's counsel for a less aggressive approach, however, caused Eisenhower to tone down his speech. Ultimately, it was still more of a propaganda effort than a genuine peace-making one.

241.   Larson, George A. "General Eisenhower's Modified B-25J Used During World War II." *American Aviation Historical Society Journal* 49, no. 1 (Spring 2004): 66-70.

Author Info	Lt. Col., USAF (Ret.)
Bibliography	References listed.
Index	No.
Notes	No.
Photographs	Yes (8).
Appendix	No.
Tables	No.

Key Words	Military- WWII, Technology
Other Notes	
Annotation	Details the specifications of and modifications to the B-25J airplane that was modified into a VIP transport for General Eisenhower. Includes anecdotes and information from interviews with people on Eisenhower's staff. Also details post-WWII history of the plane.

242. Layton, Azza Salama. "International Pressure and the U.S. Government's Response to Little Rock." *Arkansas Historical Quarterly* 66, no. 2 (Summer 2007): 243-257.

Author Info	Associate professor at DePaul University (Chicago). Ph.D. in Dept of Government from the University of Texas at Austin. CV at http://las.depaul.edu/psc/docs/Vitae/LaytonCV09JanZ.pdf
Bibliography	No.
Index	No.
Notes	Footnotes (57).
Photographs	No.
Appendix	No.
Tables	No.
Key Words	Presidency, Civil Rights, Foreign Relations, Domestic Policy
Other Notes	
Annotation	The significant world-wide criticism that the situation at Little Rock attracted convinced the Eisenhower Administration, cognizant of the importance of America's international reputation, to advance the civil rights cause. Layton provides numerous examples of the criticism from international newspapers, as well as ambassadors' and consulates' dispatches back to the U.S. Article originally appeared in the fall 1997 issue of the same journal.

243. Lesch, David W. "When the Relationship Went Sour: Syria and the Eisenhower Administration." *Presidential Studies Quarterly* 28, no. 1 (Winter 1998): 92-107.

Author Info	"David W. Lesch is Professor of Middle East History in the Department of History and Coordinator of the Middle East Concentration in the International Studies Program at Trinity University in San Antonio. He received his M.A. and Ph.D. (1991) in History and Middle Eastern Studies from Harvard University." From http://www.trinity.edu/departments/history/faculty/Lesch/lesch.html
Bibliography	No.
Index	No.
Notes	Endnotes (45).
Photographs	No.
Appendix	No.
Tables	No.
Key Words	Presidency, Middle East, Cold War, Foreign Relations

Other Notes

Annotation   Author traces the development of the hostile relationship between Syria and America to the Eisenhower Administration. The Administration's attempts to impose a globalist foreign policy of containment ignored the area's unique regional dynamics. America's failure to recognize Arab nationalism as an alternative to communism in the area led to a spiral of antagonistic actions between the countries, the effects of which linger today.

244.   Lehman, Kenneth. "Revolutions and Attributions: Making Sense of Eisenhower Administration Policies in Bolivia and Guatemala." *Diplomatic History* 21, no. 2 (Spring 1997): 185- 213.

Author Info	History professor at Hampden-Sydney College (VA).
	http://people.hsc.edu/faculty-staff/klehman/personal.htm
Bibliography	No.
Index	No.
Notes	Footnotes (65).
Photographs	Yes (2).
Appendix	No.
Tables	No.
Key Words	Presidency, Foreign Relations, Cold War
Other Notes	
Annotation	Lehman attempts to determine why, when the revolutionary movements in Bolivia and Guatemala were so similar, the Eisenhower Administration treated the countries so differently. He relies on cognitive or attribution theory to perform his analysis. Attribution theory, "holds that individuals… are 'naive scientists' seeking, in an apparently rational way, to understand the behavior of others." It also "gives attention to the intuitive process by which one often infers the motives of others, as well as to the attendant biases of intuitive thinking." Using this framework, Lehman examines how and why the U.S. supported the Bolivians while working against the Guatemalans.

245.   Little, Douglas. "His Finest Hour?: Eisenhower, Lebanon, and the 1958 Middle East Crisis." *Diplomatic History* 20, no. 1 (1996): 27-54.

Author Info	"Dr. Little received a B.A. from the University of Wisconsin in 1972, and an M.A. and Ph.D. in 1975 and 1978, respectively, from Cornell University. He has been at Clark [University] since that time and is also affiliated with the program in Peace Studies… His current research focuses on the U.S. response to radical Islam between the 1967 Six Day War and the 1979 Iranian Revolution. " From:
	http://www.clarku.edu/academiccatalog/facultybio.cfm?id=362#ixzz0r1fh1cQh
Bibliography	No.
Index	No.

Notes	Footnotes (111).
Photographs	No.
Appendix	No.
Tables	No.
Key Words	Presidency, Middle East, Foreign Relations, Cold War
Other Notes	
Annotation	Though contemporary observers and some diplomatic historians consider Eisenhower's handling of the 1958 crisis in the Middle East to be the president's finest hour, Little argues that "the short-term risks and the long-term costs" were far higher than the Eisenhower Administration realized. Short-term risks included the risk to U.S. Marines in Beirut. Long-term costs included setting a dangerous precedent that future U.S. presidents would carry into Vietnam, including "emphasizing the importance of the United State's credibility as a guarantor…, misrepresenting Third World nationalism as Soviet inspired, and… waging what amounted to a limited but undeclared presidential war." Further, the entire crisis could have been avoided had not personal connections between the Eisenhower administration and pro-Western Lebanese leaders complicated matters.

246. Little, Douglas. "The Making of a Special Relationship: The United States and Israel, 1957-68." *International Journal of Middle East Studies* 25, no. 4 (November 1993): 563-585.

Author Info	See information in Entry #245.
Bibliography	No.
Index	No.
Notes	Endnotes (118).
Photographs	No.
Appendix	No.
Tables	No.
Key Words	Presidency, Foreign Relations, Middle East, Cold War
Other Notes	
Annotation	Traces America's relations with Israel through three presidential administrations: Eisenhower, Kennedy, and Johnson. Then-newly declassified materials showed that the beginnings of a strong US-Israeli relationship were forged, not with Johnson's Administration, but with Eisenhower's and Kennedy's Administrations. Both believed that a strong Israel would be a powerful asset in America's fight against communism and Arab nationalism in the Middle East, whereas a weak Israel might develop nuclear weapons.

247. Loayza, Matthew. "An 'Aladdin's Lamp' for Free Enterprise: Eisenhower, Fiscal Conservatism, and Latin American Nationalism, 1953-61." *Diplomacy & Statecraft* 14, no. 3 (September 2003): 83-105.

Author Info	Teaches at Minnesota State University. Fields of Study are U.S. History, Foreign Relations, and Cold War. Ph.D. from Purdue University (1999). http://sbs.mnsu.edu/history/faculty/loayza.html
Bibliography	No.
Index	No.
Notes	Endnotes (37).
Photographs	No.
Appendix	No.
Tables	No.
Key Words	Presidency, Foreign Relations, Economics
Other Notes	
Annotation	Explores the Eisenhower Administration's economic policies towards Latin America and the Administration's understanding of the potential threat posed by economic nationalism. A strict believer in fiscal conservatism, Eisenhower advocated private capital development in the region over U.S. foreign aid, believing that: "private capital had the power to accelerate Latin America's economic development; more pressing needs in other regions of the world precluded spending large sums of U.S. public funds in Latin America; and agreeing to Latin American aid requests would saddle the United States with perpetual economic obligations that would drag down the economy." Because of the importance the Administration placed on the flow of private capital into the region, it opposed economic nationalism but was unable to successfully thwart it.

248.   Lombardo, Johannes R. "Eisenhower, The British and the Security of Hong Kong, 1953-60." *Diplomacy & Statecraft* 9, no. 3 (November 1998): 134-153.

Author Info	The author also published "A Mission of Espionage, Intelligence and Psychological Operations: The American Consulate in Hong Kong, 1949-64," 64-81 in *Intelligence and National Security*
Bibliography	No.
Index	No.
Notes	Endnotes (66).
Photographs	No.
Appendix	No.
Tables	No.
Key Words	Presidency, Cold War, Foreign Relations
Other Notes	
Annotation	Traces the evolution of America's commitment to the security of British Hong Kong over Eisenhower's two terms as President. Lombardo examines multiple contributing factors for America's gradual increase of commitment, including: "the intensity of the conflict between Washington and Beijing, the American desire for a strong Allied effort against Communism, American perceptions of the threat to Hong Kong, the colony's increased value to the U.S. as an intelligence 'listening post' and a symbol of the free world, the apparent

resolve of the British to defend Hong Kong, and the state of Anglo-American relations." He finds that, "the most significant determinant was the conflict between the UK and U.S. approaches to the [People's Republic of China]" and that America's "special relationship" with the British was an important element in the countries' formal and informal agreements regarding the security of Hong Kong.

M's

249.   MacKenzie, S. P. "Essay and Reflection: On the 'Other Losses' Debate." *International History Review* 14, no. 4 (December 1992): 717-731.

Author Info	Professor of History at the University of South Carolina. "Teaches military history, with special emphasis on war and society in the modern age outside of the United States." http://www.cas.sc.edu/hist/faculty/mackenzie.html
Bibliography	No.
Index	No.
Notes	Footnotes (mis-numbered 37).
Photographs	No.
Appendix	No.
Tables	No.
Key Words	Military- WWII
Other Notes	
Annotation	MacKenzie summarizes the debate among historians surrounding the accuracy of James Bacque's *Other Losses* (1989), which argues that Eisenhower had engineered the deaths of almost one million German POWs at the end of WWII. MacKenzie finds that: "It is from basic differences in the outlook of the people concerned that the *Other Losses* debate really springs," and that conclusions drawn from statistical and non-statistical evidence are to some degree dependent on the viewpoint of the historian analyzing the evidence. He postulates that the ultimate consensus will be that Bacque's conclusions rest "on shaky foundations" but that the book will continue to intrigue the public because parts of the book, including descriptions of camp conditions, are undisputed and because it is an emotionally charged read.

250.   Maddock, Shane. "The Fourth Country Problem: Eisenhower's Nuclear Nonproliferation Policy." *Presidential Studies Quarterly* 28, no. 3 (Summer, 1998): 553-572.

Author Info	Professor of History at Stonehill College. "Professor Maddock's general area of interest is Cold War America, both domestically and internationally. More specifically, he is interested in the interaction between culture (both popular and elite) and politics during this period." http://www.stonehill.edu/x8637.xml

Bibliography	No.
Index	No.
Notes	Endnotes (112).
Photographs	No.
Appendix	No.
Tables	No.
Key Words	Presidency, Cold War, Foreign Relations, NATO, Nuclear, Military Policy, Technology
Other Notes	
Annotation	Maddock examines Eisenhower's nuclear policies over his two terms in office and finds that: "Despite Eisenhower's desire to control the arms race, he left office having done more to encourage nuclear proliferation than to prevent it." Maddock cites several reasons for this, including Cold War tensions and suspicions preventing the U.S. and the Soviet Union from agreeing on nonproliferation, the complicated, multi-country acceleration of the nuclear arms race, and some failures on Eisenhower's part, including his failure to view nuclear spread from a non-American perspective, his lack of knowledge concerning the dangers of sharing of nuclear technology through Atoms for Peace aid and NATO, and his problems with bureaucracy.

251. Maranto, Robert. "The Administrative Strategies of Republican Presidents from Eisenhower to Reagan." *Presidential Studies Quarterly* 23, no. 4 (Fall, 1993): 683-697.

Author Info	"21st Century Chair in Leadership at the Department of Education Reform at the University of Arkansas, and previously served as associate professor of political science and public administration at Villanova University. He has taught at Lafayette College, James Madison, and Southern Mississippi, and served President Clinton's administration." (http://www.uark.edu/ua/der/People/maranto.php)
Bibliography	No.
Index	No.
Notes	Endnotes (61).
Illustrations	No.
Photographs	No.
Appendix	No.
Tables	Yes (4).
Key Words	Presidency, Politics, White House
Other Notes	
Annotation	Maranto outlines the efforts of presidents Eisenhower, Nixon, and Reagan to manage bureaucracy, with the heaviest focus on Reagan. He finds that all three men, "tried to foster unity among political appointees to dominate the executive at the expense of career bureaucrats and outside political interest groups," but that their success rate at doing so differed. Of Eisenhower's attempts, he concludes that his Administration "fashioned a coherent strategy, but was limited by the popularity of the New Deal programs and the

Democrats' success in congressional elections."

252.   Marchio, Jim. "Resistance Potential and Rollback: US Intelligence and the Eisenhower
       Administration's Policies Toward Eastern Europe, 1953-56." *Intelligence & National
       Security* 10, no. 2 (April 1995): 219-241.

Author Info	"James D. Marchio serves in the Office of the Director of National Intelligence. He is a retired Air Force officer who served in a range of intelligence assignments, including chief of the Defense Intelligence Agency's Russia, Eurasia & Africa Office. He is a Studies in Intelligence award winner and frequent contributor to historical journals." (https://www.cia.gov/library/center-for-the-study-of-intelligence/csi-publications/csi-studies/studies/vol51no4/).
Bibliography	No.
Index	No.
Notes	Endnotes (96).
Illustrations	No.
Photographs	No.
Appendix	No.
Tables	No.
Key Words	Presidency, Cold War, Military Policy
Other Notes	
Annotation	Article examines the importance of intelligence in the national security state, beginning in 1947. Marchio finds that intelligence's "role in shaping policy, directly and indirectly, was clearly evident during the Eisenhower administration's first term." Intelligence informed policy makers that: "Despite widespread dissatisfaction, the Communist hold on Eastern Europe remained firm," and that resistance would need outside assistance to achieve its goals. Information, in the form of intelligence and vulnerability studies, was available to policy makers and used, though used at varying levels within in the Administration, and sometimes only indirectly. U.S. intelligence "assessments of East European resistance potential and satellite vulnerabilities" did shape policy-maker's perceptions, policy objectives, and the way these policy objectives were pursued. Marchio finds, however, that: "Intelligence helped shape the world view of policy-makers; yet intelligence was affected as well by the world view, beliefs, and experiences of those it served."

253.   Marchio, James. "The Planning Coordination Group: Bureaucratic Casualty in the Cold
       War Campaign to Exploit Soviet-Bloc Vulnerabilities." *Journal of Cold War Studies* 4,
       no. 4 (Fall 2002): 3-28.

Author Info	See information in Entry #252.
Bibliography	No.
Index	No.

Notes	Footnotes (105).
Photographs	No.
Appendix	No.
Tables	No.
Key Words	Presidency, Foreign Relations, Cold War
Other Notes	
Annotation	Marchio describes the short life of the Planning Coordination Group (PCG) and examines why it was established, what it did, why it failed, and what insight it provides into Eisenhower's policies towards the Soviet bloc. He finds that it was formed to overcome bureaucratic infighting in the waging of psychological warfare against the Soviet bloc and contributed advice to senior officials on how best to wage the Cold War. It failed, however, for a number of reasons, including: its lack of a clear mission, structure, and resources; its failure to overcome the bureaucracy it was meant to unite; a clash of egos and personalities; and a changing international environment. The PCG "reflected the contradictions in the administration's policies toward the Soviet bloc," and a "disconnect between the ends the Eisenhower administration sought in Eastern Europe and the means it was willing to use in their pursuit." Finally, the case study of the PCG, "casts doubt on Eisenhower's support for psychological warfare."

254. Marsh, Steven. "Continuity and Change: Reinterpreting the Policies of the Truman and Eisenhower Administrations toward Iran, 1950–1954." *Journal of Cold War Studies* 7, no. 3 (Summer 2005): 79-123.

Author Info	At Cardiff School of European Studies. "Principal research interests lie in post World War Two international relations, specifically American foreign policy, Anglo-American relations and European Union foreign and security policies." http://www.cardiff.ac.uk/euros/contactsandpeople/profiles/marshsi.html
Bibliography	No.
Index	No.
Notes	Footnotes (171).
Photographs	No.
Appendix	No.
Tables	No.
Key Words	Presidency, Foreign Relations, Middle East
Other Notes	Substantially similar to Marsh's 2003 article, "The United States, Iran and Operation 'Ajax': Inverting Interpretative Orthodoxy."
Annotation	Arguing against the traditional interpretation that America's policy towards Iran changed because of the transition between Truman's Administration and Eisenhower's Administration, Marsh asserts that there was great continuity between the administrations and that this continuity was attributable to strongly shared principles and assumptions which guided both administrations. He argues that: "Greater U.S. assertiveness in Iran resulted not from the change in administration but from a process spurred by the ineffectiveness of U.S. policy

as of early 1952, by waning British power, and by the systematic closure of options in Iran that led to the ascendancy of policymakers favoring a stronger U.S. approach." Finally, he argues that the coup orchestrated by the Eisenhower Administration is best explained by policy continuity rather than change, stating that "the Eisenhower administration's quest to overthrow the regime in Iran was the consequence not of a random choice but of its decision to stick with its predecessor's policy until a coup seemed the only remaining option."

255.   Marsh, Steve. "The United States, Iran and Operation 'Ajax': Inverting Interpretative Orthodoxy." *Middle Eastern Studies* 39, no. 3 (July 2003): 1-38.

Author Info	See information in Entry #254.
Bibliography	No.
Index	No.
Notes	Endnotes (169).
Photographs	No.
Appendix	No.
Tables	No.
Key Words	Presidency, Foreign Relations, Middle East
Other Notes	Substantially similar to Marsh's 2005 article (Entry #254).
Annotation	Marsh inverts the interpretative orthodoxy of the 1953 Iranian coup, which holds that the coup was a result of a policy change stemming from the transfer of administrations from Truman to Eisenhower. He argues instead, that it was a result of policy continuity between the administrations: "Ultimately the stark choice between orchestrating a military coup or passively abandoning Iran to communism was thrust upon [the Eisenhower Administration] by the systematic closure of all other policy options in Iran that were consonant with the objectives, assumptions, and complicating factors that it shared so strongly with the Truman administration."

256.   Marston, Adrian. "Did President Eisenhower Have Crohn's Disease?" *Journal of Medical Biography* 10, no. 4 (November 2002): 237-239.

Author Info	Emeritus Consultant Surgeon, Middlesex Hospital in London.
Bibliography	References.
Index	No.
Notes	No.
Photographs	Yes (1).
Appendix	No.
Tables	No.
Key Words	Presidency, Personal Life
Other Notes	
Annotation	After a review of Ike's available medical history, Marston concludes that: "Although previous authors acquainted with the President's illness have been

quite confident of the diagnosis of Crohn's disease, it is quite possible that this was an ischaemic stricture, secondary to hypotension and peripheral vasoconstriction resulting from his myocardial infarction."

257. Martin, Don T. "Eisenhower and the Politics of Federal Aid to Education: The Watershed Years, 1953-1961." *Journal of the Midwest History of Education Society* 25, no. 1 (January 1998): 7-12.

Author Info	Associate Professor Administrative and Policy Studies at the University of Pittsburg. https://www.education.pitt.edu/people/DonMartin/index.aspx
Bibliography	List of references at end of article.
Index	No.
Notes	Internal citations.
Photographs	No.
Appendix	No.
Tables	No.
Key Words	Presidency
Other Notes	
Annotation	States that the "Eisenhower years constitutes a watershed for federal aid to education policies." Discusses Eisenhower's conflict between his fiscal conservatism and his recognition of the poor condition of American education in the 1950s. Also discusses the effects of Sputnik on the federal government's willingness to spend money on education.

258. Mayer, Michael S. "The Eisenhower Administration and the Desegregation of Washington, D.C." *Journal of Policy History* 3, no. 1 (January 1991): 24-41.

Author Info	History professor at the University of Montana.
Bibliography	No.
Index	No.
Notes	Endnotes (46).
Photographs	No.
Appendix	No.
Tables	No.
Key Words	Presidency, Civil Rights, Domestic Policy
Other Notes	
Annotation	Mayer argues that the liberal bias of most historians has resulted in a failure to acknowledge the Civil Rights achievements of Eisenhower, including his work to desegregate Washington DC. Although his goals were limited, and his approach gradualist, Eisenhower's Administration made real progress in desegregating the nation's capital and, "[t]aken in the context of his time, Eisenhower's efforts to desegregate Washington were notable, and his undertaking deserves more recognition than historians have accorded it."

259.   McCoy, Donald R. "Eisenhower and Truman: Their Flawed Relationship." *Midwest Quarterly* 34, no. 1 (September 1992): 30-41.

Author Info	Was a University Distinguished Professor of History at the University of Kansas and author of *Quest and Response: Minority Rights during the Truman Administration.*
Bibliography	Short paragraph regarding sources at the end of the article.
Index	No.
Notes	No.
Photographs	No.
Appendix	No.
Tables	No.
Key Words	Military- WWII, Presidency, Personal Life
Other Notes	
Annotation	In this article, McCoy recounts the disintegration of the relationship between Truman and Eisenhower. Though it was never warm, it had been one of fruitful collaboration and some degree of respect. The temperaments of the two men and politics, especially during Ike's election campaign for his first term, drove a wedge between them.

260.   McIntosh, David. "In the Shadow of Giants: U.S. Policy Toward Small Nations: The Cases of Lebanon, Costa Rica, and Austria in the Eisenhower Years." *Contemporary Austrian Studies* 4, (January 1996): 222-279.

Author Info	
Bibliography	No.
Index	No.
Notes	Endnotes (193).
Photographs	No.
Appendix	No.
Tables	No.
Key Words	Presidency, Foreign Relations, Cold War
Other Notes	
Annotation	McIntosh uses three case studies—Lebanon, Costa Rica, and Austria—to show that, "Washington's preoccupation with avoiding psychological setbacks on the battlefield of world opinion compelled U.S. policy makers to oppose all foreign developments, even in small nations like [the aforementioned countries] that might be viewed elsewhere as a gain for international communism." The case of Lebanon shows "that the administration sometimes jeopardized U.S. interests in states of secondary importance in order to forestall psychological defeats in more vital theaters." In Costa Rica, the U.S. intervened to "ensure the credibility of American democracy in the region." Austria, however, "shows that top policy makers in the Eisenhower administration... could, even when viewing a small country that lay squarely

in the crossfire of U.S.-Soviet image-warfare, free their decision-making from the influence of knee-jerk anti-communism and world opinion." Taken together, the three case studies show that: "Degrees of manipulation and accommodation occurred on both sides, and the balance of benefits varied among the cases." Article is a shortened version of the thesis McIntosh submitted to Harvard College's Department of History in 1994.

261.   McManus, James. "Presidential Poker." *American History* 45, no. 1 (April 2010): 46-51.

Author Info	"James McManus is an author and professional poker player. His most recent book is "Cowboys Full" an account of poker's role in American history. His bestselling memoir, "Positively Fifth Street" was based on his coverage of a Las Vegas trial and his participation in the 2000 World Series of Poker. His journalism has appeared in *The New York Times*, *Harper's Magazine*, and *The New Yorker*. A teacher at The Art Institute of Chicago, he lives in Kenilworth, Illinois." http://bigthink.com/jamesmcmanus
Bibliography	No.
Index	No.
Notes	No.
Photographs	Yes (8).
Appendix	No.
Tables	No.
Key Words	Early Life, Military- Pre WWII, Personal Life
Other Notes	
Annotation	In this brief article, McManus discusses the poker playing of FDR, Truman, Eisenhower, and Nixon. Of Eisenhower, he states that as a young man, Eisenhower used poker winnings to supplement his income and even to buy Mamie her engagement ring. Despite his love of the game, he quit playing as an officer, because, McManus quotes Ike: "it had become clear that it was no game to play in the Army."

262.   Medhurst, Martin J. "Atoms for Peace and Nuclear Hegemony: The Rhetorical Structure of a Cold War Campaign." *Armed Forces & Society* 23, no. 4 (Summer 1997): 571-593.

Author Info	Distinguished Professor of Rhetoric and Communication and Professor of Political Science at Baylor University. Published extensively. CV at http://www.baylor.edu/content/services/document.php?id=50268+
Bibliography	No.
Index	No.
Notes	Endnotes (48).
Photographs	No.
Appendix	No.
Tables	No.
Key Words	Presidency, Speechmaking, Politics, Cold War, Foreign Relations

Other Notes

Annotation   Medhurst argues that Eisenhower's Atoms for Peace speech was "a carefully designed—and highly successful—component of the basic defense and foreign policy stance of the Eisenhower administration," and that it "contributed directly to the implementation of the New Look doctrine." The author focuses on the military/security dimensions of the Atoms for Peace campaign and argues that it, "functioned rhetorically to: 1) divert the attention of both foreign and domestic audiences from the ongoing nuclear arms buildup; 2) persuade the U.S. Congress to amend the Atomic Energy Act of 1946, a necessary prelude to the nuclearization of NATO forces; and 3) invite foreign governments to request U.S. technological assistance in atomic energy in return for certain raw materials—primarily uranium and thorium—as well as access to their markets."

263.   Medhurst, Martin J. "Eisenhower and the Crusade for Freedom: The Rhetorical Origins of a Cold War Campaign." *Presidential Studies Quarterly* 27, no. 4 (Fall 1997): 646-661.

Author Info	See information in Entry #262.
Bibliography	No.
Index	No.
Notes	Endnotes (33).
Photographs	No.
Appendix	No.
Tables	No.
Key Words	Foreign Relations, Politics, Cold War, Speechmaking
Other Notes	

Annotation   Medhurst examines the rhetorical origins of the Crusade for Freedom (1948-1950) with a focus on the involvement of Eisenhower. He finds that the idea for the Crusade sprung from a variety of interrelated factors, including fear of the spread of Communism and a commitment to psychological warfare. The purpose of the Crusade was to create a "voice of opposition to the Communist governments," under the "guise of a bipartisan citizens' committee… whose only motive, ostensibly, was to promote democracy in central-east Europe." The Crusade involved both private and public rhetorical resources and the "rhetorical agent who most clearly linked the private rhetorics to the public sphere was [Eisenhower]." Medhurst analyzes Ike's September 4, 1950 address in Denver to launch the Crusade and finds that Ike's speech was "an archetypal example of Cold War discourse."

264.   Medhurst, Martin J. "Reconceptualizing Rhetorical History: Eisenhower's Farewell Address." *Quarterly Journal of Speech* 80, no. 2 (May 1994): 195-218.

Author Info	See information in Entry #262.
Bibliography	No.
Index	No.

Notes	Endnotes (74).
Photographs	No.
Appendix	No.
Tables	Yes (1).
Key Words	Presidency, Speechmaking
Other Notes	
Annotation	Medhurst provides a revisionist reading of Eisenhower's Farewell Address, the theme of which he finds to be "balance" and not a warning against the military industrial complex. He characterizes the speech as "a carefully planned piece of strategic discourse intended to accomplish several goals simultaneously." These goals were: "to restate the basic themes and philosophies that had characterized Eisenhower's public life; to link the president historically, conceptually, and attitudinally to the persona of George Washington; and to advance, under the rubric of a warning about the military-industrial complex, an indirect and implicit critique of [Kennedy] while making a direct and explicit appeal for citizen involvement to thwart the designs of the newly elected administration." The author provides a rhetorical analysis of the speech and shows that Eisenhower's warning against the military-industrial complex was not new to this speech, was balanced with recognition of the need for defense spending, and was intended as an example of his overall theme of balance. Argues that Ike was a "strategic communicator".

265. Medhurst, Martin J. "Robert L. Scott plays Dwight D. Eisenhower." *Quarterly Journal of Speech* 81, no. 4 (November 1995): 502-506.

Author Info	See information in Entry #262.
Bibliography	No.
Index	No.
Notes	Endnotes (4).
Photographs	No.
Appendix	No.
Tables	No.
Key Words	Presidency, Speechmaking
Other Notes	
Annotation	Responds to Scott's critique of Medhurst's earlier essay in his article, "Eisenhower's Farewell Address: Response to Medhurst." *Quarterly Journal of Speech* 81, no. 4 (November 1995): 496-501. Medhurst states that Scott's argument (that Ike's Farewell Address was either about the military-industrial complex (MIC), or if about balance as Medhurst had claimed, poorly written as it was widely interpreted to be about the MIC) is fundamentally flawed as the speech was not widely understood to be about the MIC by Ike's contemporaries. Additionally, Medhurst defends his characterization of "balance" as the theme generally and clarifies his statements about Ike's warnings to and about Kennedy and his administration. Medhurst also responds to and engages with Scott regarding ideas of rhetorical criticism.

266.   Medhurst, Martin J. "Text and Context in the 1952 Presidential Campaign: Eisenhower's 'I Shall Go to Korea' Speech." *Presidential Studies Quarterly* 30, no. 3 (Sep, 2000): 464-484.

Author Info	See information in Entry #262.
Bibliography	List of references.
Index	No.
Notes	Internal citations.
Photographs	No.
Appendix	No.
Tables	No.
Key Words	Presidency, Speechmaking, Politics, Cold War, Korea, Elections, Foreign Relations
Other Notes	
Annotation	Medhurst argues that Ike's "I Shall Go to Korea" speech resonated with voters not only because of Eisenhower's military background but because of four overlapping contextual discourses—the discourses of the cold war, Korea, the Eisenhower persona, and foreign policy—"that shaped the symbolic environment within which that pledge was heard." Medhurst also discusses the dramatic, courtroom structure of the speech, and provides a history of its drafting.

267.   Melissen, Jan. "The Politics of US Missile Deployment in Britain, 1955-59." *Storia delle Relazioni Internazionali* 13, no. 1 (1998): 151-185.

Author Info	"Prof. Jan Melissen is Head of Clingendael's Diplomatic Studies Programme and Professor of Diplomacy at the University of Antwerp (Belgium). He is founding co-editor of peer-reviewed *The Hague Journal of Diplomacy* and editor of the Diplomatic Studies Series... He has a wide-ranging research interest in contemporary diplomacy. Among his seven books are... *The New Public Diplomacy* (Palgrave-Macmillan, 2005 and 2007), which was translated [into] three other languages... Before moving to the Clingendael Institute Jan Melissen was Director of the Centre for the Study of Diplomacy at the University of Leicester (UK). He graduated in politics and international relations at the University of Amsterdam and holds a doctorate from Groningen University." http://www.clingendael.nl/staff/?id=47
Bibliography	No.
Index	No.
Notes	Footnotes (70).
Photographs	No.
Appendix	No.
Tables	No.
Key Words	Presidency, Foreign Relations, Cold War, Military Policy, Technology

Other Notes

Annotation   Examines the political, technological, economic, and military factors that drove the discussions and negotiations of the United States and the United Kingdom in the conceptualization and development of intermediate-range ballistic missiles, Thor missiles, based in Britain. The negotiations over the missiles lasted over a year and ultimately required concessions from both the British and the Americans. The Soviet Union's launch of Sputnik greatly impacted these negotiations as it increased pressure on the United States and gave Britain greater bargaining power. Ultimately, the Thor missiles were based in Britain but the warheads remained under U.S. control.

268.   Metz, Steven. "Eisenhower and the Planning of American Grand Strategy." *Journal of Strategic Studies* 14, no. 1 (February 1991): 49-71.

Author Info   "Dr. Steven Metz is Chairman of the Regional Strategy and Planning Department and Research Professor of National Security Affairs at the Strategic Studies Institute. He has been with SSI since 1993, previously serving as Henry L. Stimson Professor of Military Studies and SSI's Director of Research. Dr. Metz has also been on the faculty of the Air War College, the U.S. Army Command and General Staff College, and several universities… He is the author of more than 100 publications including articles in journals such as Washington Quarterly, Joint Force Quarterly, The National Interest, Defence Studies, and Current History….Dr. Metz holds a Ph.D. from the Johns Hopkins University." http://www.strategicstudiesinstitute.army.mil/pubs/people.cfm?authorID=22

Bibliography	No.
Index	No.
Notes	Endnotes (137).
Photographs	No.
Appendix	No.
Tables	No.
Key Words	Presidency, Cold War, Foreign Relations

Other Notes

Annotation   Metz analyzes Eisenhower's New Look policy and finds it to be a partial success. Metz finds that it "was not markedly worse than the strategies which preceded and followed it, but then again, it was not fundamentally different." He argues that the New Look's focus on "managerial features such as solvency" as opposed to "entrepreneurial features" such as vision and creativity, made it inflexible and "meant that the New Look postponed difficult strategic decisions rather than confronting them."

269.   Miller, William Lee. "Two Moralities." *Miller Center Journal* 2, (January 1995): 19-39.

Author Info   "Scholar in Ethics and Institutions at the Miller Center. From 1992 until his retirement in 1999, Mr. Miller was Thomas C. Sorensen Professor of Political and Social Thought and Director of the Program in Political and Social Thought at the University of Virginia. He was professor of religious studies from 1982 to 1999, and chaired the Department of Rhetoric and Communication Studies from 1982 to 1990.... [He] served as a speech writer for U.S. presidential candidate Adlai Stevenson's campaign in 1956." From http://millercenter.org/about/staff/miller

Bibliography	No.
Index	No.
Notes	No.
Photographs	No.
Appendix	No.
Tables	No.
Key Words	Presidency, Election, Politics, Personal Life, Religion
Other Notes	
Annotation	Miller describes the similarities in the moral groundings of Eisenhower and Truman, including their Midwestern backgrounds, shared sense of duty and loyalty, and firm religious beliefs. He notes that despite their similarities, "in their most intense encounter with each other, in the events surrounding the 1952 campaign, they would severely disapprove of each other." For example, Eisenhower faulted Truman for scandals during his presidency, and Truman was very critical of Eisenhower for yielding to Senator McCarthy by dropping a paragraph from a Wisconsin speech which praised Marshall.

270.   Millett, Allan R. "Dwight D. Eisenhower and the Korean War: Cautionary Tale and Hopeful Precedent." *Journal of American-East Asian Relations* 10, no. 3/4 (Fall-Winter 2001): 155-174.

Author Info	Faculty Emeritus of military history at The Ohio State University.
Bibliography	No.
Index	No.
Notes	Footnotes (37).
Photographs	No.
Appendix	No.
Tables	No.
Key Words	Presidency, Korea, Military Policy, Cold War, Foreign Relations
Other Notes	
Annotation	Millett traces Eisenhower's involvement with the Korean War from its beginning to its end. He finds that the, "war never became a defining experience for [Ike], nor did it play an inordinate role in his foreign and defense policies," however, he does note that, "the resolution of the Korean War and the development of the Eisenhower administration's national security policy ran in parallel courses in 1953." Millett finds that "the core lesson of the Korean War was how little personal influence Eisenhower had on the war's causes, conduct, and consequences." He concludes that the legacy of Korea, "combined active policies like mutual security agreements and military

assistance with negative lessons on the costs of putting the American armed forces into combat in regions of national interest, but not national survival."

271. Milum, Betty. "Eisenhower, ALA, and the Selection of L. Quincy Mumford." *Libraries & Culture*, 30, No. 1 (Winter, 1995): 26-56.

Author Info	Faculty Emeritus at Ohio State University Libraries.
Bibliography	No.
Index	No.
Notes	Endnotes (132).
Photographs	Yes (2).
Appendix	No.
Tables	No.
Key Words	Presidency, Politics
Other Notes	
Annotation	Milum chronicles how Eisenhower came to a decision to appoint L. Quincy Mumford as Librarian of Congress in 1954. Eisenhower "did seek the involvement of the library profession, he did give some serious consideration to two librarians on the American Library Association's preferred list, and he did ultimately appoint [Mumford], thus continuing a truce in the recurring debate between presidents and professional librarians in the selection of the Librarians of Congress." Milum provides biographical information on the three other strong candidates for the position, and the political and/or personal reasons they were not chosen and Mumford was selected.

272. Moores, Simon. "'Neutral on our Side': US Policy towards Sweden during the Eisenhower Administration." *Cold War History* 2, no. 3 (April 2002): 29-62.

Author Info	"Dr Simon Moores is widely recognised as one of the UK's most respected technology columnists and broadcasters." http://www.bigwales.com/398227.htm See also http://www.zentelligence.com/mall/Zentelligence/page4.htm
Bibliography	No.
Index	No.
Notes	Endnotes (109).
Photographs	No.
Appendix	No.
Tables	No.
Key Words	Presidency, Foreign Relations, Cold War
Other Notes	
Annotation	Moores argues that rather than Sweden's military non-aligned status being a source of concern for Eisenhower, "Washington wholly accepted Swedish armed neutrality and regarded it as the policy that best served U.S. aims." He draws a distinction between "political Sweden" and "military Sweden":

"Whilst the former pronounced its neutrality, eschewed the notion of joining a military alliance, and called for a relaxation in tensions between the two blocs, the latter remained throughout the Eisenhower period the West's neutral first life of defense in the Scandinavian region." U.S. decision makers were aware of this distinction and accepted it as Sweden's armed neutrality helped to "keep Scandinavia an area of low-level superpower tension."

273. Morgan, Thomas. "The Making of a General: Ike, the Tank, and the Interwar Years." *On Point: The Journal of Army History* 9, no. 2 (March 2003): 11-15.

Author Info   LTC Thomas Morgan, USA-Ret.
Bibliography   There is a paragraph on further reading at the end of the article.
Index   No.
Notes   No.
Photographs   Yes (5).
Appendix   No.
Tables   No.
Key Words   Military—B/w the Wars, Personal Life
Other Notes
Annotation   Morgan surveys Ike's professional, and to a lesser extent his personal, life between the Wars and argues that: "During those years, Eisenhower was sorely tested and strengthened by adversity. These trials and tribulations, however, prepared him for [WWII and the Cold War]." Morgan discusses Ike's work with tanks and his relationships with Patton, Conner, and Marshall.

274. Morris, Kenneth E. and Barry Schwartz, "Why They liked Ike: Tradition, Crisis, and Heroic Leadership, *The Sociological Quarterly*, 34, no. 1 (Spring, 1993): 133-151.

Author Info   Morris was in the Department of Sociology at the University of Georgia. Schwartz is an Emeritus faculty at the University of Georgia in the Sociology Department.
Bibliography   List of references.
Index   No.
Notes   Endnotes (8).
Photographs   No.
Appendix   No.
Tables   No.
Key Words   Presidency
Other Notes
Annotation   Authors examine why Eisenhower was so popular during his lifetime and why his popularity declined so sharply after his death. They find that "Eisenhower's achievements and public conduct resonated with the concerns and values of his generation," and that this contributed to his popularity. Eisenhower symbolized three important traditional values—"liberty, equality,

and community"—that drew the public to him. After Ike's death, subsequent generations' views of the 1950s as a time of peace and prosperity (as opposed to the turbulent 1940s and 1960s) "rendered Eisenhower dull and forgettable."

275. Morrison, Robert. "Faith Fights Communism: The United States and Islam in Saudi Arabia During the Cold War." *Journal of the North Carolina Association of Historians* 17, (April 2009): 81-113.

Author Info	Was at the University of North Carolina, Wilmington.
Bibliography	No.
Index	No.
Notes	Footnotes (79).
Photographs	No.
Appendix	No.
Tables	No.
Key Words	Presidency, Foreign Relations, Middle East, Economics
Other Notes	
Annotation	Morrison, "examines the U.S. interpretation and mobilization of Islam in Saudi Arabia as a bulwark against the spread of Soviet influence in the geographic Middle East." He finds that the tactic, on the surface, appeared to be a success as, for the most part, communism failed to make major inroads in the Middle East. Other factors, however, especially economic, played a major role in the relationship between the U.S. and Saudi Arabia during this time. Morrison also notes that the American understanding of Islam was, "at the very least, misinformed." American officials in the Eisenhower administration, and Eisenhower himself, "saw Islam as a unified global phenomenon rather than a complicated set of religious beliefs… [and] mistakenly assumed that Islam was the dominant force in every Muslim's life."

N's

276. Nadaner, Jeffrey M. "Strife Among Friends and Foes: The 1958 Anglo-American Military Interventions in the Middle East." *UCLA Historical Journal* 17, (January 1997): 82-123.

Author Info	In 1997 he was a John M. Olin Foundation doctoral fellow in diplomacy at the Yale University Department of History. His dissertation is entitled "Shifting Sands: John F. Kennedy and the Middle East."
Bibliography	No.
Index	No.
Notes	Yes (160).
Photographs	No.

Appendix	No.
Tables	No.
Key Words	Presidency, Middle East, Cold War, Military Policy
Other Notes	
Annotation	Nadaner explores lessons learned during the 1958 Middle East crisis, which "marked an important stage in United States' relations with Great Britain and with the Arab world." He examines events in Lebanon, Jordan, and Iraq and finds that over the course of the crisis, the U.S. became more discerning of the differences between communism and Arab nationalism than it had been. The Eisenhower Administration, "became less prone to label a government or individual anti-Western by shallow and mistaken criteria," and began to demand less public show of support by pro-Western Arab states. He argues that the Eisenhower Doctrine "died a quiet death during the '58 Crisis."

277.   Nash, Philip. "Jumping Jupiters: The US Search for IRBM Host Countries in NATO, 1957-59." *Diplomacy & Statecraft* 6, no. 3 (November 1995): 753-786.

Author Info	Assistant Professor of History at Pennsylvania State Shenango. CV available at http://www.personal.psu.edu/pxn4/
Bibliography	No.
Index	No.
Notes	Endnotes (56).
Photographs	No.
Appendix	No.
Tables	No.
Key Words	Presidency, Military Policy, NATO, Technology, Foreign Relations, Cold War
Other Notes	
Annotation	Nash analyzes America's search for IRBM host countries after the 1957 NATO Heads of Government meeting in Paris; the search, which took 22 months to complete, resulted, in addition to the 60 Thors in Britain, 30 Jupiters in Italy and 15 in Turkey. Nash concludes that the search took so long, despite the desire for a speedy resolution on the part of the U.S. for multiple reasons, the most basic of which was that, "the 1957 NATO offer necessitated bilateral agreements between independent, sovereign states." On the European side, domestic politics and self-interest exacerbated delays. On the American side, the tactic of pursuing host countries sequentially rather than simultaneously, multi-departmental involvement, and funding difficulties complicated the process. Nash questions why the strategy went forward despite the doubts of Eisenhower's Administration of the efficacy of the program. He posits that the U.S. did not want to abandon the program because it did not want to appear to be giving into Soviet pressure and did not want to threaten its credibility in NATO.

278.   Nichols, David A. "'The Showpiece of Our Nation': Dwight D. Eisenhower and the Desegregation of the District of Columbia." *Washington History* 16, no. 2, (Fall/Winter, 2004/2005): 44-65.

Author Info	"David A. Nichols, a leading expert on the Eisenhower presidency, holds a Ph.D. in history from William and Mary. A former professor and academic dean at Southwestern College, he is the author of A Matter of Justice: Eisenhower and the Beginning of the Civil Rights Revolution, and Lincoln and the Indians. He lives in Winfield, Kansas." http://authors.simonandschuster.com/David-A-Nichols/42263792. See also Entry #19.
Bibliography	No.
Index	No.
Notes	Endnotes (74).
Photographs	Yes (8).
Appendix	No.
Tables	No.
Key Words	Presidency, Civil Rights, Domestic Policy
Other Notes	
Annotation	Chronicles Eisenhower's efforts to desegregate the District of Columbia from 1953-1954. Eisenhower focused on what he believed he had the legal authority to accomplish as President and his "determined leadership… produced significant civil rights advances in D.C. in the areas of public accommodations, fair employment practices, and school desegregation". Nichols also addresses Ike's appointment of pro-civil rights men to important positions, including the Supreme Court, his reaction to *Brown vs. Board of Education* and the resultant push to desegregate D.C. schools, and his handling of political issues due to his desegregation efforts.

279.   Nolan, Cathal J. "The Last Hurrah of Conservative Isolationism: Eisenhower, Congress, and the Bricker Amendment." *Presidential Studies Quarterly* 22, no. 2 (Spring 1992): 337-349.

Author Info	Associate Professor of History and Executive Director of International History Institute at Boston University. CV at http://www.bu.edu/history/nolan.pdf
Bibliography	No.
Index	No.
Notes	Endnotes (63).
Photographs	No.
Appendix	No.
Tables	No.
Key Words	Presidency, Politics, Bricker Amendment, Domestic Policy, Foreign Relations
Other Notes	
Annotation	Nolan argues that while the Bricker Amendment was supported by people concerned about states' rights and worried about constitutional liberties, its

main driving force was isolationism. Eisenhower recognized this and fought against it, largely against the conservative element in his own party. Through "hard lobbying and the tactic of sacrificing human rights treaties," Ike defeated the Bricker Amendment. His victory, "meant that U.S. foreign policy would not... be reduced to a weak state comparable to its condition under the Articles of Confederation," but "US policy and interests within a variety of international organizations suffered badly," especially in the realm of human rights. Nolan concludes that: "Most fundamentally... the Bricker controversy represented more the eclipse than the strength of isolationism in the postwar period."

280. Norpoth, Helmut. "From Eisenhower to Bush: Perceptions of Candidates and Parties." *Electoral Studies* 28, no. 4 (Dec, 2009): 523-532.

Author Info	Professor in the Department of Political Science at Stony Brook University (NY) http://www.stonybrook.edu/polsci/hnorpoth/
Bibliography	References.
Index	No.
Notes	Footnotes (4).
Photographs	No.
Appendix	No.
Tables	Yes (9).
Key Words	Presidency, Elections
Other Notes	
Annotation	Norpoth compares the perceptions of Eisenhower and Bush and their respective political parties in the 1952 and 2004 elections, as reported by two books which pioneered "the large-scale use of a survey technique that relied on open-ended questions about the political parties and presidential candidates." Norpoth found that "both Eisenhower and Bush earned praise for their ability to lead and being decisive," and that Ike's military service "proved to be no net plus," and Bush's "lack of frontline service barely registered" with voters. Norpoth also examines voters' perceptions of parties and the use of open-ended survey questions.

281. Nwaubani, Ebere. "Eisenhower, Nkrumah and the Congo Crisis." *Journal of Contemporary History* 36, no. 4 (Oct, 2001): 599-622.

Author Info	Was at the University of Colorado at Boulder as an Assistant professor in the Department of History.
Bibliography	No.
Index	No.
Notes	Footnotes (118).
Photographs	No.
Appendix	No.

Tables	No.
Key Words	Presidency, Foreign Relations
Other Notes	
Annotation	Traces the relationship of the United States with Ghana from a friendly one of mutual need in the late 1950s to a chilled relationship by 1960. Nwaubani argues that the worsening of American's relations with Ghana were due to Ghana's increasing assertiveness in African diplomacy and politics and the emergence of other independent African nations, a development that made Ghana less strategically important to the US. He concludes that by 1960, America had sufficient reason to redefine its relationship with Ghana and that: "The Congo crisis provided the convenient excuse to do so, although in an acrimonious manner."

O's

282. O'Reilly, Kenneth. "Racial Integration: The Battle General Eisenhower Chose Not to Fight." *The Journal of Blacks in Higher Education*, No. 18 (Winter, 1997/1998): 110-119.

Author Info	"Prior to joining the [University of Alaska Anchorage] faculty in 1983, Dr. O'Reilly taught at Marquette University, where he did his doctoral work, and at the University of Wisconsin at Milwaukee. Dr. O'Reilly has received Chancellor's Awards for Excellence in Research and Teaching." Has written books on race, the presidency, and the FBI. http://www.uaa.alaska.edu/bookstore/authors/oreilly.cfm
Bibliography	No.
Index	No.
Notes	No.
Photographs	Yes (3).
Appendix	No.
Tables	No.
Key Words	Presidency, Civil Rights, Domestic Policy
Other Notes	
Annotation	In this article, pulled from his book *Nixon's Piano: Presidents and Racial Politics from Washington to Clinton* (1995) O'Reilly characterizes Eisenhower as a "nineteenth-century man" with regard to racial issues. O'Reilly argues that Eisenhower exhibited racism (for example, telling racist jokes) and did little to nothing to advance the rights of African Americans. Further, he argues that when Eisenhower did take such actions, they were because of domestic and/or political considerations and narrowly circumscribed.

283. Osgood, Kenneth A. "Form before Substance: Eisenhower's Commitment to Psychological Warfare and Negotiations with the Enemy." *Diplomatic History* 24, no. 3 (Summer 2000): 405-433.

Author Info	Assistant Professor of History at Florida Atlantic University. Wrote *Total Cold War: Eisenhower's Secret Propaganda Battle at Home and Abroad* (2006). http://wise.fau.edu/~kosgood/
Bibliography	No.
Index	No.
Notes	Footnotes (60).
Photographs	Yes (2).
Appendix	No.
Tables	No.
Key Words	
Other Notes	Presidency, Cold War, Foreign Relations, Military Policy
Annotation	Osgood argues that "Eisenhower's commitment to psychological warfare exerted a profound influence on the overall direction of his foreign policy, especially in the fields of peace and disarmament." He contends and that "Eisenhower placed political warfare consideration over his concern for effective arms control." He states that Eisenhower had a broad view of "psychological warfare" that included not only propaganda, but also diplomacy, policy coordination, and initiative, and believed that "the totality of U.S. policies should reflect political warfare considerations." Osgood uses Eisenhower's "Atoms for Peace" as a case study to show the importance of psychological warfare in Ike's foreign policy.

P's

284. Parker, Jason. "Cold War II: The Eisenhower Administration, the Bandung Conference, and the Reperiodization of the Postwar Era." *Diplomatic History* 30, no. 5 (Nov, 2006): 867-892.

Author Info	Associate professor of history at Texas A&M. "Jason Parker joined the A&M History Department in 2006, after teaching for four years at West Virginia University. He is the author of *Brother's Keeper: The United States, Race, and Empire in the British Caribbean, 1937-1962* (Oxford University Press, 2008).... His broad research interests are U.S. foreign relations, decolonization and the Cold War, race and diplomacy, and Caribbean/inter-American affairs." http://www.tamu.edu/history/faculty/parker.htm
Bibliography	No.
Index	No.
Notes	Footnotes (80).
Photographs	Yes (3).
Appendix	No.

Tables	No.
Key Words	Presidency, Foreign Relations, Cold War
Other Notes	
Annotation	Parker argues that the 1955 Bandung Conference, a Conference of Afro-Asian Peoples in Indonesia, "represented the crossroads of several key Cold War trends: the old specter of communism and the new one of neutralism; the vectors of anticolonialism and Third World nationalism, and a stirring consciousness of changes in inter- and intranational race relations." He deems the Eisenhower Administration's handling of the conference, "at least a partial success, and arguably much more," and describes the Administration's use of psychological maneuvers and behind the scenes work with the use of proxies. Parker also, however, believes that Bandung was a missed opportunity to the Administration. It signaled to the U.S. that "European colonialism was becoming more of a Western liability than an asset," but efforts to react to this new understanding "ran aground on British intransigence, American inertia, and fear of communism spreading in… the Third World" and were not fully realized until Suez. Earlier versions of this material were presented at the 2003 University of San Diego conference on "Eisenhower and the Third World" and at the SHAFR meeting that same year. A portion of the text also appears in the Eisenhower conference volume (ed. Statler and Johns). See entry #101.

285.   Parker IV, Jerome H. "Fox Conner and Dwight Eisenhower: Mentoring and Application." *Military Review* 85, no. 4 (July 2005): 92-95.

Author Info	As of 2005: "Jerome H. Parker IV is an adjunct instructor at Tarrant County College, Fort Worth, Texas. He received a B.A. and an M.P.A. from the University of Texas." In 2006, Parker was with the Peace Corps in Albania, working with a microcredit lender.
Bibliography	No.
Index	No.
Notes	Endnotes (44).
Photographs	No.
Appendix	No.
Tables	No.
Key Words	Military- Pre WWII, Personal Life, Leadership
Other Notes	
Annotation	Describes the mentoring relationship between Conner and Eisenhower. Parker describes Conner as "a masterful leader who believed leadership could be taught by delegating authority, providing instruction and example, setting high standards, and holding everyone to those standards without fear or favor." He discusses how Conner mentored Ike and how Ike absorbed and utilized the lessons he learned from Conner.

286.	Parry-Giles, Shawn J. "'Camouflaged' Propaganda: The Truman and Eisenhower Administrations' Covert Manipulation of News." *Western Journal of Communication* 60, no. 2 (Spring 1996): 146-167.

Author Info	Assistant Professor, Department of Communication, University of Maryland. CV at http://terpconnect.umd.edu/~spg/CV.htm
Bibliography	List of references.
Index	No.
Notes	Internal citations and endnotes (9).
Photographs	No.
Appendix	No.
Tables	No.
Key Words	Presidency, Media, Cold War, Domestic Policy
Other Notes	
Annotation	Examines the domestic "camouflaged" propaganda of the Truman and Eisenhower Administrations and the news media's role in "willing and unwittingly serving national communication objectives." Parry-Giles describes "camouflaged" propaganda as existing where "not only the source is concealed but the propagandistic nature of the material is unknown." He explains how both administrations assured the American public that they would be immune to propaganda, but "these public promises were merely smokescreens serving to mask the covert activities of the Truman and Eisenhower presidencies." Such activities included shared personnel and subsidization of private media. He argues that while the media was willing to participate, they, "apparently did not fully recognize the depths of their manipulation." He suggests that this type of "camouflaged" propaganda was more subtle, and potentially had greater power than propaganda in totalitarian regimes because it was masked as free, objective press.

287.	Parry-Giles, Shawn J. "The Eisenhower Administration's Conceptualization of the USIA: The Development of Overt and Covert Propaganda Strategies." *Presidential Studies Quarterly* 24, no. 2 (Spring 1994): 263-276.

Author Info	See information in Entry #286.
Bibliography	No.
Index	No.
Notes	Endnotes (70).
Photographs	No.
Appendix	No.
Tables	No.
Key Words	Presidency, Media, Cold War, Domestic Policy
Other Notes	
Annotation	Parry-Giles details Eisenhower's use of propaganda in the Cold War and his formation, based on the recommendation of the Jackson committee, of the United States Information Agency (USIA). Under Eisenhower, "propaganda

strategy became more centralized, with the president acting as commander in chief of propaganda operations." The number of official propaganda channels was decreased, and the remaining channels used a more positive tone, while the "more explicitly polemical material was relegated to organizations not publicly identified with the [government] so as to cultivate the perception of a 'news' station." The Chance for Peace and Atoms for Peace campaigns, "revealed how the Eisenhower administration used the presidential addresses to set the themes and tone of the USIA program."

288. Patterson, Bradley H., Jr. "Teams and Staff: Dwight Eisenhower's Innovations in the Structure and Operations of the Modern White House. *Presidential Studies Quarterly* 24, no. 2 (Spring 1994): 277-298.

Author Info	"Bradley H. Patterson Jr. has lived and worked in Washington for 55 years, fourteen of them in the White House, where he served on the staffs of three presidents. He has worked in the Department of State, the Peace Corps, the Treasury Department, and the Brookings Institution. He is a graduate of the University of Chicago and of the National War College. A senior fellow of the National Academy of Public Administration, he is past president of the American Society for Public Administration." From http://www.brookings.edu/press/Books/2000/white_house_staff.aspx
Bibliography	No.
Index	No.
Notes	Endnotes (36).
Photographs	No.
Appendix	No.
Tables	No.
Key Words	Presidency, White House
Other Notes	
Annotation	Patterson, Deputy Cabinet Secretary under Eisenhower, argues that Ike was "perhaps the President who did the most to shape the structures of the modern White House" and notes that many of his innovations are still used today. These include the positions of Staff Secretary and Chief of Staff. He describes the eighteen new White House staff elements introduced by Eisenhower, the creation of which were influenced by: "(1) the tremendously expanded American role in the world following World War II, (2) the work of the first Hoover Commission and (3) the success of the secretariat idea in the senior-most of the Cabinet Departments." A longer version of this essay appeared in *Reexamining the Eisenhower Presidency*, ed. Shirley Anne Warshaw (1993). See Entry #112.

289. Payne, Rodger A. "Public Opinion and Foreign Threats: Eisenhower's Response to Sputnik." *Armed Forces and Society* 21, no. 1 (Fall 1994): 89-112.

Author Info	Professor of political science at the University of Louisville. http://louisville.edu/politicalscience/faculty/rodger-a-payne.html
Bibliography	No.
Index	No.
Notes	Endnotes (68).
Photographs	No.
Appendix	No.
Tables	No.
Key Words	Presidency, Cold War, Foreign Relations, Military Policy
Other Notes	
Annotation	Payne uses Eisenhower's reaction to public opinion after the Soviet's launch of Sputnik as a case study to further the conversation between "realists" who "mostly ignore so-called social dimensions of state behavior, focusing on the capabilities and external actions of states… [or] argue that national leaders can manipulate domestic politics as needed," and "social theorists" who "claim realism 'seriously undervalues' the role public opinion plays in the 'formation and conduct of a democratic nation's foreign policy.'" Payne finds that Eisenhower did respond to public opinion, as predicted by social theorists. Despite the fact that Eisenhower did not perceive the threat to be as dire as did the public, his administration, "announced and implemented changes in science and military programs that assured public audiences that Soviet threats were not overwhelming and that the U.S. would mitigate them." Payne concludes: "Despite what realists believe, policymakers respond to public perceptions about threats, even when they do not believe the external context merits specific actions."

290.   Pedaliu, Effie G. H. "Truman, Eisenhower and the Mediterranean Cold War, 1947-57." *Maghreb Review* 31, no. 1/2 (2006): 2-20.

Author Info	Senior Lecturer in International History at the University of the West of England. "Dr Pedaliu studied at the London School of Economics obtaining a MA in International History and her Ph.D.. Before joining the History Department at UWE in 2003, she was a lecturer in International History at the LSE, (1990-94) and at King's College London (1997-2002). She was also a Jean Monnet Fellow in European History at Luton University (1995-1997).… Dr Pedaliu's main research interest is the history of international relations since 1945. In particular she specialises in American and British Cold War policy and strategy with particular reference to issues of European and Mediterranean security, human rights and European Integration." http://www.uwe.ac.uk/hlss/history/staff_epedaliu.shtml
Bibliography	No.
Index	No.
Notes	Footnotes (91).
Photographs	No.
Appendix	No.

Tables	No.
Key Words	SACEUR, Presidency, Cold War, Military Policy, Foreign Relations.
Other Notes	
Annotation	Examines America's involvement with and policies towards the Mediterranean during the Truman and Eisenhower presidencies. Pedaliu argues that "the incorporation of the whole of the Mediterranean basin in American Cold War 'grand strategy' and defense planning after [WWII] was at first gradual and that it accelerated during 1946 to compensate for Britain's weakness in fulfilling its responsibilities as the hitherto, pre-eminent Mediterranean power." She describes the Mediterranean region as important as: "It was the region where the Soviets probed the limits of American tolerance and America stumbled upon a policy of containment that was to become its mainstay during the Cold War years."

291.   Perret, Geoffrey. "Ike the Pilot" *MHQ: Quarterly Journal of Military History* 12, no. 2 (Winter 2000): 70-78.

Author Info	Perret, "served in the U.S. Army from 1958-1961 and attended the University of Southern California, Harvard, and the University of California at Berkeley. His first book was the award-winning *Days of Sadness, Years of Triumph*, his account of America's home front during World War II. He is also the author of *Ulysses S. Grant, Old Soldiers Never Die: The Life of Douglas MacArthur*, and *Winged Victory*." From *Eisenhower* by Perret. See Entry #82.
Bibliography	No.
Index	No.
Notes	No.
Photographs	Yes (11).
Appendix	No.
Tables	No.
Key Words	Military- Pre WWII, Military—B/w the Wars, Military- WWII, Presidency, Military Policy
Other Notes	
Annotation	Describes how Ike obtained his pilot's license late in life (age 48) because of Mamie's objection to his flying, and how his training as a pilot influenced him as a general and as President. For example, "what made Eisenhower unique among WWII army officers was not so much his faith in air power as his deep understanding of it." Further, as President, he pushed the U-2 program over air force objections.

292.   Pfeiffer, David A. "Ike's Interstates at 50." *Prologue* 38, no. 2 (Summer 2006): 13-19.

Author Info	Article notes that he was "an archivist with the Civilian Records Staff, Textual Archives Services Division, of the National Archives at College Park. He specializes in transportation records and has published articles and given

numerous presentations concerning railroad records in the National Archives."

Bibliography	Note on sources.
Index	No.
Notes	
Photographs	Yes (3).
Appendix	No.
Tables	No.
Key Words	Military—B/w the Wars; Transportation
Other Notes	
Annotation	Eisenhower's participation in the 1919 convoy across America and his observation of German autobahns in WWII influenced Ike's interest in an interstate highway system in America. Also discusses presidential, legislative, and budgetary efforts to achieve national highway construction.

293.   Pharo, Per F. I. "Revising Eisenhower Revisionism?" *Newsletter of the Society for Historians of American Foreign Relations* 30, no. 4 (September 1999): 18-22.

Author Info	Deputy Director, The Government of Norway's International Climate and Forest Initiative, The Norwegian Ministry of Environment. From http://www.law.harvard.edu/programs/about/pifs/symposia/fcfs/09-fcfs-participants.pdf
Bibliography	No.
Index	No.
Notes	Footnotes (8).
Photographs	No.
Appendix	No.
Tables	No.
Key Words	Presidency, Cold War, Foreign Relations
Other Notes	
Annotation	Responding to Suri's 1997 article in *Diplomatic History* ("America's Search for a Technological Solution to the Arms Race: The Surprise Attack Conference of 1958 and a Challenge for 'Eisenhower Revisionists'."), Pharo states that Suri's "perspective is too narrow to sustain the broadness of his conclusions" and that Suri's arguments are flawed by unspoken assumptions: "first, that President Eisenhower *wanted* to be more compromising with the Soviets on arms control, and that the insistence upon inspection was mainly a bureaucratic construction to prevent progress towards arms control and disarmament; second, that the lack of progress in limiting the US-Soviet arms race was due to a failure of leadership."

294.   Pickett, William. "Eisenhower, Clausewitz, and American Power." *Newsletter of the Society for Historians of American Foreign Relations* 22, no. 4 (September 1991): 28-40.

Author Info	Professor Emeritus of History at the Rose-Hulman Institute of Technology in

Terre Haute, Indiana. CV at http://www.rose-hulman.edu/~pickett/

Bibliography	No.
Index	No.
Notes	Footnotes (31).
Photographs	No.
Appendix	No.
Tables	No.
Key Words	Military- WWII, Presidency, Foreign Relations, Cold War
Other Notes	
Annotation	Pickett cites the importance of the philosophy of nineteenth-century philosopher of war Karl Von Clausewitz (that war is merely a means to an end) to Eisenhower's formulation of his strategies as a military commander and as President. Eisenhower read Clausewitz before WWII, and: "Everywhere [Ike] went he drew upon the ideas of Clausewitz, especially the importance of ends and means." Eisenhower's "ends" were "to preserve democracy and free enterprise" and his "means" were "strength... national unity, and the will to prevail." Pickett examines some of Ike's major political strategies, including the "New Look," under the rubric of "means and ends."

295. Prados, John. "Ike, Ridgway, and Dien Bien Phu." *MHQ: Quarterly Journal of Military History* 17, no. 4 (Summer 2005): 16-23.

Author Info	Prados "directs the Archive's Iraq Documentation Project as well as its Vietnam Project and is a Senior Research Fellow on national security affairs, including foreign affairs, intelligence, and military subjects. He holds a Ph.D. in International Relations from Columbia University and has authored many books, most recently *Vietnam: The History of an Unwinnable War* and the forthcoming *How the Cold War Ended....* His books *Unwinnable War*, *Keepers of the Keys* (on the National Security Council) and *Combined Fleet Decoded* (on intelligence in the Pacific in World War II) were each nominated for the Pulitzer Prize... ." http://www.gwu.edu/~nsarchiv/nsa/arc_staff.html
Bibliography	No.
Index	No.
Notes	No.
Photographs	Yes (4).
Appendix	No.
Tables	No.
Key Words	Presidency, Military Policy, Vietnam
Other Notes	
Annotation	Examines disagreements among Eisenhower and his Joint Chiefs of Staff over military intervention in Vietnam in 1954. Eisenhower's position on intervention wavered, other JCS were in favor of intervention, and Ridgway was staunchly cautious. Prados argues that the disagreement hurt the relationship between Eisenhower and Ridgway.

296.   Price, Kevin S. "The Partisan Legacies of Preemptive Leadership: Assessing the Eisenhower Cohorts in the U.S. House." *Political Research Quarterly* 55, no. 3 (Sep, 2002): 609-631.

Author Info   "A summa cum laude graduate of the University of Puget Sound and a University of Wisconsin Ph.D., Kevin S. Price directs the investment practice at Interlake Capital Management (http://www.interlakecapital.com/index.php), an investment advisory firm located in Madison, Wisconsin. Before co-founding Interlake in 2006, Kevin held a faculty position at the University of Washington and worked in the Global Wealth Management group at Merrill Lynch & Co." From http://seekingalpha.com/author/kevin-s-price

Bibliography   References listed.
Index   No.
Notes   Internal citations, Footnotes (9).
Photographs   No.
Appendix   No.
Tables   Yes (7).
Key Words   Presidency, Politics, Elections, Leadership
Other Notes
Annotation   Casting Eisenhower as a "preemptive" president, under Stephen Skowronek's classification, Price examines the success of Eisenhower's New Republicanism, using House elections and lawmaking records. He finds that, "Eisenhower's preemptive leadership affected the partisan and ideological composition of the congressional cohorts elected during his Presidency," but he also finds that Ike's legacy was a complicated one. Eisenhower's presidency, "reshuffled party commitments in the House by leaving more-moderate but numerically decimated Republicans to battle ideologically galvanized and numerically strengthened Democrats in the 1960s." Earlier version of this article was presented at the 2000 Annual Meeting of the Midwest Political Science Association in Chicago.

R's

297.   Rabe, Stephen G. "Eisenhower Revisionism: A Decade of Scholarship." *Diplomatic History* 17, no. 1 (January 1993): 97-115.

Author Info   "…[G]raduated from Hamilton College (B.A., 1970) and the University of Connecticut (Ph.D., 1977), Stephen G. Rabe is now a professor of history at The University of Texas at Dallas. His field of research interest is in U.S. foreign relations, with a special interest in U.S. relations with Latin America. Rabe has written… *Eisenhower and Latin America: The Foreign Policy of Anticommunism* (1988)…" From http://www.utdallas.edu/~rabe/

Bibliography   No.
Index   No.

Notes	Footnotes (84).
Photographs	No.
Appendix	No.
Tables	No.
Key Words	Presidency
Other Notes	
Annotation	In this historiographical essay, Rabe examines postrevisionist responses to revisionist work and finds that "the majority of case studies have not sustained Eisenhower revisionism." He describes postrevisionists as "believ[ing] that historians accept the revisionist case that Eisenhower was a thoughtful, decent leader committed to international peace and prosperity. But the avoidance of war is not peace [and] Eisenhower's rigid anticommunism led him to sanction unwise, globalist adventures."

298.   Rempe, Dennis M. "An American Trojan Horse? Eisenhower, Latin America and the Development of US Internal Security Policy 1954-1960." *Small Wars & Insurgencies* 10, no. 1 (Spring 1999): 34-64.

Author Info	External researcher for the Strategic Studies Institute. Bio from their website: "[Rempe] is a consultant for an engineering firm. He served as an infantry officer in the Canadian Armed Forces (Reserve) and was a member of the Canadian National Team Military Pentathlon. Mr. Rempe has written numerous articles on counterinsurgency, intelligence, and foreign international defense… Mr. Rempe is completing his Ph.D. on U.S.-Colombian internal security issues at the University of Miami's School of International Studies." http://www.strategicstudiesinstitute.army.mil/pubs/people.cfm?authorID=11
Bibliography	No.
Index	No.
Notes	Endnotes (112).
Photographs	No.
Appendix	No.
Tables	No.
Key Words	Presidency, Foreign Relations, Cold War, Military Policy
Other Notes	
Annotation	Rempe examines the formulation and difficult implementation of Eisenhower's Overseas Internal Security Program (OISP) in Latin America. OISP, "sought to strengthen host-nation security forces, judicial systems, and public information media in an effort to combat indirect communist intervention strategies," and linked internal security efforts to aid programs. Eisenhower had difficulty implementing the program for domestic and international reasons. Domestically, he faced criticism for working with and supporting dictatorial regimes with questionable human rights records. Bureaucratic inefficiencies and disorganization and personnel and budget shortages slowed the process. In Latin American countries, there was a fear, "that the new program would be used as a 'Trojan Horse' to penetrate their security structures" and political

resistance. Fear sparked by the Cuban Revolution helped to propel the OISP policy to primacy.

299. Roman, Peter J. "Eisenhower and Ballistic Missiles Arms Control 1957-1960: A Missed Opportunity?" *Journal of Strategic Studies* 19, no. 3 (Sep, 1996): 365-380.

Author Info	Senior associate at the Stimson Center. "Prior to joining the Stimson Center, Dr. Peter Roman was a Senior Fellow at the ANSER Institute for Homeland Security, where he directed the Biological and Agro Anti-Terrorism Partnership Project. He has published widely on homeland and national security issues. Dr. Roman served as a Distinguished Visiting Professor at the National War College in Washington, DC and has taught at the University of Wisconsin-Madison, the University of Alabama, the University of Colorado-Boulder, and Duquesne University." His MA and Ph.D. are from the University of Wisconsin-Madison. http://www.stimson.org/experts/expert.cfm?ID=72
Bibliography	No.
Index	No.
Notes	Endnotes (54).
Photographs	No.
Appendix	No.
Tables	No.
Key Words	Presidency, Military Policy, Foreign Relations
Other Notes	
Annotation	Roman argues that there were limits to arms control during the Eisenhower Administration, and that the failure to limit ballistic missiles was not a "missed opportunity" but a "mirage." Three main factors "prevented consideration by the Eisenhower administration of constraining ballistic missiles through arms control." These were: 1) limitations of intelligence capabilities which caused overestimations of the Soviet ICBM threat; 2) a limited arms control agenda, which was already focused on nuclear testing; and 3) the "requirements of stability during the transition from bombers to missiles."

300. Rosenau, William. "The Eisenhower Administration, US Foreign Internal Security Assistance, and the Struggle for the Developing World, 1954-1961." *Low Intensity Conflict and Law Enforcement* 10, no. 3 (Autumn 2001): 1-32.

Author Info	Rosenau, "is a political scientist in the Rand Corporation's Washington Office, where he specializes in the study of insurgency, terrorism, intelligence, and military special operations. He is also the chairman of RAND's Insurgency Board. Dr. Rosenau has served in the US State Department's counterterrorism office (S/CT); as a congressional legislative assistant; on the U.S. Department of Defense Commission on the Roles and Missions of the Armed Forces (CORM); and in the office of the U.S. assistant secretary of defense for special

operations and low-intensity conflict (OASD/SOLIC). In October 2009 he will join the Strategic Studies Division at the Center for Naval Analyses." From http://explore.georgetown.edu/people/wr29/

Bibliography	No.
Index	No.
Notes	Endnotes (155).
Photographs	No.
Appendix	No.
Tables	No.
Key Words	Presidency, Foreign Relations, Cold War
Other Notes	
Annotation	With an eye toward offering lessons to America's then-President, George W. Bush, Rosenau examines Eisenhower's counter-subversive campaign which provided assistance to the police and paramilitary forces of friendly governments of the developing world to help them resist communist incursions. He finds that "despite Washington's attempts to revamp the foreign internal security program," by the late 1950s, Administration officials "concluded that the [U.S.] had failed to stem the tide of communist subversion in the developing world." Rosenau notes that the Administration understood that measuring success or progress in foreign security was difficult. The goal itself ("of helping friendly Third World governments to maintain internal order and security") was a difficult one to achieve, especially in light of the mix of foreign and domestic problems within each of the countries assisted. He also acknowledges other obstacles that the program faced, including bureaucracy and organizational conflict, recruitment difficulties, and institutional cultures. Finally, he argues that is difficult to state whether or not Eisenhower devoted sufficient resources to the program.

301. Rottinghaus, Brandon. "Rethinking Presidential Responsiveness: The Public Presidency and Rhetorical Congruency, 1953–2001." *Journal of Politics* 68, no. 3 (August 2006): 720-732.

Author Info	Assistant professor, department of political science at the University of Houston. CV at http://www.polsci.uh.edu/faculty/rottinghaus/rottinghaus%20cv.pdf
Bibliography	List of references.
Index	No.
Notes	Internal citations.
Photographs	No.
Appendix	No.
Tables	Table (1); Figure (1).
Key Words	Presidency, Politics, Speechmaking
Other Notes	
Annotation	Rottinghaus develops "a direct measure of presidential congruency between public opinion and public presidential rhetoric on policy" and uses it to analyze

the presidential policy statements of nine presidential administrations (Eisenhower to Clinton). He finds that "across all administrations, public presidential policy rhetoric is highly congruent with public opinion," and that Eisenhower, during his second term, was the most congruent with public opinion, and was the most hypercongruent with public opinion in both of his terms. Rottinghaus also discusses differences in rhetoric between first and second terms.

302.   Ruddy, T. Michael. "U.S. Foreign Policy, the 'Third Force,' and European Union: Eisenhower and Europe's Neutrals." *Midwest Quarterly* 42, no. 1 (September 2000): 67-80.

Author Info	Professor and Director of Graduate Studies in the History Department of St. Louis University. From his university profile: "My primary area of research is Modern America, more specifically U.S. foreign policy from the time of World War II. In recent years, my research has focused on two topics. First, I have been examining America's Cold War relations with the neutral states of Europe. Relatively little work has been done on relations with nations like Sweden, Finland, and Austria, which tried to steer an independent course as Europe divided into the two blocs dominated by the Soviet Union and the United States.... My second area of interest is in the McCarthy era...." http://www.slu.edu/x19409.xml
Bibliography	Yes, brief.
Index	No.
Notes	Internal citations.
Photographs	No.
Appendix	No.
Tables	No.
Key Words	Presidency, Foreign Relations, Cold War
Other Notes	
Annotation	Examines America's pragmatic relationship with European neutrals, specifically Finland, Sweden, and Austria, during the Cold War. Ruddy differentiates between "neutrality" ("a government policy or nation's status in foreign relationships") and "neutralism" ("'essentially... an attitude or psychological tendency'"). He argues that the Eisenhower Administration concluded that, "these states could maintain their neutrality and at the same time through political and economic ties indirectly contribute to collective security." Ruddy also examines America's work to integrate these neutral countries into the European Union. He concludes that, "America's neutral policy represented a dynamic, positive influence on the changing international situation."

S's

303. Saeki, Chizuru. "The Cancellation of Eisenhower's Visit to Japan and the U.S.-Japan Centennial Festival of 1960." *New England Journal of History* 63, no. 2 (Spring 2007): 1-14.

Author Info	Associate Professor of History at the University of North Alabama. http://www.una.edu/history/faculty-staff/saeki.html
Bibliography	No.
Index	No.
Notes	Endnotes (31).
Photographs	No.
Appendix	No.
Tables	No.
Key Words	Presidency, Foreign Relations, Cold War
Other Notes	
Annotation	Saeki recounts the cancellation of Eisenhower's visit to Japan to participate in the U.S.-Japan Centennial Festival of 1960. The main purpose of Ike's visit was political—Eisenhower wanted to support the Japanese passage of the revised U.S.-Japan Mutual Security treaty. The cultural Centennial Festival served to camouflage this political reason from the Japanese leftist protest movement, comprised of intellectuals, workers, and students. Mass demonstrations of the leftist movement ultimately resulted in the Japanese government's cancellation of Ike's trip because they could not assure his safety. The cancellation "was a symbolic communist victory" and the "Eisenhower administration's cultural diplomacy resulted in a disastrous failure." The Centennial Festival was still held, however, and it was used by the Japanese government to apologize to Eisenhower and America, and to help "to normalize U.S.-Japan relations after the bitter incident." The treaty was eventually passed, however, "there was no way to make up the loss of U.S. credibility and prestige that the U.S. suffered in this incident."

304. Saulnier, Raymond J. "Recollections of a 1948 Visit with General Eisenhower." *Presidential Studies Quarterly* 24, no. 4 (Fall, 1994). 865-867.

Author Info	See information in Book Entry #93.
Bibliography	No.
Index	No.
Notes	No.
Photographs	No.
Appendix	No.
Tables	No.
Key Words	Army Chief of Staff, Presidency, Elections, Politics
Other Notes	
Annotation	Saulnier remembers a discussion he had with Eisenhower on January 28, 1948, "in which [Ike] spoke at some length on how he came to see himself as a

Republican." They discussed political and economic philosophy and, "it was evident as we talked that his views on public policy fitted him indisputably into the Republican scheme of things." Saulnier also recalls that Ike discussed his values, learned from his family, and stated that he "'figured'" that he "'must be a Republican.'"

305. Schapsmeier, Edward. L. and Frederick. H. Schapsmeier. "Eisenhower and Agricultural Reform: Ike's Farm Policy Appraised." *American Journal of Economics and Sociology* 51, no. 2 (April 1992): 147-159.

Author Info	Edward Schapsmeier is a distinguished professor emeritus in history at Illinois State University. Frederick Schapsmeier was at the University of Wisconsin, Oshkosh, when this was published. Brief educational histories of the brothers at http://www.fordlibrarymuseum.gov/library/guides/Finding%20Aids%5CSchapsmeier_-_Papers.htm. Prolific scholars, they have worked together on many studies of U.S. agricultural history and policy.
Bibliography	No.
Index	No.
Notes	Endnotes (40).
Photographs	No.
Appendix	No.
Tables	No.
Key Words	Presidency, Domestic Policy
Other Notes	
Annotation	Schapsmeier & Schapsmeier explore Eisenhower's efforts to reform farm policy during his administration, with the assistance of his controversial Secretary of Agriculture Ezra Taft Benson. Eisenhower successfully increased the flexibility in agricultural price supports and his Administration's agricultural programs, "took cognizance of technological advances, the need for American agricultural products to compete in world markets, and the fact that farmers should be reacting to consumer preferences rather than producing for government warehouses." The authors conclude that Ike helped to modernize American agriculture and that his farm policy legacy, "was to establish firmly the principle of perpetual flexibility and relative freedom for farmers to react realistically to changing conditions."

306. Scheele, Henry Z. "President Dwight D. Eisenhower and the U.S. House Leader Charles A. Halleck: An Examination of an Executive-Legislative Relationship." *Presidential Studies Quarterly* 23, no. 2 (Spring 1993): 289-299.

Author Info	Associate Professor of Communication at Purdue University. http://www.cla.purdue.edu/communication/People/index.cfm?p=Henry_Scheele
Bibliography	No.

Index	No.
Notes	Footnotes (74).
Photographs	No.
Appendix	No.
Tables	No.
Key Words	Presidency, Politics
Other Notes	
Annotation	Scheele describes the close relationship between Eisenhower and Halleck, whom Eisenhower described as "indispensable throughout my service in the presidency." Scheele uses this legislative-executive relationship to argue that Ike, "possessed great organizational ability, notable political acumen and a keen sense for the importance of communication." His weekly meetings with congressional leaders, including Halleck, "fostered better understanding and helped to keep in balance the exquisite tension between the executive and legislative branches."

307.   Schlesinger, Arthur Jr. "Effective National Security Advising: A Most Dubious Precedent." *Political Science Quarterly* 115, no. 3 (Fall 2000): 347-351.

Author Info	"[H]istorian whose more than 20 books shaped discussions for two generations about America's past and who himself was a provocative, unabashedly liberal partisan, most notably in serving in the Kennedy White House… . Twice awarded the Pulitzer Prize and the National Book Award, Mr. Schlesinger exhaustively examined the administrations of two prominent presidents, Andrew Jackson and Franklin Delano Roosevelt, against a vast background of regional and economic rivalries. He strongly argued that strong individuals like Jackson and Roosevelt could bend history." He died in 2007. Obituary at http://www.nytimes.com/2007/03/01/washington/01schlesinger.html?pagewanted=print
Bibliography	No.
Index	No.
Notes	Footnotes (7).
Photographs	No.
Appendix	No.
Tables	No.
Key Words	Presidency
Other Notes	
Annotation	Schlesinger, a former member of Kennedy's White House, is highly critical of Eisenhower's national security advising system, stating that it "quite failed to bring planning and coherence into his conduct of foreign affairs" and arguing that it is "surely not" a "precedent for effective national security advising." It was, he says, "wrong too in theory." Schlesinger favors the models of FDR and JFK which he says were more flexible and informal and have a more horizontal structure better suited for our digital age.

308. Scott, George W. "The Culmination of the Great Columbia Power War: The CVA, Governor Arthur B. Langlie and Eisenhower's 'Partnership.'" *Journal of the West* 44, no. 1 (Winter 2005): 27-37.

Author Info	"George W. Scott, Ph.D., served in both houses of the Washington State Legislature from 1969 to 1983, as a caucus chair, and chair of the budget-writing Ways and Means Committee during his 12 years in the Senate. He was WSBA director of public affairs (1985-88), then state archivist. Scott is author of *A Majority of One: Legislative Life* (Seattle: Civitas Press, 2002, 2003), *Governors of Washington* (2007), and *Turning Points in Washington's Public Life*, (2007)." http://www.wsba.org/media/publications/barnews/octscott.htm
Bibliography	No.
Index	No.
Notes	Endnotes (42).
Photographs	Yes (7).
Appendix	No.
Tables	No.
Key Words	Presidency, Politics, Domestic Policy
Other Notes	One illustration.
Annotation	Discusses the political battles over the formation of the Columbia Valley Authority (CVA) on the Pacific Northwest's Columbia River. The article focuses mainly on the governors and local officials of Pacific Northwest states, but also discusses the roles of Roosevelt, Truman, and Eisenhower. Federalism and states' rights concerns played a large role in the disputes over the CVA.

309. Scott, Robert L. "Eisenhower's Farewell Address: Response to Medhurst." *Quarterly Journal of Speech* 81, no. 4 (November 1995): 496-501.

Author Info	Professor Emeritus at the University of Minnesota. "Although Dr. Scott is Professor Emeritus, he remains an active member of the graduate program and the Communication Studies Department, currently serving as the Honors Representative to the College of Liberal Arts and advising Honors undergraduate students and a few graduate majors." http://www.comm.umn.edu/faculty/profile.php?UID=scott033
Bibliography	No.
Index	No.
Notes	No.
Photographs	No.
Appendix	No.
Tables	No.
Key Words	Presidency, Speechmaking
Other Notes	
Annotation	Responds to Medhurst's 1994 article (see Entry #264). Scott believes that Medhurst was wrong in stating that Eisenhower's Farewell Speech was

primarily about a philosophy of balance rather than a warning against the military-industrial complex. He notes that if the speech was as well crafted as Medhurst states and had been about balance, then it would not make sense that it would be widely interpreted as being about the complex. He also disagrees with Medhurst's characterization of the speech as a warning to and about Kennedy.

310.   Scowcroft, Brent. "Eisenhower and a Foreign Policy Agenda." *Presidential Studies Quarterly* 22, no. 3 (Summer 1992): 451-454.

Author Info   "[H]as served as the National Security Advisor to both Presidents Gerald Ford and George H.W. Bush. From 1982 to 1989, he was Vice Chairman of Kissinger Associates, Inc., an international consulting firm…. His prior extraordinary twenty-nine-year military career began with graduation from West Point and concluded at the rank of Lieutenant General following service as the Deputy National Security Advisor. His Air Force service included Professor of Russian History at West Point; Assistant Air Attaché in Belgrade, Yugoslavia; Head of the Political Science Department at the Air Force Academy; Air Force Long Range Plans; Office of the Secretary of Defense International Security Assistance; Special Assistant to the Director of the Joint Chiefs of Staff; and Military Assistant to President Nixon. Out of uniform, he continued in a public policy capacity by serving on the President's Advisory Committee on Arms Control, the Commission on Strategic Forces, and the President's Special Review Board, also known as the Tower Commission…. He earned his masters and doctorate in international relations from Columbia University." http://www.scowcroft.com/html/staff/scowcroft.html

Bibliography   No.
Index   No.
Notes   No.
Photographs   No.
Appendix   No.
Tables   No.
Key Words   Presidency
Other Notes
Annotation   Essay based on Scowcroft's 1992 address "as the first recipient of the Eisenhower Leadership Prize awarded by The Eisenhower Institute, Gettysburg College." Scowcroft emphasizes the importance of Eisenhower's legacy and his model of leadership. He states that for the future, we must succeed on three fundamentals: "democracy, liberal trade, U.S. leadership."

311.   Secrest, Clark. "The Picture that Reassured the World." *Colorado Heritage* (Winter 1996): 31-35.

Author Info   Historian in Denver. Wrote a book on prostitution in early Denver.

Bibliography	No.
Index	No.
Notes	No.
Photographs	Yes (3).
Appendix	No.
Tables	No.
Key Words	Presidency, Personal life.
Other Notes	
Annotation	In this short article, Secrest recounts the fear that gripped America following the heart attack Eisenhower suffered while enjoying a working vacation in Denver in 1955. Secrest also discusses the lengths reporters went to in order to obtain a photograph of the convalescing president.

312.   Sewell, Bevan. "A Perfect (Free-Market) World? Economics, the Eisenhower
       Administration, and the Soviet Economic Offensive in Latin America." *Diplomatic
       History* 32, no. 5 (Nov, 2008): 841-868.

Author Info	Lecturer in American Foreign Relations, Faculty of Arts at the University of Nottingham School of American and Canadian Studies. http://www.nottingham.ac.uk/American/People/bevan.sewell
Bibliography	No.
Index	No.
Notes	Footnotes (129).
Photographs	No.
Appendix	No.
Tables	No.
Key Words	Presidency, Economics, Cold War, Foreign Relations
Other Notes	
Annotation	Sewell argues that historians have been wrong to dismiss the Soviet Economic Offensive ("SEO") in Latin America as insignificant. The Eisenhower Administration's response to the Soviet offer of economic and technical assistance to Latin American countries was to enact a "short-term solution based on meeting the immediate political threat" rather than make drastic changes in its economic approach toward the region. Latin American countries wanted "wide-ranging economic assistance from Washington" and this "was too radical a step for U.S. officials." The Administration's adherence to the expansion of free-market capitalism in the area clashed with rising anti-American sentiment. Although short-term measures were relatively successful, "by prioritizing its strategic aims in the region and failing to address the economic grievances of the Latin Americans, the Eisenhower administration inadvertently undermined the long-term stability of the U.S. position."

313. Sewell, Bevan. "The Problems of Public Relations: Eisenhower, Latin America and the Potential Lessons for the Bush Administration." *Comparative American Studies* 6, no. 3 (September 2008): 295-312.

Author Info	See information in Entry #312.
Bibliography	Yes
Index	No.
Notes	Internal citations; endnotes (4).
Photographs	No.
Appendix	No.
Tables	No.
Key Words	Presidency, Cold War, Economics, Foreign Relations, Media
Other Notes	
Annotation	Sewell finds Bush's 2007 visit to Latin America reminiscent of Eisenhower's public relations campaign in the region in the 1950s and offers the Bush Administration advice based on the lessons learned from Ike's efforts. After noting similarities and differences in the domestic and foreign contexts in which the two Presidents worked to improve relations with Latin America, Sewell describes the Eisenhower Administration's experiences and finds in them two major lessons: "First, that a short-term propaganda or PR operation can achieve very little in an atmosphere of hostility, and second, that 'words' have, to some extent, to be matched by 'deeds' if any PR approach is going to be successful."

314. Smith-Norris, Martha. "The Eisenhower Administration and the Nuclear Test Ban Talks, 1958–1960: Another Challenge to 'Revisionism'." *Diplomatic History* 27, no. 4 (September 2003): 503-541.

Author Info	Associate professor of history at the University of Saskatchewan http://www.arts.usask.ca/college/directory/display.php?bioid=620
Bibliography	No.
Index	No.
Notes	Footnotes (234).
Illustrations	No.
Photographs	No.
Appendix	No.
Tables	No.
Key Words	Presidency, Cold War, Nuclear, Foreign Relations
Other Notes	
Annotation	In this postrevisionist article based on declassified documents in the U.S. and Great Britain, Smith-Norris examines the Nuclear Test Ban Talks in Geneva among Great Britain, America, and the Soviet Union as a case study to show "that the United States did not seriously seek an arms-control agreement in the late 1950s." She finds that British documents lay the blame on the U.S. for the failure of the talks to produce a comprehensive test-ban treaty and that two

themes emerge: 1) American bureaucratic infighting had an important impact on the process; and 2) Eisenhower failed to resolve that infighting or provide real leadership until the last year of his presidency.

315.   Spaulding, Robert Mark Jr. "'A Gradual and Moderate Relaxation': Eisenhower and the Revision of American Export Control Policy, 1953-1955." *Diplomatic History* 17, no. 2 (April 1993): 223-249.

Author Info	Professor of history at the University of North Carolina at Wilmington. http://appserv02.uncw.edu/DASAPPS/directory/results.aspx?fn=&ln=spauldin g&d=&sw=ALL&fnst=beginsWith&lnst=beginsWith&qtpval=D7A663A9D6 8EB1037400296F7A81188DDEB1A756684207E63D154671031CA97435339 E8FC61F9D7849ADFDC3C637E1B48A2301F467E899A8B3EC0C8EA4445 8ED
Bibliography	No.
Index	No.
Notes	Footnotes (88).
Photographs	No.
Appendix	No.
Tables	No.
Key Words	Presidency, Foreign Relations, Politics, Cold War
Other Notes	
Annotation	Spaulding argues against the European-centered view of the relaxation of Western export controls and contends that it was the Americans, specifically Eisenhower, who acted as the impetus for the export control reduction. Eisenhower fundamentally changed America's trade policies because he was "[c]onvinced the embargo policy was imposing unacceptable economic sacrifices on the Europeans and that American pressure for more restrictive export controls was undermining NATO unity, and [he was] skeptical of the embargo's ability to affect the Soviets." Once the controls were relaxed, "it became clear that the real impediment to East-West trade growth was not U.S. intransigence but the limited export abilities of the Soviet bloc countries." An earlier version of this paper was presented in 1987 at Harvard University at a conference entitled "The United States and Western European Society, 1950-1955" hosted by the Charles Warren Center for American Studies.

316.   Spaulding, Robert Mark. "Eisenhower and Export Controls Revisited: A Reply to Førland." *Newsletter of the Society for Historians of American Foreign Relations* 25, no. 1 (January 1994): 9-16.

Author Info	See information in Entry #315.
Bibliography	No.
Index	No.
Notes	Footnotes (11).
Photographs	No.

Appendix	No.
Tables	No.
Key Words	Presidency, Foreign Relations, Politics, Cold War
Other Notes	
Annotation	Countering Førland's critique in his article, Entry #184, Spaulding argues that Førland has confused the "British short list idea" with the "British short list proposal". He concedes that the British short list idea *may* have occurred prior to Eisenhower's altering the course of the U.S. export control policy, but he says that the idea itself is not as meaningful as the British short list proposal, which did not arise "until *well after* the U.S. had outlined its new policy." (Emphasis in original). Spaulding also contests Førland's "explanatory dichotomy of the United States versus Britain," which he argues "no longer makes very much sense after September 1953 when the U.S. invited British participation in discussing a new export control policy aimed at reducing the International Lists."

317. Spaulding, Robert Mark. "Once Again- Eisenhower and Export Controls: A Reply to Tor Forland." *Newsletter of the Society for Historians of American Foreign Relations* 25, no. 4 (September 1994): 36-40.

Author Info	See information in Entry #315.
Bibliography	No.
Index	No.
Notes	Footnotes (7).
Photographs	No.
Appendix	No.
Tables	No.
Key Words	Presidency, Foreign Relations, Politics, Cold War
Other Notes	
Annotation	Final response to Førland in their debate concerning the 1954 relaxation of Western export controls. (See Article Entries 315 and 316). Spaulding reiterates his earlier points, namely and in chronological order: 1) between March and July of 1953 American export control underwent a fundamental revision at Eisenhower's initiative; this program relaxed the embargo restrictions; 2) the U.S. informed the British of their new policy and invited them to engage in bilateral talks with America on the relaxed embargo; and 3) "having consciously waited for an 'appropriate moment' which was now provided by the American invitation for consultation, the U.K. subsequently... presented its own ideas on how best to reduce the control lists." Spaulding states that Førland has failed to produce any "evidence to refute the central points of chronology and causation". Spaulding also finds fault with Førland's imprecise term "list reduction".

318. Spiliotes, Constantine J. "Conditional Partisanship and Institutional Responsibility in Presidential Decision Making." *Presidential Studies Quarterly* 30, no. 3 (September 2000): 485-513.

Author Info	Author of *Vicious Cycle: Presidential Decision Making in the American Political Economy* (2002). Was assistant professor of government at Dartmouth College.
Bibliography	List of References.
Index	No.
Notes	Footnotes (86).
Photographs	No.
Appendix	No.
Tables	No.
Key Words	Presidency
Other Notes	
Annotation	Spiliotes examines the interaction of institutional structures and political incentives on presidential decision-making. He finds that the interaction produces "institutional responsibility" which "substantially constrains presidential response to partisan and electoral incentives present in the policy-making environment". He uses two case studies—economic policy making decisions of Eisenhower and Carter—to illustrate his point. He finds that, "Eisenhower, a Republican president, temporarily appropriates a Democratic logic for stabilization policy, while Carter, a Democrat, is captured doing the same in reverse." These cases, "suggest not only are presidential decisions regarding macroeconomic outcomes *not* immutably partisan *nor* largely stimulative in election years; they respond systematically to changes in institutional context in ways that actually work against these incentives."

319. Stern, Mark. "Eisenhower and Kennedy: A Comparison of Confrontations at Little Rock and Ole Miss." *Policy Studies Journal* 21, no. 3 (Autumn 1993): 575-588.

Author Info	Vice President for Academic Affairs and professor of political science at Shepherd University. CV at www.shepherd.edu/aaweb/vpaa/currvita.doc
Bibliography	References.
Index	No.
Notes	Internal citations and endnotes (5).
Photographs	No.
Appendix	No.
Tables	No.
Key Words	Presidency, Civil Rights, Domestic Policy
Other Notes	
Annotation	Stern compares Eisenhower's use of federal troops to Little Rock in 1957 with Kennedy's deployment of federal troops to the University of Mississippi (Ole Miss) in 1962. Both presidents were reluctant to call in the troops to enforce desegregation, but both ultimately felt forced to do so to enforce federal orders.

Though Kennedy had characterized Ike's use of troops as a failure, he was unable to avoid the same fate. Stern argues that: "The employment of armed federal force was traumatic to the nation, and it permanently altered the federal-state relationship."

320.   Strong, Robert A. "Eisenhower, Reagan, and Escaping the Dilemmas of Deterrence." *White House Studies* 4, no. 1 (January 2004): 19-29.

Author Info	Associate Provost, Director, The Rupert H. Johnson, Jr. Program in Leadership and Integrity, and Professor of Politics at Washington and Lee University. CV at http://williams.wlu.edu/whatwestudy/poli/vitae/Strong.pdf
Bibliography	No.
Index	No.
Notes	Endnotes (26).
Photographs	No.
Appendix	No.
Tables	No.
Key Words	Presidency, Cold War, Military Policy, Nuclear, Technology
Other Notes	
Annotation	Strong cites Eisenhower's Atoms for Peace speech and Reagan's Star Wars speech as examples of "popular and powerful presidents making dramatic proposals in widely noted speeches that may owe part of their origin to a presidential sense of powerlessness and desperation in the face of implacable technological realities". He argues that both men felt "a sense of frustration about the helplessness and hopelessness that accompanied life in the age of nuclear armaments" and refused to believe that deterrence was the best way to provide long-term security for the nation. Both prepared their speeches with only a small cadre of advisors and on their own initiative. Strong cites these two initiatives, "as evidence of presidential power and as products of forces that constrain that power." Ultimately, both failed to provide the security promised in the speeches.

321.   Suri, Jeremi. "America's Search for a Technological Solution to the Arms Race: The Surprise Attack Conference of 1958 and a Challenge for 'Eisenhower Revisionists'." *Diplomatic History* 21, no. 3 (Summer 1997): 417- 451.

Author Info	Self description from his website: "Jeremi Suri is the E. Gordon Fox Professor of History, the Director of the European Union Center of Excellence, and the Director of the Grand Strategy Program at the University of Wisconsin. He is the author of three books on contemporary politics and foreign policy." For additional information, see his CV at http://jeremisuri.net/doc/2009/03/cv911.pdf
Bibliography	No.
Index	No.

Notes	Footnotes (67).
Photographs	Yes (2).
Appendix	No.
Tables	No.
Key Words	Presidency, Foreign Relations, Cold War
Other Notes	
Annotation	Suri finds fault with Eisenhower's handling of the 1958 "Surprise Attack Conference" between the East and West on arms control. Contrary to revisionist ideas of Ike, Suri states that a reading of the history of the Conference shows Eisenhower as "an ambivalent, confused, and passive chief executive" who can be criticized, "for his inability to formulate organized, logical, coordinated, and practical arms control policies." Suri focuses on three themes that emerge in his analysis of the Eisenhower administration's failures in arms control: 1) "the administration's belief in a technical panacea for a largely political problem"; 2) "America's emphasis on inspection as the only true point of consensus on arms control within Washington and the Western alliance"; and 3) "Eisenhower's attempts to redress through legal reconnaissance the Soviet advantages derived from greater secrecy".

322. Sylvester, John A. "Taft, Dulles and Ike: New Faces for 1952." *Mid America* 76, no. 2 (Sprng/Summer 1994): 157-179.

Author Info	Sylvester was on the faculty at Oklahoma State University.
Bibliography	No.
Index	No.
Notes	Footnotes (59).
Photographs	No.
Appendix	No.
Tables	No.
Key Words	SACEUR, Presidency, Elections
Other Notes	
Annotation	Examines the foreign policy positions of Taft, Dulles, and Eisenhower in the 1952 election, as well as efforts to forge a Republican Party foreign policy platform. Taft could not overcome his previous isolationist positions and Ike's internationalist stance was ultimately successful.

T's

323. Tal, David. "Eisenhower's Disarmament Dilemma: From Chance for Peace to Open Skies Proposal." *Diplomacy and Statecraft* 12, no. 2 (June 2001): 175-196.

Author Info	Professor of History at the University of Calgary. Specialization: Israel,

American nuclear disarmament. http://hist.ucalgary.ca/profiles/david-tal

Bibliography	No.
Index	No.
Notes	Endnotes (77).
Photographs	No.
Appendix	No.
Tables	No.
Key Words	Presidency, Nuclear, Cold War, Military Policy, Foreign Relations, Speechmaking
Other Notes	
Annotation	Tal argues that Eisenhower's "Atoms for Peace" and "Chance for Peace," speeches and his "Open Skies" proposal need to be read in the context of Eisenhower's understanding of the relationship between arms, war, and disarmament. Ike believed that disarmament itself would not prevent war: "In Eisenhower's eyes, the real threat was not the arms race, but the Soviet Union's political and ideological structure, which he perceived as the root cause of the Cold war and its persistence." Eisenhower also saw America's nuclear arsenal as the best prevention to a world war. Because of pressure from America's allies, especially Britain, and the Soviet Union's disarmament initiatives, however, Eisenhower could not avoid disarmament talks. To respond to this "Disarmament Dilemma," Ike made speeches and proposals which, "implicitly suggest[ed] that any agreement on disarmament must entail the removal of the true cause of current tensions and of the Cold War: the political and social structure of the Soviet Union."

324. Thompson, Robert J. "Contrasting Models of White House Staff Organization: The Eisenhower, Ford, and Carter Experiences." *Congress & the Presidency* 19, no. 2 (Autumn 1992): 113-137.

Author Info	Political Science professor at East Carolina University. CV at http://www.ecu.edu/polsci/faculty/vita/thompson_vita.pdf
Bibliography	List of references.
Index	No.
Notes	No.
Photographs	No.
Appendix	No.
Tables	Yes (5).
Key Words	Presidency, White House
Other Notes	
Annotation	Using the Presidents' daily diaries, Thompson compares the interaction patterns of Presidents Eisenhower, Ford and Carter with their senior White House staff. The purpose of his study is to contrast his comparison with the typical models of White House staff organization to gauge the models' accuracy. Eisenhower is understood as having used a hierarchical (or formalistic) model, Ford and Carter as having used a collegial model. He

provides a general breakdown of each President's day, as well as a more specific breakdown of the time spent with senior staff. Thompson finds that the differences among the Presidents' interaction patterns are not as great as was expected, given the polar nature of the organizational models. The models did "not [hold] up in terms of expected access patterns," nor did they "appear to hold up entirely in terms of expected time demands placed on the president."

325. Trace, Howard. "In Public and Behind Closed Doors: President Eisenhower and 'Sputnik'." *Quest: History of Spaceflight* 14, no. 4 (October 2007): 46-51.

Author Info	Oral history editor for *Quest* magazine.
Bibliography	No.
Index	No.
Notes	No.
Photographs	Yes (4).
Appendix	No.
Tables	No.
Key Words	Presidency, Space Exploration, Cold War
Other Notes	
Annotation	Provides transcription of documents and oral histories relating to the "actions, attitudes, and plans of [Eisenhower] and [the] U.S. government" after the launch of Sputnik. White House Transcript of Eisenhower's October 9, 1957 press conference, the minutes of the October 10, 1957 meeting of the National Security Counsel, and transcriptions of oral histories are included.

326. Tudda, Chris. "'Reenacting the Story of Tantalus': Eisenhower, Dulles, and the Failed Rhetoric of Liberation." *Journal of Cold War Studies* 7, no. 4 (Fall 2005): 3-35.

Author Info	Historian in the Office of the Historian at the U.S. Department of State (2003-present). Visiting/Part time faculty with a focus on U.S. Diplomacy at George Washington University. CV at www.gwu.edu/~history/docs/ChrisTuddaCV.doc
Bibliography	No.
Index	No.
Notes	Footnotes (112).
Photographs	No.
Appendix	No.
Tables	No.
Key Words	Presidency, Foreign Relations, Cold War, Military Policy
Other Notes	
Annotation	Tudda argues that Eisenhower and Dulles simultaneously pursued two contradictory diplomatic strategies. On the one hand, they advocated "liberation policy"—freeing Eastern Europeans from Soviet control—through "rhetorical diplomacy" ("the use of belligerent rhetoric in private meetings

with allied and Soviet officials and in public speeches, addresses, and press conferences"). On the other hand, Eisenhower and Dulles, "believed that actual liberation might induce the Soviet Union to react violently." Because of this concern, "they *confidentially* rejected military liberation as impractical and dangerous." Tudda argues that the "schizophrenic nature of U.S. policy" had unintended consequences and caused "increased tensions" between America and the Soviet Union, and America and its allies. It also caused confusion among Americans and may have contributed to the 1956 Hungarian revolt.

W's

327.   Walcott, Charles and Karen Hult. "White House Organization as a Problem of Governance: The Eisenhower System." *Presidential Studies Quarterly* 24, no. 2 (Spring 1994): 327-339.

Author Info	Walcott—professor at Virginia Tech in the Political Science Department. Bio at http://www.psci.vt.edu/main/faculty/walcott.html including: "Professor Walcott's research over the past two decades has focused principally upon understanding the structural evolution and workings of the White House Office." Hult—professor at Virginia Tech in the Political Science Department. Bio at http://www.psci.vt.edu/main/faculty/hult.html including: "Her research and teaching interests include organization theory, the U.S. presidency and executive branch bureaucracy, the U.S. judiciary, and research methodologies."
Bibliography	No.
Index	No.
Notes	Endnotes (45).
Photographs	No.
Appendix	No.
Tables	No.
Key Words	Presidency, White House
Other Notes	
Annotation	Walcott and Hult challenge the classification of Eisenhower's management of the White House as "formalistic". They argue that classification of entire White House systems as "formal" or "informal" is too narrow and that, "more attention needs to be paid to the diversity of decision structures in the White House." The authors propose a more refined theoretical model and examine three different policy-relevant decision processes in the Eisenhower Administration using this model. They conclude that "given the President's political and policy objectives, staff structuring was largely appropriate." Earlier version of this essay was presented at the Gettysburg College Eisenhower Symposium in 1990.

328.   Warner, Geoffrey. "Eisenhower and Castro: US-Cuban Relations, 1958-60."
        International Affairs [London] 75, no. 4 (October 1999): 803-817.

Author Info   As of 2007: "GEOFFREY WARNER is professor of European Humanities at
                   the Open University, Milton Keynes, England. A graduate of Cambridge
                   University, he did postgraduate work at the University of Paris and has taught
                   in Australia and at the Bologna Center of the Johns Hopkins University, as well
                   as in the United Kingdom. Author of Pierre Laval and the Eclipse of France
                   (1968)". (From
                   http://www3.interscience.wiley.com/journal/120005541/abstract)
Bibliography   No.
Index   No.
Notes   Footnotes (22).
Photographs   No.
Appendix   No.
Tables   No.
Key Words   Presidency, Foreign Relations, Cold War
Other Notes
Annotation   Primarily using the documents in Volume VI of the Foreign Relations of the
                   United States series for the period of 1958-1960, Warner examines the origins
                   of the antagonism between the U.S. and Castro's regime in Cuba. He recounts
                   the Administrations' interactions with Castro prior to and after his ascension to
                   power. Warner finds a host of reasons for the U.S.'s decision that the Cuban
                   regime should be overthrown, including those from a memo to Eisenhower
                   from the Secretary of State: "the fomenting of anti-American sentiment in Cuba
                   and the rest of Latin America; the move towards a 'neutralist' foreign policy;
                   the support of other revolutionary movements in the Caribbean; the toleration
                   and encouragement of communist infiltration into key sectors of the
                   government and administration; and the increasing tendency towards the
                   establishment of a statist economy". He concludes that: "It is hard to escape
                   the conclusion that what really infuriated the [U.S.] about the Castro regime
                   was not whether it was communist or not, or even whether it expropriated
                   American assets, but that it stood for the opposite of everything the [U.S.] stood
                   for: pluralist democracy, free market capitalism, 'free world' solidarity against
                   'international communism' and, above all, American supremacy in the western
                   hemisphere."

329.   Weatherford, M. Stephen. "Presidential Leadership and Ideological Consistency: Were
        There 'Two Eisenhowers' in Economic Policy?" *Studies in American Political
        Development* 16, no. 2 (Fall 2002): 111-137.

Author Info   Political Science professor at the University of California, Santa Barbara.
                   "Professor Weatherford's research has ranged over questions of representation,
                   political behavior and political economy, mainly in the context of U.S. politics.
                   On public opinion and participation, his publications include articles on

economic voting, political trust, party realignment, and democratic deliberation. On political economy, he has written on presidential leadership in economic policy-making and on economic policy coordination between the U.S. and Japan." http://www.polsci.ucsb.edu/content/view/136/195/

Bibliography	No.
Index	No.
Notes	Footnotes (122).
Photographs	No.
Appendix	No.
Tables	One figure.
Key Words	Presidency, Economics, Domestic Policy
Other Notes	
Annotation	Weatherford challenges the notion held by some historians that there were "two Eisenhowers"—a more liberal Eisenhower in the first part of his presidency and a more conservative Eisenhower at the end. He instead argues that Eisenhower was more consistent than the "two Eisenhowers" advocates suggest and uses analyses of four of Eisenhower's decisions from early in his administration—relating to wage and price controls, social security, taxes, and the Taft-Hartley Act—to demonstrate his point. He states that Eisenhower's "ideological positions were not as liberal at the beginning of his presidency as these advocates suggest, nor were they as conservative at the end." He suggests that the primary reason some might see a shift in Ike's core political views is because "the level of conflict between Eisenhower and Congress took an unmistakable upturn in the second term," largely due to "a substantial shift in the liberal direction on the part of members of [Congress]."

330.   Wells, Wyatt. "Public Power in the Eisenhower Administration." *Journal of Policy History* 20, no. 2 (April 2008): 227-262.

Author Info	Professor of history at the University of Auburn, Montgomery (Alabama) http://www.aum.edu/profile_ektid5608.aspx
Bibliography	No.
Index	No.
Notes	Endnotes (124).
Photographs	No.
Appendix	No.
Tables	Yes (1).
Key Words	Presidency, Politics, Domestic Policy
Other Notes	
Annotation	Wells argues that President Eisenhower and his administration came to understand that they could not reverse New Deal federal policy toward electric utilities and thus worked to contain public power. Wells examines Ike's approach to projects such as the Tennessee Valley Authority and the Rural Electrification Administration, as well as the emerging nuclear energy field. He concludes that Ike was successful in preventing public power's expansion at

the expense of private utilities. He argues that Eisenhower "occupied a central place in this drama" and that he was driven by ideological conviction—he "believed that public power threatened the free enterprise system and local self-government, which he valued and considered integral to political democracy." One table.

331. Wenger, Andreas. "Eisenhower, Kennedy, and the Missile Gap: Determinants of US Military Expenditure in the Wake of the Sputnik Shock." *Defense and Peace Economics* 8, no. 1 (1997): 77-100.

Author Info	"Professor of International and Swiss Security Policy and Director of the Center for Security Studies. He holds a doctoral degree from the University of Zurich and was a guest scholar at Princeton University (1992-94), Yale University (1998), the Woodrow Wilson Center (2000), and, recently, at the George Washington University (2005). His research team is part of the Center for Security Studies, which is integrated in the Center for Comparative and International Studies (CIS) at ETH Zurich and the University of Zurich." For more information see Book Entry #116 and http://www.css.ethz.ch/people/stafflist/wengeran
Bibliography	List of references.
Index	No.
Notes	Footnotes (19) and internal citations.
Photographs	No.
Appendix	No.
Tables	No.
Key Words	Presidency, Cold War, Military Policy, Economics
Other Notes	
Annotation	Wenger examines the impact that Sputnik had on America's defense policy and the debate over the military budget during the Eisenhower and Kennedy Administrations. He concludes that "both Eisenhower and Kennedy for political purposes proposed bigger defense expenditure to Congress than they thought was justified from a military standpoint." Wenger examines multiple pressures the Presidents faced but emphasizes foreign policy pressures: "both administrations perceived large military expenditure to be important politically and psychologically to reassure allies and deter adversaries." Increased defense expenditures were tied to "the creditability of the status of the United States as a superpower and security guarantor."

332. Williamson, Daniel C. "Understandable Failure: The Eisenhower Administration's Strategic Goals in Iraq, 1953-1958." *Diplomacy and Statecraft* 17, no. 3 (September 2006): 597-615.

Author Info	Associate Professor of History at the University of Hartford. See also Book Entry #119.

Bibliography	No.
Index	No.
Notes	Endnotes (62).
Photographs	No.
Appendix	No.
Tables	No.
Key Words	Presidency, Foreign Relations, Middle East, Cold War
Other Notes	
Annotation	Williamson offers a defense of the Eisenhower Administration's actions in Iraq and concludes that the Administration's "policies towards Iraq demonstrate that Washington followed a reasonable strategy, even if it failed to achieve the goal of helping to keep Iraq as a stable Western ally." He argues that critics of Ike's Iraq policies fail to take into account the constraints of Great Britain's and Iraq's political and diplomatic goals, the limited aims of American military aid to Iraq, and America's economic concerns. Williamson further argues that the 1958 Iraq Revolution may have been sparked by Iraq's participation in the Baghdad Pact, but he notes that this alliance was not simply an American creation but one involving Britain and the Iraqi monarchy. Finally, Williamson praises "the Eisenhower administration for its very moderate response to the violent overthrow of the Iraqi monarchy."

333. Wilson, Hugh A. "President Eisenhower and the Development of Active Labor Market Policy in the United States: A Revisionist View." *Presidential Studies Quarterly* 39, no. 3 (September 2009): 519-548.

Author Info	There is an award named in his honor at Adelphi: "Hugh Wilson, Emeritus Professor of Political Science, taught courses on American Government at Adelphi for 35 years. Before working at Adelphi and through his early years at the university, Professor Wilson was an organizer of poor people's movements in Nassau, Suffolk, and Westchester counties. His work focused on economic, social, and racial justice issues including welfare, housing, and employment rights. His justice work transitioned as he became a consultant to nonprofits and served as a trainer for nonprofit boards and staff. Professor Wilson was also a participant in the 1960s civil rights and anti-war movements. He published numerous articles on Black politics, the suburbs, the politics of nuclear power, and Black families. He is still an active member of the Adelphi community having served as interim director of African, Black and Caribbean Studies (spring 2007). He also returns to teach." http://academics.adelphi.edu/artsci/pol/awards.php
Bibliography	List of references.
Index	No.
Notes	Internal citations.
Photographs	No.
Appendix	No.
Tables	No.

Key Words   Presidency, Domestic Policy, Economics

Other Notes

Annotation   Wilson analyzes Eisenhower's active labor market policies over his two terms as President. He finds that Eisenhower's administration "had a vigorous active labor market policy" in both terms and that Ike "was an active and knowledgeable participant and director of this policy" who "actively lobbied for or defended his legislative initiatives." Ike used predominantly demand-orientated strategies (such as road building and college housing) during both terms. During the first term, these strategies involved substantial new funding, and in the second term when Ike was more financially conservative, they emphasized, "increasing the tempo of existing funding to fight unemployment." Wilson finds that existing literature on active labor market policies largely ignores Ike's contributions.

Y's

334.   Yaqub, Salim. "Imperious Doctrines: U.S.–Arab Relations from Dwight D. Eisenhower to George W. Bush." *Diplomatic History* 26, no. 4 (Fall 2002): 571-591.

Author Info   "Salim Yaqub is an Associate Professor of History at the University of California at Santa Barbara. He received his B.A. from the Academy of Art College and an M.A. at San Francisco State University, continuing on to Yale University, where he earned an M. Phil and a Ph.D. in American History. Dr. Yaqub specializes in the History of American Foreign Relations, 20th-Century American Political History, and Modern Middle Eastern History since 1945." Profile from http://www.teach12.com:80/tgc/professors/professor_detail.aspx?pid=268 See also Book Entry #122.

Bibliography   No.

Index   No.

Notes   Footnotes (45).

Photographs   No.

Appendix   No.

Tables   No.

Key Words   Presidency, Middle East

Other Notes

Annotation   Yaqub compares U.S.-Arab relations during the Eisenhower and G. W. Bush Administrations. He finds "striking parallels" between the Eisenhower Doctrine (freedom vs. communism) and Bush's war on terrorism (civilization or terror). He also finds, however, "vast and alarming changes in the psychological and moral content of U.S.-Arab relations and in the ways in which the two people have come to regard one another." The lack of respect that the Americans and Middle Eastern Arabs have come to have for one another has greatly exacerbated relations.

335.   Young, Jeffrey R. "Eisenhower's Federal Judges and Civil Rights Policy: A Republican 'Southern Strategy' for the 1950s." *Georgia Historical Quarterly* 78, no. 3 (Fall 1994): 536-565.

Author Info	Article notes that he was then "a Ph.D. candidate in history at Emory University and a research assistant at the Martin Luther King, Jr. Papers Project".
Bibliography	No.
Index	No.
Notes	Footnotes (115).
Photographs	Yes (4).
Appendix	No.
Tables	No.
Key Words	Presidency, Civil Rights, Domestic Policy, Politics
Other Notes	
Annotation	Young argues that Eisenhower deserves none of the credit for the civil rights achievements made by the judges he appointed: "While [Ike's] appointees to the bench courageously reshaped the southern racial status quo, the president catered to that region's fears about the impending demise of Jim Crow" and also demonstrated, "heartfelt sympathy for white southerners alarmed by desegregation." Young refers to Eisenhower as "racially conservative" and characterizes his appointments of liberal judges to the southern federal bench as "ironic," stating that Ike "never anticipated their advocacy of the civil rights cause." The judges were appointed not because of their racial ideas, but because of political considerations—the appointed judges had been active in Ike's campaign in the South. Young also examines Eisenhower's legacy in the Republican party, stating that: "Far from providing a moral alternative to the one-party South, Eisenhower's 'modern' Republicanism catered to an enduring and ignoble tradition of racial prejudice."

Z's

336.   Zhai, Qiang. "Crisis and Confrontations: Chinese-American Relations During the Eisenhower Administration." *Journal of American-East Asian Relations* 9, no. 3/4 (September 2000): 221-249.

Author Info	History professor at Auburn University, Montgomery (Alabama). Zhai was born in Nanjing, China, and went to Auburn in 1991. He holds both the BA (1981) and MA (1984) degrees from Nanjing University. "After coming to the United States, he earned a Ph.D. from Ohio University in 1991. Within the

Department of History, Dr. Zhai serves as liaison to the university's Library Committee and he is currently the chair of the department as well. Dr. Zhai has published widely within his field including two books…. [and] many articles in scholarly journals…. In recognition of these many publications, Dr. Zhai was recognized as one of AUM's Distinguished Research Professors in 1997." http://www.aum.edu/profile_ektid5730.aspx

Bibliography	No.
Index	No.
Notes	Yes (73).
Photographs	Yes (5).
Appendix	No.
Tables	No.
Key Words	Presidency, Cold War, Foreign Relations, Military Policy
Other Notes	
Annotation	Using American and Chinese documents, Zhai examines American-Chinese relations and the U.S.-Taiwan alliance during the Eisenhower Administration. He argues that the Administration was hostile to the People's Republic of China and that the benefits of this policy included satisfaction of anti-Communist right wingers at home, and the possibility that a "hard-line approach" might drive a wedge in the Sino-Soviet alliance. Zhai also examines the Eisenhower Administration's de facto "two-China" policy (Taiwan permanently separated from mainland China) and the reactions of the leaders of the PRC and Taiwan to the policy.

337. Zachariou, Stelios. "The Road to the Garrison State: An Overview of Greek-American Relations During the Eisenhower and Kennedy Administrations (1952-1963)." *Modern Greek Studies Yearbook* 14, (January 1998): 241-260.

Author Info	Master's degree from University of New Orleans, continued his graduate studies at the University of Athens. Currently, "working as a scientific advisor for the U.N. Division of the Hellenic Ministry of Foreign Affairs, following matters relevant to disarmament and proliferation of Weapons of Mass Destruction." Bio at http://history.uno.edu/alumni/fall07--zachariou.cfm
Bibliography	No.
Index	No.
Notes	Endnotes (94).
Photographs	No.
Appendix	No.
Tables	No.
Key Words	Presidency, Foreign Relations, Cold War
Other Notes	Zachariou's master's thesis from the University of New Orleans had an identical title to this article.
Annotation	Examines Greek-American relations during the Eisenhower and Kennedy Administrations. Also begins with a discussion of relations during the Truman Administration. Greece needed financial assistance that Britain was no longer

able to provide. America began providing aid to Greece because of its strategic position as a buffer from the Soviet Union and as a passage to the Middle East. Zachariou finds that from 1952 to 1963, "Greece had experienced a period of apparent political stability under American influence," but the Greek public came to resent the policies and restrictions of the U.S., which entrenched a conservative, pro-American government. Thus: "During those years of relative stability, the conditions for future upheaval were gradually structured."